# THE GENERALS

THE BATTLE OF NEW ORLEANS

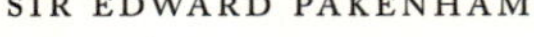

SIR EDWARD PAKENHAM

ANDREW JACKSON

# *The* Generals

## ANDREW JACKSON, SIR EDWARD PAKENHAM, *and the Road to* THE BATTLE OF NEW ORLEANS

Benton Rain Patterson

NEW YORK UNIVERSITY PRESS
*New York and London*

NEW YORK UNIVERSITY PRESS
New York and London
www.nyupress.org



Library of Congress Cataloging-in-Publication Data
Patterson, Benton Rain, 1929–
The generals : Andrew Jackson, Sir Edward Pakenham, and the road to the Battle of New Orleans / Benton Rain Patterson.
p. cm.
Includes bibliographical references and index.
ISBN 0–8147–6717–6 (cloth : acid-free paper)
1. New Orleans, Battle of, New Orleans, La., 1815. 2. Jackson, Andrew, 1767–1845. 3. Pakenham, Edward Michael, 1778–1815. 4. Generals—United States—Biography. 5. Generals—Great Britain—Biography. 6. United States. Army—Biography. 7. Great Britain. Army—Biography. I. Title.
E356.N5P36 2005
973.5'239'0922—dc22 2004026811

New York University Press books are printed on acid-free paper, and their binding materials are chosen for strength and durability.

Manufactured in the United States of America

10 9 8 7 6 5 4 3 2 1

*To Louise,*

*who restored my soul*

# CONTENTS

*All illustrations appear as an insert following p. 130.*

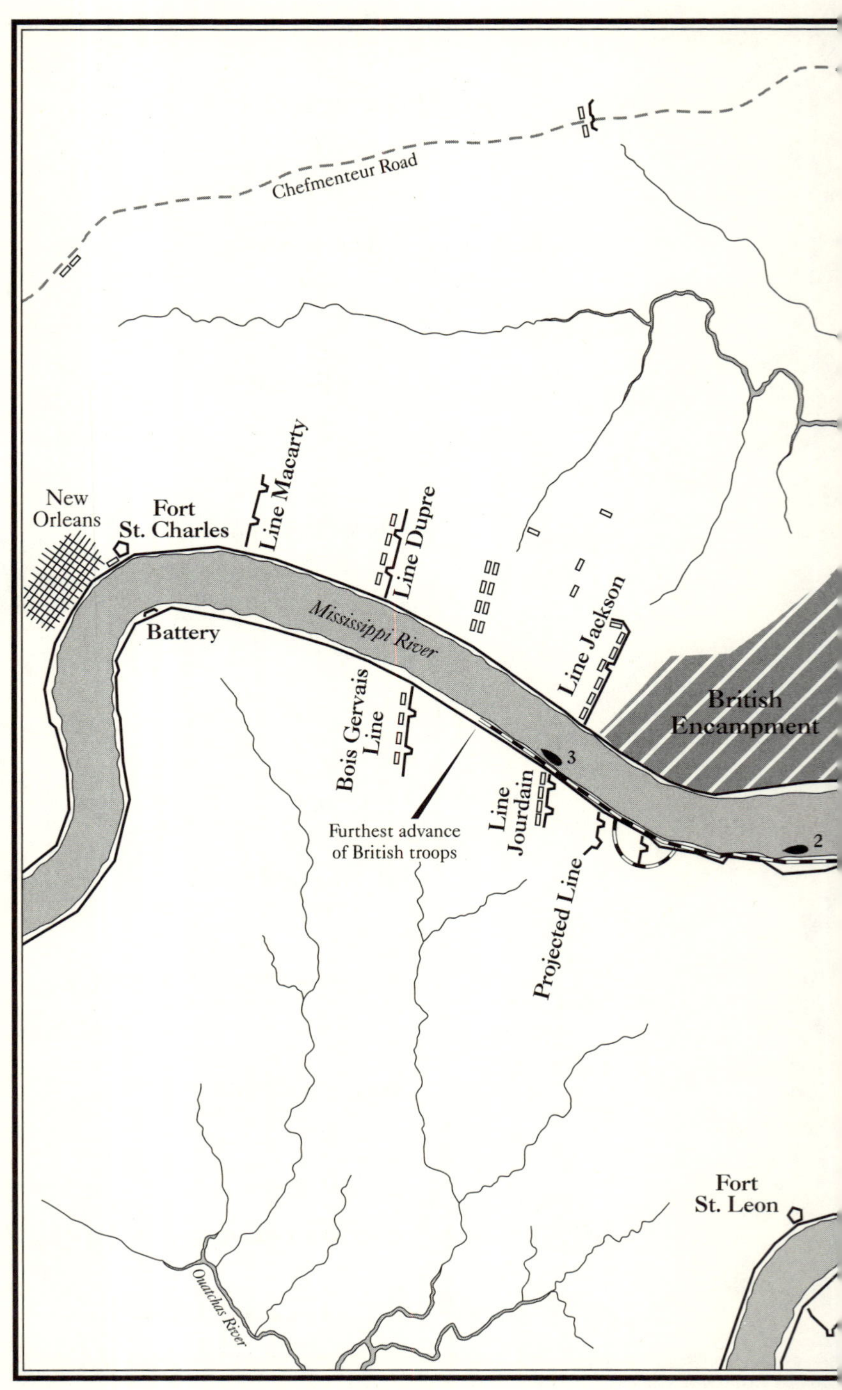

Chefmenteur Road
New Orleans
Fort St. Charles
Line Macarty
Line Dupre
Battery
Mississippi River
Bois Gervais Line
Line Jackson
British Encampment
3
2
Line Jourdain
Furthest advance of British troops
Projected Line
Fort St. Leon
Ouatchas River

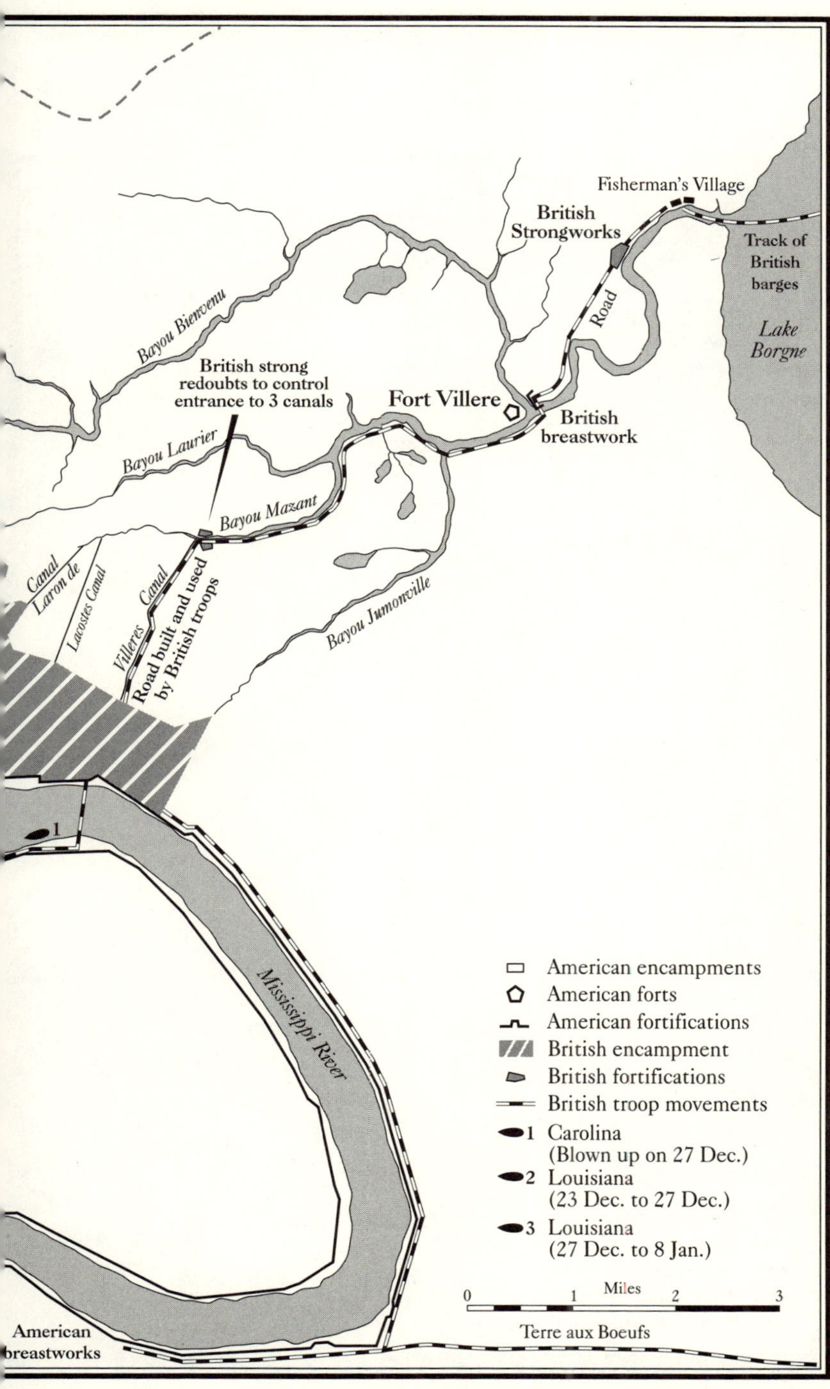


Map showing the site of the Battle of New Orleans and the adjacent areas along the Mississippi River.

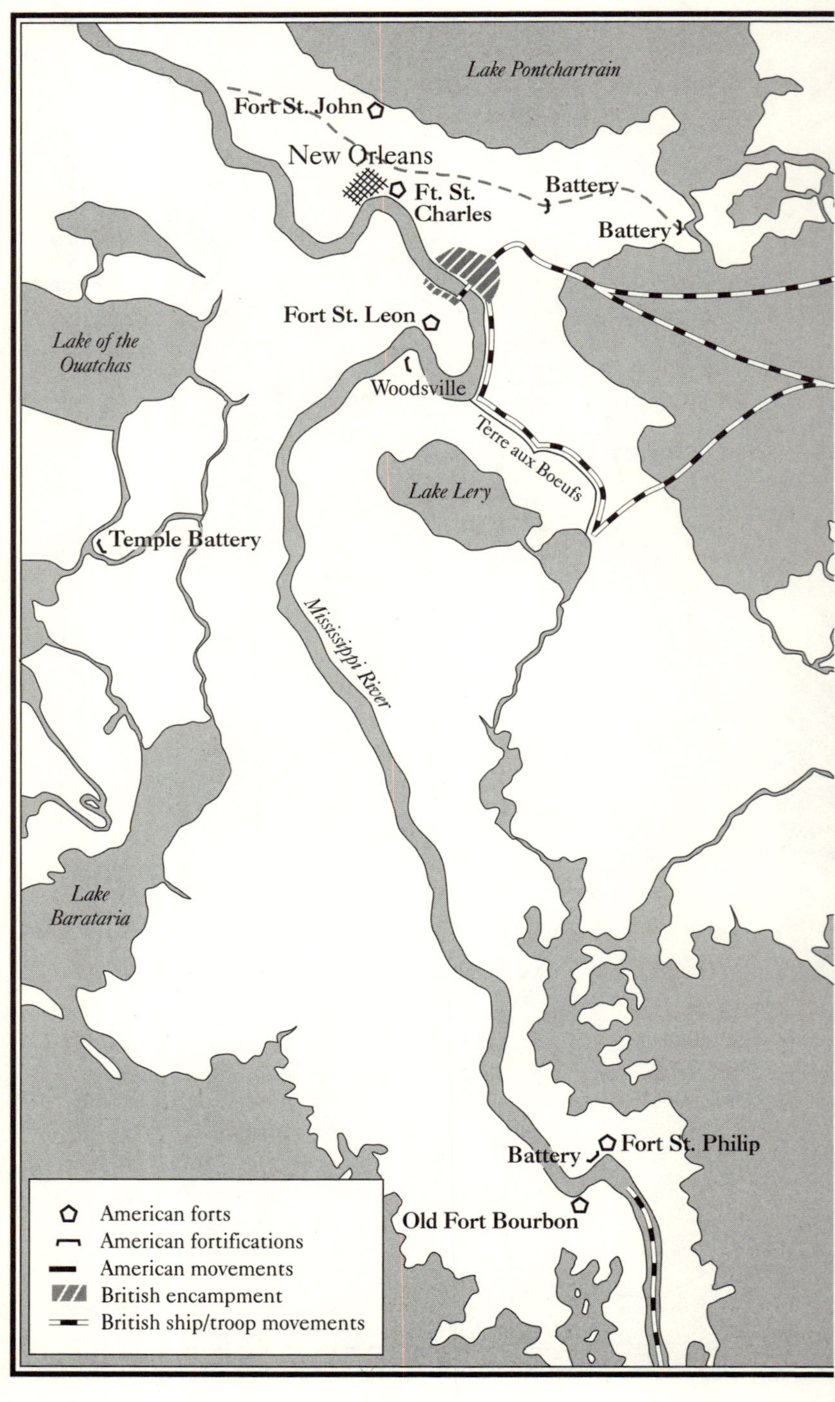
Lake Pontchartrain
Fort St. John
New Orleans
Ft. St. Charles
Battery
Battery
Fort St. Leon
Lake of the Ouatchas
Woodsville
Terre aux Boeufs
Lake Lery
Temple Battery
Mississippi River
Lake Barataria
Battery
Fort St. Philip
Old Fort Bourbon
American forts
American fortifications
American movements
British encampment
British ship/troop movements

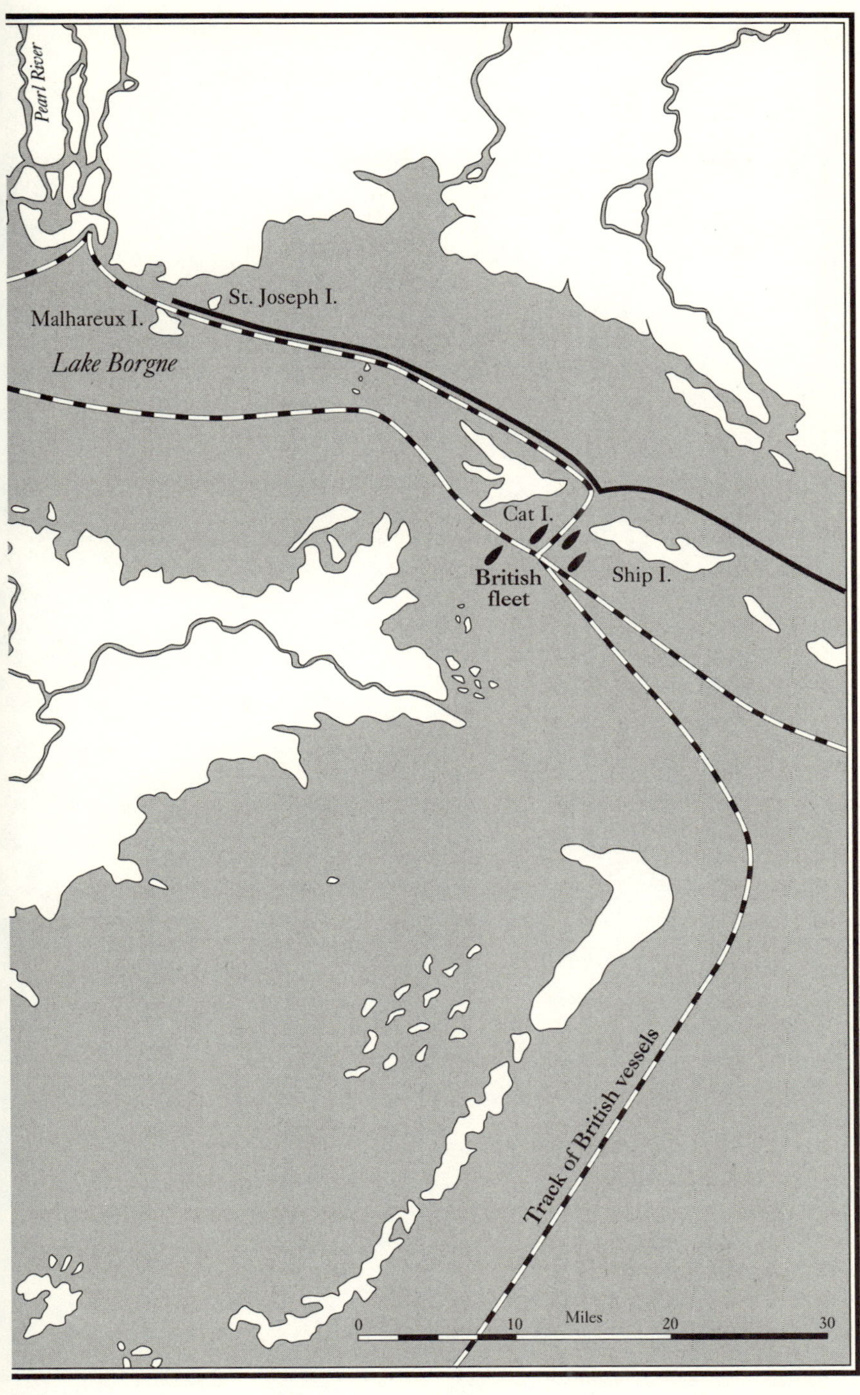

Map showing the British approach to New Orleans from the Gulf of Mexico, through Lake Borgne and Bayou Bienvenue.

# Introduction

THE War of 1812, not America's most familiar conflict, is probably best known for three events—the burning of Washington, D.C., by the British, the composition of America's national anthem in the dawn's early light at Baltimore, and the battle at New Orleans that proved for the first time the legitimacy of the American nation. In that battle, which threatened not only the city of New Orleans but the strategic lifeline of the nation, the elite troops of Great Britain, victors over the dreaded armies of Napoleon, confronted a makeshift American army of defenders patched together from regular troops, militias, French-speaking Louisiana Creoles, free blacks, Indians, Kentucky mountaineers, miscellaneous volunteers, and the pirates of Barataria.

Because of its drama and its significance in American history, and because it came as the conclusion to the conflict, the Battle of New Orleans is for history writers the war's most compelling story. All the war's events prior to December 1814, when the battle began, seem no more than a preface to it.

For a long time I have wanted to tell that story. I have known much of it ever since I was boy growing up in the old New Orleans suburb of Gentilly, some three hundred yards from the Chef Menteur highway, the route by which General Andrew Jackson thought the British must come to assault the city. I knew Chalmette, the site of the battle, and Pakenham Oak, the hoary, mossy tree under which, according to tradition, the valorous British commander died of his wounds. I knew Jackson Square, the French Quarter's old Place d'Armes, the place where New Orleans's defenders first assembled and which had had its name changed in memory of the indomitable American general who saved the city—and the honor of his country as well.

I knew, too, of many of the characters who played parts in the drama—Governor William C. C. Claiborne, Jean Lafitte, Dominique You, the Villeres. Tales of those men were—and still are—vital pieces of New Orleans folklore.

Most fascinating, to me, of all the characters in the drama were the two major figures, Jackson and Pakenham, one made hugely famous by his victory at New Orleans, the other made less so by his failure there. To tell the story of the battle, I would focus as best I could on those two men, showing them coming from two very different backgrounds, each making his own way, each moving toward the spot where their paths converged in the cane fields below New Orleans, between the river and the swamp.

There was much to be discovered and shared about Jackson, a man of many accomplishments and an extraordinarily colorful person whose life is recorded in elaborate detail in many sources. Pakenham, however, was a different case entirely. There was little information available about him. Not only were there great gaps in the story of his career, but, worse, little was known about him as a person. The richest source of personal material about Pakenham was a slender biography written for the celebration of the 150th anniversary of the battle, authored by Valerie Pakenham, a relative of the general. With that volume, at last the bits and pieces started to come together, forming the portrait of a man far different from his foe.

To Lady Pakenham and the many others whose works provided the details of the story told here, I am deeply indebted and truly grateful.

What I have attempted is not merely the story of two historic figures and the conflict that made them adversaries, for the real story is much larger than that. It is, as I hope the book will show, the story of the triumph of a great cause. It is the story of a diverse people, championed by a heroic leader, joined together in a fierce struggle to preserve those precious things they held in common—their citizenship in a free country and their own personal freedom—and to do so against enormous odds.

# ∴ 1 ∴

# The Immigrants' Son

TWENTY-SEVEN-YEAR-OLD Andrew Jackson and his wife, Elizabeth, must have known that leaving their home and familiar surroundings, perhaps forever, would be painful and that the voyage from northern Ireland to the other side of the Atlantic would be long and hard on them and their children. Others had certainly imagined the pain of emigration. So daunting were the prospects of the journey and the separation that all but two of the nineteen families who had agreed to sail with the Jacksons in the spring of 1765 changed their minds as the time to depart drew near.

For Andrew and Elizabeth, though, the reasons to go were more compelling than the reasons to stay. They were tenant farmers, bound in obligation to their landlord and made desperate by the lack of hope of improving their lives or the lives of their children beyond the state of their own. They determined to look elsewhere for something more promising.

For five generations Andrew's family had lived in the vicinity of Carrickfergus, on the Irish Sea, above Belfast in County Antrim, having first settled there, like many others in northern Ireland, after emigrating from Scotland more than a hundred years earlier. Andrew's father was a linen weaver in Carrickfergus, but Andrew, disdaining his father's trade, had decided he wanted to work outside and had become a farmer. His brothers, Sam and Hugh, had gone their own way, too, Sam becoming a world-traveled sailor and Hugh having joined the British army and having served with His Majesty's forces in America during the French and Indian War. As a member of the Forty-ninth Regiment of Foot, he had seen action with General Edward Braddock in Virginia and with

General James Wolfe at Quebec. He had also fought Indians along the North Carolina–South Carolina border, in the Waxhaws region, an area that stuck in his memory.

It was Hugh Jackson who had organized a group of young families to migrate to America. Out of the army and back in Ireland, he had recruited the twenty families who were to sail together, his own and Andrew's included, and he had made preparations for shipping their belongings and buying passage. His new wife, however, refused to leave Ireland, and Hugh had to back out of the plan, as did most of the others.

Andrew's wife, red-haired Elizabeth Hutchinson Jackson, more adventuresome, was undeterred. Four of her sisters had already emigrated, had married, and were living in the Waxhaws area, where there was a settlement of Scotch-Irish immigrants like themselves and where Hugh Jackson had intended to lead his band of immigrants. In April 1765 Elizabeth and Andrew, with their two young sons, Hugh, two years old, and Robert, six months, boarded a ship and sailed from Larne, Ireland, leaving the Old World behind, bravely heading for the New. Sailing with them were the two other families who were all that remained of the original twenty families Hugh Jackson had recruited.

After nearly two months at sea the Jacksons landed in Philadelphia in May 1765.[1] From there, in a wagon loaded with their possessions, they traveled southwestward, creeping down into Virginia and then into North Carolina, moving in a stream of immigrants who were bound for the promising land of the Carolinas. Elizabeth's sister Jane and her husband, James Crawford, had established a farm and built a large house near the center of the Waxhaw settlement some five years earlier; the Jacksons intended to find a place near them and near the families of Elizabeth's other sisters, who also lived in the area.

The settlement, on Waxhaw Creek, a tributary of the Catawba River, was about 150 miles northwest of Charleston, South Carolina, and had swelled with Scotch-Irish immigrants to the point where it included a Presbyterian meetinghouse. The area was mostly grassy fields and piney woods growing from red clay soil. Its most arable land, where farming was the most profitable, was along the Catawba River and along Waxhaw Creek, but by 1765 most, if not all, of it had been claimed by earlier settlers.

At last reaching their destination, Andrew and Elizabeth chose a two-hundred-acre tract on Ligget's Branch, near the headwaters of Twelve Mile Creek, another tributary of the Catawba. The tract was about four miles off the post road, isolated and rugged, about ten miles from the Crawfords' prosperous farm on Waxhaw Creek and about seven miles from the farm of Elizabeth's sister Margaret and her husband, George McKemey. The land nourished only a stand of scrub pine, hickory, and oak trees, its soil thin and unpromising. Better land was available some twenty miles more distant, but proximity to Elizabeth's sisters, as well as the price of land, was apparently a big consideration in Andrew and Elizabeth's decision.

When the Jacksons had arrived in the Waxhaws, Thomas Ewing was living on the land they chose, evidently without legal title. Whatever right he had to the two hundred acres, however, he apparently conveyed to Andrew and Elizabeth. When a crew of government surveyors turned up at the property during the spring after Andrew and Elizabeth took possession of it, they ran a line around the Jackson tract and described it as "beginning at a White Oak South side of the creek by a small Branch & thence N 10 E 180 Poles to a Red Oak . . . enclosing 200 acres being in . . . the county of Mecklenburgh Province of North Carolina."[2]

Andrew went to work hewing trees and fashioning a log cabin to house his family. He cleared several acres and put in a crop, all backbreaking work, and managed to eke out a living, looking forward to better times ahead. Then, late in the winter of 1767, less than two years after arriving in America with high hopes, Andrew fell gravely ill. In March of that year, at age twenty-nine, he died, leaving Elizabeth, then nine months pregnant, and their two young sons to survive as best they could without him.

Following a traditional Irish wake for Andrew, the coffin containing his body was loaded onto a mule-drawn sled and laboriously hauled across the snow-covered ground, through an icy ford of Waxhaw Creek, and to its eventual resting place in the Waxhaw Presbyterian churchyard.

When the funeral service and burial were over, Elizabeth and her children moved into the home of her sister Jane. Days later, on March 15, 1767, while still at the home of James and Jane Crawford,[3] she gave birth to her third son. She named him Andrew, after the father he would never see or know.

The Crawfords had eight children, and Jane, who is described in some accounts as an invalid,[4] needed help with domestic responsibilities. The Crawfords were apparently well off by frontier standards, perhaps because of the relative prosperity of their farm, and James was easily able to afford someone to relieve his wife of the burden of running a household. Offered the job, Elizabeth agreed to become the Crawfords' live-in housekeeper, an arrangement no doubt welcomed by both Elizabeth and Jane.

Though she moved out of the cabin Andrew had built, Elizabeth kept her claim to the property on Ligget's Branch. In 1770, when young Andrew (who came to be called Andy) was three years old, Elizabeth gained a clear title to the two hundred acres and had the deed made out to her three sons.

When it was time for Andy to start school, Elizabeth used her earnings from spinning flax, at which she was recognized in the Waxhaws as an expert, to pay for him to attend the "academy" that held classes at the Presbyterian church, conducted by the pastor. The other Jackson boys attended a community school that offered not much more than reading, writing, and arithmetic. Elizabeth wanted Andy to become a Presbyterian clergyman, and at the academy he received instruction in Latin and Greek, among other subjects.

Andy was not much of a scholar, but he was bright enough and had a quick mind. He could read when he was five years old and could write in a neat, legible hand when he was eight. His grammar and syntax were not as bad as his spelling, which was atrocious. History, math, science, and political science held little interest for him.

His physical energy made Andy gravitate toward sports, especially wrestling, foot races, and horse races. He was described as "a wild, frolicsome, willful, mischievous, daring, reckless boy, generous to a friend but never content to submit to a stronger enemy."[5] Although he loved wrestling, Andy's slim build and light weight put him at a disadvantage in the sport. He was nevertheless a determined competitor. "I could throw him three times out of four," one of his classmates said, "but he would never stay throwed. He was dead game and never would give up."[6] Andy gained a reputation for being quick to fight and for refusing to admit defeat. He also became well known for his cursing and rough language, which, along with his lack of application to his studies, eventually ended his mother's dream of his becoming a man of the cloth.

Andy was eight years old when war broke out between Britain and its thirteen rebellious American colonies in April 1775. He was twelve when his sixteen-year-old brother, Hugh, serving in the militia, died of heat exhaustion following the Battle of Stono Ferry, South Carolina, in June 1779. He was thirteen when the war at last came to the Waxhaws in May 1780. Lieutenant Colonel Banastre Tarleton, under the command of Lieutenant General Charles Cornwallis, led a mounted pursuit of Colonel Abraham Buford's regiment of Virginia Continentals, who were retreating toward Hillsborough, North Carolina, after the capture of Charleston, and inflicted a bloody defeat on them near the Waxhaw settlement on May 29, 1780. The battle turned into a savage massacre as Tarleton's troops refused quarter to the outmaneuvered and outfought Americans. They sabered the officer who raised a white surrender flag and bayoneted the wounded in a merciless slaughter that killed 113 American troops and wounded as many as 203, of whom 150 were wounded so severely that Tarleton was unable to carry them off as prisoners but instead left them lying where they had fallen.

Upon Tarleton's withdrawal from the field, the people of the Waxhaw settlement lifted their wounded countrymen from the bloodied ground and carried them in wagons to the Waxhaw Presbyterian meetinghouse, turning it into a hospital. Elizabeth Jackson was one of the settlement women who ministered to the mangled, maimed, and mutilated. Andy and his brother Robert helped her.

Three of the survivors of the massacre were Andy's Crawford cousins—Joseph, William, and James Jr. From them Andy and Robert heard firsthand about the barbarity of Tarleton and his troopers. Those and other accounts of the battle sent a wave of rage throughout the Carolinas. Colonel Thomas Sumter and Major William Davie (the adopted son of the late Waxhaw Presbyterian pastor, William Richardson) marshaled their Carolina militiamen to wreak vengeance on the British. Thirteen-year-old Andy Jackson and sixteen-year-old Robert offered their services to Davie, who was recruiting cavalrymen in the Waxhaws. Andy became, as he later described his assignment, "a mounted orderly or messenger." It was a job for which he felt, as he said, "well fitted, being a good rider and knowing all the roads."[7] Davie armed him with a pistol.

At dawn on August 6, 1780, after virtually wiping out three companies of loyalist militia occupying a farmhouse near the British outpost at Hanging Rock, South Carolina, north of Camden, Davie's force joined Sumter's in a combined assault on the Hanging Rock outpost itself. Riding with Davie's cavalry in those attacks were Andy and Robert Jackson. Davie's and Sumter's troopers overwhelmed the Hanging Rock garrison, composed of British regulars and loyalist militiamen, in a hard-fought, four-hour battle in which the British lost at least 192 men, counting killed and wounded, and Davie and Sumter lost 12 killed and 41 wounded. At Hanging Rock Andy Jackson witnessed mortal combat for the first time.

Following the raid, both Sumter and Davie withdrew their forces, and Andy and Robert Jackson returned to the Waxhaws with their wounded comrades, among whom was their cousin James Crawford Jr. There they were caught up in more of the war's conflict. Loyalists continually harassed their patriot neighbors, hostile bands of loyalist militia attacking farmhouses, burning them, destroying crops, and running off cattle, engaging the revolutionaries in combat when they could. As did the countryside of other states, the Waxhaws became a battleground in a war between partisan militias. The homes of patriot militia leaders became garrisoned outposts in the internecine struggle. The home of Robert Crawford, a militia major and the brother of Andy and Robert's uncle James Crawford, was one such outpost. When the Jackson boys sought a new assignment after returning home, they were posted at the home of another militia leader, a Captain Land.

News reached the Waxhaw settlement that a force of British dragoons had been dispatched from their post at Camden to assist loyalist militia in their efforts to terrorize and neutralize their patriot neighbors in the Waxhaws. A force of patriot volunteers was quickly called out to confront the British, and the Waxhaw Presbyterian meetinghouse was designated as the rendezvous point for the gathering patriots. About forty of them, including the Jackson brothers, assembled with their horses and weapons in a grove next to the meetinghouse, awaiting the arrival of additional patriot volunteers from a settlement nearby. Tipped off that the patriots were gathering at the meetinghouse, the commander of the British force marched directly on it, placing the loyalist militiamen in his forward element as he approached the grove and keeping his uniformed dragoons in the rear.

When the patriots saw the loyalists coming toward them at a distance, they mistook them for the company of patriot militia coming to assist them. By the time they discovered their mistake, it was too late. The loyalists were suddenly upon them, and eleven of the forty patriots were quickly taken prisoner. Most of the rest hurriedly mounted their horses and, pursued by the British dragoons, desperately fled down a road, then into a field, then into a marsh, their mounts struggling through the mire and shallow water. In the confusion, Andy and Robert had been separated, but beside Andy in flight was his cousin Thomas Crawford, a militia lieutenant.

When Andy reached the other side of the marsh, his horse coming up on firm, dry land, he looked back to see where his cousin was. Thomas's mount had stumbled in the morass, and Thomas had gone down with it. Before he could get up and run, a British cavalryman caught up with him and struck him in the head with his saber. Severely wounded by the blow, Thomas surrendered. Andy sped off, unable to help.

Andy made it safely to the woods, where he found Robert also hiding. They spent the night there, tense and hungry. The next morning they left to find food at the home of their captured cousin, Thomas Crawford. A loyalist neighbor, however, had discovered their hiding place and notified a detail of dragoons, who rode straight for the Crawford house and quickly surrounded it, with the Jackson boys and Thomas's wife and baby inside. Andy and Robert were eating breakfast when the dragoons burst into the house and began wildly smashing furniture, dishes, crockery, and glasses, destroying the contents of the house and ripping apart the Crawfords' clothes, including those of the infant child.

While the wreckage was going on, the British officer in charge ordered Andy to clean his mud-spattered jackboots. Andy refused. "I am a prisoner of war," he reportedly told the officer, "and claim to be treated as such."[8] The officer swung at Andy's head with his saber, and Andy instinctively raised his left hand to ward off the blow. The blade slashed his hand, cutting it to the bone, and gashed his head as well. The officer then turned to Robert and ordered him to clean the boots. When Robert also refused, the officer struck him in the head with his saber, knocking him senseless to the floor.

Bleeding from his wounds, Andy was ordered, under threat of death, to mount a horse and lead the detail of dragoons to the home of a prominent patriot named Thompson. Andy complied with the demand but took the British a roundabout way that allowed Thompson to see them coming across a field a half mile away. As the dragoons approached to within a hundred yards, Thompson burst through the door of his house, leaped onto his saddled horse, sped from the farmyard, and plunged his mount and himself into the swollen creek that streamed in a torrent past his house. He escaped on the far side of the creek while the dragoons, unwilling to hazard the flooded stream, reined up on the near side.

Andy was then returned to where his brother Robert and cousin Thomas were being held along with other patriots who had been taken prisoner. With the others, he was marched off to the British post at Camden, some forty miles away, a trip made without food or water. At Camden, Andy, Robert, and Thomas were separated and placed in a building that served as a jail, surrounded by an enclosure. Inside, some 250 men were crammed into a confined space, with no beds, no medicine, no medical treatment for the wounded, and a meager ration of stale bread, provided once a day. Their loyalist enemies stripped them of much of their clothing, Andy losing his shoes and his coat, which he needed to keep warm during the chill nights of the early spring of 1781.

Not long after they were herded into the prison, smallpox broke out, with nothing to check its spread, nothing to ameliorate its effects, and no one to care for its victims. Both Andy and Robert, whose head wound had not been treated and had not healed, soon developed the early flulike symptoms—high fever, vomiting, intense headaches, and backache.

Elizabeth Jackson, meanwhile, was attempting to free her sons. She had made her way to Camden while negotiations for a prisoner exchange were going on between a patriot militia captain and the British commander at Camden, Lieutenant Colonel Francis Rawdon, a twenty-six-year-old Irish nobleman. Elizabeth talked Rawdon into having her two boys included among the seven patriot fighters, all from the Waxhaws, to be released in exchange for thirteen British soldiers taken captive by the Americans.

Elizabeth had two horses on which to make the journey home. On one rode Robert, so sick from smallpox and his infected wound that he had to be held in the saddle by his comrades as they strode beside his horse. On the other mount rode Elizabeth. At the tail end of the forlorn little caravan walked Andy, tormented by fever, plodding barefoot and coatless for forty miles, much of the trip being made in a driving rain.

When they at last reached home, Elizabeth put both boys to bed and struggled to keep them alive. Despite her efforts, Robert succumbed two days later. She then devoted all her energy to saving her one remaining son, now wildly delirious, his body covered with foul-smelling, suppurating sores.

Remarkably, Andy survived. For months, however, into the summer of 1781, he was an invalid. While he was recovering, Elizabeth, apparently satisfied that her son was out of danger, volunteered her nursing services in a heroic effort to save the lives of two of her Crawford nephews, William and Joseph, and other American prisoners of war who were being held by the British aboard two prison ships in Charleston harbor. An epidemic of "ship's fever"—cholera—had swept through the vessels.

Realizing the danger she would face by exposing herself to the cholera victims, Elizabeth bade Andy good-bye with words that sounded like a final farewell. She told him to make friends by being honest and to keep them by being steadfast. "Never tell a lie," she said, "nor take what is not your own . . . nor sue for slander. . . . Settle them cases yourself."[9]

With two other women from the Waxhaws, Elizabeth then set out on her mission of mercy. She never returned. She died of cholera, and the disease also took the life of Joseph Crawford. William Crawford survived. In November 1781, a month after General George Washington's decisive victory over the British at Yorktown, Virginia, Elizabeth Hutchinson Jackson was buried along with other cholera victims in an unmarked grave outside Charleston.

Andy received the news of his mother's death along with a package containing her spare clothes. At age fourteen, having already lost his two brothers, he was now an orphan. "I felt utterly alone," he said later, remembering that awful day, "and I tried to recall her last words to me."[10]

## .·. 2 .·.

# A Life on His Own

ANDY tried living with some of his relatives—the McKemeys (Elizabeth's sister Margaret and her husband), the Thomas Crawfords, and Joseph White, who was Mrs. Crawford's uncle. None of these arrangements lasted long. At the Crawfords' he got into a scrape with another houseguest, a Captain Galbraith, whose thick Scottish brogue Andy found amusing. When Andy mimicked it, Galbraith took offense and threatened to beat Andy with a horsewhip to teach him better manners.

Unintimidated, Andy chillingly warned Galbraith that if he lifted his whip hand to him, he had better be prepared to meet his Maker.[1] At that tense point, Crawford stepped in and broke up the confrontation. Shortly after that incident, Andy was sent to stay with Joseph White and was apprenticed to a saddle maker, whose occupation Andy cared for not at all. He quit the apprenticeship after six months.

His companions in those days were the teenage sons of Charleston residents who had fled to the Waxhaws to escape the British occupation of their city, many of them families wealthy enough to afford idleness and to indulge their children. Andy promptly adopted their lifestyle of drinking, cockfighting, horse racing, and gambling, all of which tended to alienate him from his Waxhaws relatives.

In December 1782, more than a year after Cornwallis's defeat at Yorktown, the British pulled out of Charleston, and those who had found refuge in the Waxhaws moved back to reclaim their homes and their lives. Not long after that event, a windfall came to Andy. His grandfather, Hugh Jackson, the Carrickfergus weaver, died and left him an inheritance of three to four hundred pounds sterling, enough, probably, to make something of the two-hundred-acre farm to which he now held sole title, or enough to pay his way through a school that would provide him a profession. Neither of those sensible options was in Andy's mind, however. Instead of using the money to prepare for his future, he took it and, on a fine horse he had acquired, set out in March 1783 for Charleston to rejoin his friends there and resume the frivolous life he had shared with them.

In Charleston his small fortune was soon dissipated in gambling and high living, and he fell into debt to his landlord. At the end of his financial rope, sixteen-year-old Andy wandered into a gaming house, where he was challenged to a dice game. The challenger put up two hundred dollars against Andy's good-looking horse, winner take all. Andy accepted and won.

Sobered by the discovery of how quickly his fortunes could ebb and flow, Andy took his winnings and paid off his landlord the next morning, then mounted his horse and rode back home to the Waxhaws. "My calculation," he later recalled,

> was that, if a loser in the game, I would give the landlord my saddle and bridle, as far as they would go toward the payment of his bill, ask a credit for the balance, and walk away from the city; but being successful, I had new spirits infused into me, left the table, and from that moment to the present time I have never thrown dice for a wager.[2]

Back home, he decided to return to school, this time in nearby Charlotte, North Carolina;[3] evidently he acquired enough additional education to land himself a job as a teacher in a school near home. By now Andy had developed an eye for more than horses. Girls had become a big interest to him, and he drew notice from several. Susan Smart described him as a "lank, leaning-forward fellow" and remarked that there was "something very agreeable about him."[4] Mary Massey, whose family lived on a farm adjoining that of Major Robert Crawford, thought not so well of him, while her neighbor, Mary Crawford, the major's daughter, was apparently pleased with Andy's attention toward her.[5]

Restless, Andy soon decided to give up teaching and train to become a lawyer. He applied to the most celebrated lawyer in the Carolina backcountry, Waightstill Avery of Morganton, North Carolina, asking to become his student. Avery turned him down. Andy then applied to Spruce Macay of Salisbury, North Carolina, another eminent attorney. Macay accepted him. In December 1784 Andy had what one source calls "a tender parting" with Mary Crawford on the bank of the Catawba River,[6] and he then set out for Salisbury, some fifty-five miles to the north, leaving the Waxhaws, never to return.

By Christmas 1784 he had found lodging at Rowan House, a modest tavern in Salisbury, where for four shillings a day he bought room and board for himself and his horse. He then took up his studies in Macay's law office, a small boxlike building on the front lawn of Macay's mansion. Andy joined two other young men who were reading law with Macay.

Remaining true to form, he soon reverted to his former habits. According to one commentator on his behavior in those days, "Andrew Jackson was the most roaring, rollicking, game-cocking, horse-racing, card-playing, mischievous fellow that ever lived in Salisbury . . . the head of the rowdies hereabouts . . . more in the stable than in the office."[7] His mischiefmaking, assisted presumably by his friends, included hauling off outhouses and removing signposts. His escapades included girls as well as his male drinking companions.

The girls of Salisbury welcomed Andy's company. One of them, Nancy Jarret, said that she

> often met him at parties, balls and . . . at the house of my relative, Mr. McKay. I knew him as well as I did any other young man when I was a single girl . . . for his ways and manners . . . were most captivating. . . . We all knew that he was wild . . . that he gambled some and was by no means a Christian young man. . . . When he was calm he talked slowly and with good selected language. But . . . animated . . . he would talk fast with a very marked North-Irish brogue. . . . Either calm or animated there was something about

> him I cannot describe except to say that it was a presence. . . . This I and all the other girls in Salisbury. . .talked about among ourselves.[8]

Andy had a long, thin face and reddish blond hair that grew thick and wild and fell across his high forehead. Still remarkably slender, he stood six foot one without his boots on. Although he was not conventionally handsome, there nevertheless was something compelling about his appearance. His posture was unusually erect, making his height all the more imposing, and his remarkably expressive, dark blue eyes would blaze fiercely when he became agitated. Taken together, his carriage, manner, movements, and features gave him an air of charisma.[9] He conveyed an attitude of competence, instilling in others a feeling that he was in charge and that they could look to him to handle whatever situation had arisen.

Andy did not finish his legal training with Macay but in 1786 moved from Macay's law office to that of John Stokes, another prominent North Carolina attorney. He completed his studies under Stokes six months later. On September 26, 1787, at age twenty, he appeared before Judge Samuel Ashe and Judge John F. Williams of the Superior Court of Law and Equity of North Carolina to be tested for his knowledge of the law. Following his examination, Ashe and Williams ordered that "Andrew Jackson . . . a person of unblemished moral character and . . . competent . . . knowledge of the law [be admitted to practice] in the said several courts of pleas and quarter sessions. . .with all and singular the privileges and emoluments which. . .appertain to attorneys."[10]

Andy Jackson, that wild but captivating young man from the Waxhaws, was a lawyer at last. Nancy Jarret, among others, was at the courthouse to see him licensed. He showed up, she said, in "a new suit, with broad-cloth coat [and] ruffled shirt" and with his "dark red hair combed carefully back . . . and, I suspect, made to lay down smooth with bear's oil."[11] It was a while, however, before the young attorney settled down to a practice that would earn him a steady income. For the next year he bounced around North Carolina, practicing law when he could find clients to represent, spending time with friends when he could not. In Richmond, North Carolina, he reportedly offered to defend an accused thief with a guarantee of acquittal or else there would be no fee. The accused was found guilty and sentenced to the whipping post, and Jackson slipped out of town owing a bill for his board (a matter that much later would cause him embarrassment).

After several months it became obvious to Andy that he needed to find more fertile ground for his lawyering. A friend, John McNairy, one of the two other young men who had studied law with Andy in the Macay law office, had been recently elected by the state legislature to be judge of the newly founded Superior Court in the so-called Western District. That westernmost part of North Carolina stretched all the way to the Mississippi River and would later become the new state of Tennessee. McNairy's powers as judge included the authority to appoint a public prosecutor for the district. He offered the job to Andy, who, responding to this clear call of opportunity and to his own energetic spirit of adventure, promptly accepted. McNairy appointed Thomas Searcy, another fellow student at Macay's law office, clerk of the court in the district, and the three young lawyers, in the company of others moving west, set out from Morganton, North Carolina, in the spring of 1788 to hack out of the wild frontier new lives for themselves.

The road from Morganton led northwest over and through the Great Smoky Mountains to Jonesborough, then the leading settlement in the eastern part of the district (later to become east Tennessee). Nearly three hundred miles west of Jonesborough, along the banks of the tortuous Cumberland River, rose the leading settlement of the western half of the district, at the center of which was the town of Nashville. Between the two settlements lay a mountainous, wooded wilderness wherein travelers faced almost every natural danger in addition to the constant threat of hostile Indians. It was to Nashville that Andy and his comrades intended to go. They would wait in Jonesborough, though, until enough other westward-bound immigrants gathered to form a caravan of sufficient numbers to discourage Indian attacks and to await the arrival of an armed escort from Nashville.

A settlement on the Cumberland River had been established in 1779, largely through the efforts of James Robertson and John Donelson, and had spread out some eighty-five miles along the river, where farming flourished. By 1788, when Andy and his friends were ready to ride into it, the settlement had swelled to a population of nearly five thousand inhabitants, despite the ever-present danger of Indian attacks. Before the conclusion of the Revolutionary War, in 1783, the British had fomented Indian attacks on the settlers. Later the Spanish, in hopes of halting American expansion, took a turn at having the settlers and new immigrants harassed by Indians, who generally needed little or no encouragement.

In September 1788 the wagon train that Andy and his friends had been waiting to form finally left Jonesborough, escorted by an armed guard of sixteen men provided by the state of North Carolina. The train of immigrants would be following the newly opened Cumberland Road, which would take them through a gap in the Cumberland Mountains and then on to Nashville. It was not long before the threat of an Indian attack materialized.

While the travelers slept one night on the trail, Andy and the caravan's sentries kept watch over the group. At about ten o'clock, he heard suspicious owl calls. He roused his fellow travelers and urged them to break camp and move out immediately. They quickly mounted their wagons and horses and fled into the night. Sometime later a party of five hunters happened upon the abandoned camp and decided to spend the rest of the night there. The next morning the bodies of four of the five hunters were found at the campsite. They had all been scalped.[12]

The train of immigrants finally reached its destination, Nashville, on Sunday, October 26, 1788. The town consisted of two taverns, one distillery, two stores, one courthouse, and a scattering of cabins, tents, and wagon camps, encircled by a fence to keep roaming buffalo at a safe distance.

To find a place to live, Andy tried the best lodgings available, the home of John Donelson's widow, who owned a cabin near the blockhouse in which she lived, a few miles outside Nashville. Mrs. Donelson did not really need the money that Andy would pay her for room and board; she was mainly interested in having another good gun hand to help her fight off marauding Indians. She agreed to let Andy stay there. She also took in John Overton, another lawyer, who shared the cabin with Andy and would become Andy's good friend.

It was at Mrs. Donelson's that Andy met Rachel Donelson Robards, the widow's daughter, who had recently returned home after being separated from her husband, Lewis Robards, whom she had married three years earlier, when she was seventeen. Rachel was attractive, vivacious, and bright. "She was irresistible to men," one of her relatives concluded. "Medium height, beautifully moulded form, full red lips," and an oval, olive face "rippling with smiles and dimples."[13] Another pronounced her to be "the best storyteller, the best dancer, the sprightliest companion, the most dashing horsewoman in the western country."[14]

Her marriage to Robards, from a well-to-do family in Mercer County, Kentucky, had proved a mistake. He was inordinately jealous and suspicious concerning his wife. She, being naturally outgoing and flirtatious, brought out the worst in him. While they were living with his mother in her grand house near Harrodsburg, Kentucky, the elder Mrs. Robards took in a boarder named Peyton Short, a young attorney who, attracted to Rachel, became attentive to her. Also boarding at the Robards home at the time was John Overton, who apparently was a family friend of the Robardses. One day Robards came home and found Rachel and Short on the porch chatting in a way that Robards thought much too familiar. A heated quarrel erupted, and Robards could not be mollified, even though his mother defended Rachel, and Short swore that relations between them were completely innocent. Fuming, Robards ordered Rachel never to show her face in his house again and sent word to the Donelsons, ordering them to fetch her back to Nashville. The widow Donelson sent her son Samuel to Kentucky to bring his sister home.

It did not take long for Robards to realize he had overreacted, for he found life desolate without Rachel. He asked John Overton to go to Rachel and implore her to forgive him. That mission was one of the reasons Overton was at Mrs. Donelson's at the same time Andy was. Overton's appeal evidently was effective, for Rachel gave in and allowed Robards to join her at her mother's house. She now, however, had caught Andy's eye. She, in turn, was as much attracted to him as he was to her.

Robards's jealousy soon erupted again, now with Andy as the object of his wrath. Overton happened onto Rachel and her mother crying one day and discovered that Robards had accused Rachel of carrying on with Andy. Andy, though, was unaware of the incident, and Overton could not bring himself to inform him. Another incident occurred later, and this time Andy heard about it. Robards had gone out with a group of women who were picking blackberries, accompanied by several guards who were there to protect them against hostile Indians. During the outing, Robards remarked to one of the guards that he thought Jackson was too intimate with his wife. The guard took Robards's words to Andy, who responded with characteristic fury. He confronted Robards, vowing that if he ever again associated Andy's name with Rachel's, he would cut his ears out of his head.

Robards immediately ran for help. He went to the first magistrate he could find and filed a complaint. Andy was arrested and ordered to appear in court to face the charge. On the day of the hearing, Andy, escorted by guards and followed by Robards as they all walked to the courthouse, asked one of the guards to let him borrow the hunting knife he was carrying in a sheath. When the guard handed it over, Andy, looking back at Robards and catching his eye, carefully fingered the sharp edge and point of the knife, sending a silent, threatening message. Robards understood. He broke from the group and dashed off. Andy and the guards proceeded to the courthouse, where the complaint was dismissed because the complainant, Robards, failed to appear.[15]

Once that threat was over, Robards returned to the Donelson home, where he became increasingly belligerent. Another of Mrs. Donelson's boarders, John Downing, wrote his observations of Robards's behavior toward Rachel, which, he said, "was cruel, unmanly and unkind in the extreme." He said that "Lewis Robards was in the habit within my knowledge of leaving his wife's bed and spending the night with the negro women." Downing wrote that Robards's sister-in-law "fully corroborates all I have said. She states that the breach arose from Robards own cruel and improper conduct."[16]

Andy, wishing to avoid further trouble, moved out of Mrs. Donelson's cabin and became a boarder at the home of Casper Mansker, another pioneer settler of the Cumberland. Sometime after that, Robards created another big scene with Rachel, then mounted his horse and rode off, vowing he would divorce Rachel. He headed back to Kentucky, leaving Nashville for the last time and leaving Andy without a rival for Rachel's charms.

Despite his personal problems, Andy was doing well professionally. In Nashville he found a huge backlog of cases awaiting him, most of them apparently involving debt. Within the first thirty days that he was on the job, he enforced seventy writs against debtors who had refused to pay merchants and others for goods and services provided. He quickly won the support of creditors who, thanks to Andy's vigorous prosecution, at last received the money owed them by deadbeats who had avoided payment by bribes, through the incompetence of the sheriff, and by sheer defiance of the law. He developed a private practice that soon kept him busy with cases involving debt, land titles, sales, and assaults. As his practice flourished, he traveled frequently between Nashville and Jonesborough to represent clients, despite the continuing menace of Indians.

In the autumn of 1790 (or perhaps in January 1791, as John Overton much later recalled the events), a rumor reached Nashville that Lewis Robards had changed his mind again about his wife and had announced that he was returning to Nashville to take her back to Kentucky, by force if necessary. Horrified, Rachel quickly made plans to flee to safety. A party of traders was preparing to embark from Nashville on a trip to Natchez, forming a small flotilla of barges that would float down the Cumberland to the Ohio River, then on into the Mississippi. Rachel pleaded with John Stark, the captain of one of the vessels, to take her aboard as a passenger, which Stark was reluctant to do. The voyage would be through hostile Indian country, and the party would face the possibility of having to fight off Indian attacks, in addition to facing the ordinary perils of a river journey of some two thousand miles. Stark did not want to expose the daughter of John Donelson to such dangers. In addition, he apparently did not want the responsibility of having to protect a young woman on so hazardous a venture.

Rachel, however, whom Stark knew, remained determined to go. Beginning to yield, Stark, according to Overton's account, agreed to take her if Andy Jackson—apparently commonly known to be her suitor—would accompany her and assume the role of her protector. With negligible hesitation, Andy signed on. He placed his law practice in the care of his friend John Overton, and either in the autumn of 1790 or in the "winter or spring" of 1791, as Overton later said,[17] Andy and the young woman who had won his heart shoved off into the current of the Cumberland, bound for Natchez—and for a lifetime of controversy.

∴ 3 ∴

# The Nobleman's Son

IN the autumn of 1777 Edward Michael Pakenham, the second Baron Longford, was at peace with himself and satisfied with his situation in life. At Pakenham Hall, his mansion in County Westmeath, in Ireland's midlands, he reflected on his contentment. He was, he wrote in his journal, "as happily situated as a man could be, my Home of Pakenham Hall repaired and made comfortable, the Debts into which I found my Estate encumbered nearly discharged, my circumstances easy tho' my income was not great, blessed with the best of wives and with a promising and pleasing family of a son and four daughters."[1]

In December 1777, not many weeks after he had penned those happy words, he was recalled to active duty in the navy of His Majesty King George III, then contending not only with the rebellion of his subjects in his thirteen American colonies but also with the threat presented by the formidable navy of France, now openly supporting the revolution in America. Following orders, in January 1778 Captain Lord Longford—Pakenham, that is—sailed from his home in Ireland to England to assume command of the British frigate *America* and to join the fleet of Admiral Augustus Keppel, commander of Britain's Home Fleet, which was guarding the English Channel against the French.

Pakenham was a descendant of the Edward Pakenham who had come to Ireland in 1576 and had become part of the landowning English aristocracy there. "A man of strong practical sense and decided temper who gave his opinion in few words," was the way one of his friends, Richard Lovell Edgeworth, described him, judging him to be "shrewd humoured . . . good and kind-hearted without parade . . . in short, a well born, well-bred British naval officer."[2]

Three months after Pakenham departed for duty, on April 18, 1778, Lady Longford, his wife, the former Catherine Rowley, gave birth to a sixth child, a second son. She named him Edward Michael Pakenham, after his father. (She was later to give birth to three more sons, Hercules Robert, William, and Henry.)

Pakenham returned home in 1781, in the same year that His Majesty's army under Lieutenant General Charles Cornwallis was forced to surrender to General George Washington at Yorktown, Virginia, thereby ending British hopes for success in the war with the American rebels. Back home, resuming his domestic responsibilities, Pakenham concerned himself with the education of his children, particularly his sons. He had observed the character and behavior of the sons of some of his friends, young men who apparently had been assigned to service aboard the vessels that Pakenham had commanded. He found them a sorry lot, calling them "dishonest, drunken, ignorant, self-sufficient and quarrelsome."[3] He resolved to do better by his own boys.

His eldest son, Thomas, he sent first to Diss, a well-known school in Norfolk, England. Later he sent Thomas to the Royal Classic School in Armagh, in northern Ireland. Evidently satisfied with that school, in December 1788 he sent Edward there also, when the boy was ten years old. The school, with its myriad rules and regimentation, would be a vast change from what Edward had been used to—living carefree in comfortable old Pakenham Hall (which came equipped with a wooded park, a lake for swimming and boating, and a stable of ponies) and looked after by an understanding, tolerant mother who let her children climb trees, dig holes, and build piers in the lake. Her one overarching rule for them was, "Give no extra trouble. If you make a mess, clean it up yourself."[4]

In 1792, when young Edward was fourteen years old, his father died at age forty-nine. Two years later Edward left school to begin a career in the army, which was not at all unusual for the second son of an aristocrat to do, the first son having been ordained by tradition to inherit the title and estate of the father, and the second and other sons left to find something else useful to do. Although he may have been keen on leaving school when he did, Edward came to regret having his formal education ended so early. "I should wish the boys to be removed from Armagh when a good place preparatory to Cambridge [University] can be ascertained," he later wrote concerning his nephews' education. "The system is no doubt the most expensive, but money in such a case is well laid out and, if any other means are insufficient, I am willing to turn American bear and live on my paws to give such boys the means of a gentleman's life on a gentleman's education."[5]

On May 28, 1794, less than six weeks after his sixteenth birthday, Edward became a lieutenant in the Ninety-second Foot Regiment. Three days later he was promoted to captain in the same regiment, and on December 6, still sixteen years old, he became a major in the Thirty-third Light Dragoons. His breathtakingly rapid rise in grade occurred because of the former British system of having officers buy their commissions and promotions. It was a way to ensure that the officer corps, the leaders of the nation's military forces, was composed of men of means and privilege who were presumed sympathetic to the establishment, posing no threat of armed rebellion against a government run by their own kind. Even under the purchase system, though, Edward's meteoric rise was unusual. A twentieth-century Pakenham family member, Valerie McNair Scott, commenting on Edward's quick promotions, theorized that Lady Longford, Edward's mother, may have been "exceptionally generous with purchase money."[6]

Actually, his duties in the regiment were probably not so demanding, and he had time to learn on the job. It was not until May 1798, four years after he had entered the army, that he saw active duty, when the Irish Rising of 1798 broke out. Among the British forces called out to keep Ireland under English domination was Edward's regiment. Theobald Wolfe Tone, a thirty-five-year-old Irish lawyer and patriot, had stirred his countrymen to resist continued English tyranny. He rallied Catholic and Presbyterian Irishmen alike to rise to arms against the English king, George III (who some twenty-three years earlier had vainly attempted to suppress an American rebellion), against the king's Anglo-Irish establishment, and against the sycophantic Irish parliament in which Catholics, who constituted 75 percent of Ireland's population, were precluded by law from serving, and for whose members they were not allowed to vote.[7] The Pakenham family, however, held at least two seats of their own in the Irish parliament, apparently representing none but themselves and their king. "I have now seen," Tone wrote in his journal in 1797,

> the Parliament of Ireland, the Parliament of England, the Congress of the United States of America, the *Corps Legislatif* of France and the *Convention Batave* . . . so that I have seen, in the way of deliberative bodies as many I believe as most men; and of all those I have mentioned, beyond all comparison the most shamefully profligate and abandoned of all sense of virtue, principle, or even common decency, was the legislature of my own unfortunate country. The scoundrels! I lose my temper every time I think of them![8]

The rising was halfheartedly supported by the French, whom Tone had enlisted to the cause but who promised more help than they delivered. For a time the rebels, in a burst of success, threatened to overrun the Pakenham family estates in Westmeath, advancing to within sight of Pakenham Hall, but they were eventually thrown back and dispersed by a superior pro-British force. By the end of November 1798, the king's army had succeeded in quashing the rebellion, Tone having been captured and martyred and many of his followers, as well as innocent civilians, having lost their lives in a cruel, vengeful campaign of suppression. According to a Pakenham family source, "Both Edward and his uncle, Captain Thomas Pakenham, distinguished themselves [in the suppression of the rebellion]; and General Lake [the British commander] mentioned them in his official dispatches."[9]

Following the conclusion of the rebellion, Edward received a new promotion, to lieutenant colonel, at age twenty-two, and was transferred to the Sixty-fourth Regiment, posted in Chelmsford, England. Two months later King George III visited the regiment there, an event Edward "recorded with jubilation."[10]

In January 1801 Edward's regiment received orders to march to Portsmouth and there board ships bound for the West Indies, by way of Nova Scotia. It would be Edward's first voyage to North America. His vessel set sail on February 7 and after a fifty-three-day Atlantic crossing, reached Halifax, Nova Scotia, where Edward spent some time before reembarking. During his stay in Halifax he decided the town was beautiful but its residents provincial.[11] Apparently from his contacts with people there, including the British governor, Sir George Prevost, Edward concluded that antipathy toward the British, nearly twenty years after the Revolutionary War had ended, was still running high in America. His remarks written in a letter betray something of an aristocratic hauteur on his part and a loose grip on the reality of popular feeling in the United States. "There is no saying," he offered, "how far the intrigue of Bonaparte and the hatred of Jefferson against England may mislead the ignorant and unprincipled multitude of the great Southern towns [of the United States]."[12] He was speaking as if Americans, who for years had suffered the high-handedness of British government policies (and would continue to do so for years to come), as well as the brutalities of Britain's war to keep its colonists in subjection, needed the influence of the then president Thomas Jefferson, or anyone else, to inspire enmity toward England.

After the stop in Halifax, Edward's regiment sailed to British-settled Barbados, then to the Danish island of Saint Croix, which Edward reached by midsummer of 1801 and where he was apparently happy to come comfortably to rest while in "support of his Britannic majesty's interest," as he put it.[13] From Saint Croix he went back to Barbados and in August 1802 was on Saint Kitts, where in a letter he acknowledged the gifts sent him from home—a trunkful of "books, boots and other snuggeries."[14] In February 1803 he and his regiment were back at Barbados, which Britain was using as a staging area for its troops operating in the West Indies, to which its imminent war with Napoleon's France was expected to spread.

In June 1803, following Britain's declaration of war against France, Edward's commander, General Grinfield, received orders to take the

French-held islands of Saint Lucia, Martinique, and Tobago, all in the Windward chain of islands. On June 20, 1803, Edward and his Sixty-fourth Regiment, part of a force of some three thousand British troops, sailed from Barbados for an assault on Saint Lucia.

The fleet bearing the British troops arrived off Saint Lucia at daybreak on June 21, and before the day was over, the British had taken the island's protective fortress, suffering a 138 casualties in the process, one of whom was Edward Pakenham, shot just below the neck as he led his regiment in the assault. He was carried from the fortress's glacis, where he had fallen, by a French family who took him to their home and treated his wound, repaying him, reportedly, for his kindness in saving French women from British troops' brutality following an earlier battle. On July 20, 1803, he wrote to his mother from Barbados to let her know he was making a speedy recovery. Some weeks later, in the autumn of 1803, he was ordered home to recuperate further.

During the three years that Edward had been gone, changes had occurred at home. Pakenham Hall had undergone renovation and expansion. His brother Hercules had become an ensign in the army, his brother William had become a lieutenant in the navy, and two of his sisters had married and had children.

Back in England, Edward received a promotion to brevet colonel and was transferred to the Seventh Royal Fusilier Regiment. It was about this time that he developed a love interest. According to one account, he had become engaged. The young woman who was his reported fiancée, Emily Napier, however, apparently decided against marrying him, perhaps under the influence of her mother, Lady Sarah Napier, who regarded Edward as less than a prize catch and wrote to a friend about him:

> Emily is in high beauty. Edward Pakenham is expected to-day and will interest her a great deal; it was told she was to marry Ed P., and it appeared as completely ridiculous to us all that of course if you hear it, you may contradict it; for you may guess Emily will make a more refined choice than a tiresome little P; . . . even if he is improved, it is but a Pakenham at best.[15]

Edward's sister Catherine, whom everyone called Kitty, was about to make a spectacular catch. Arthur Wellesley had met Kitty years earlier when her father was a member of the Irish parliament, in Dublin. She was a pretty, petite, chatty, vivacious girl who loved reading books of all kinds, a popular young member of Dublin society. Arthur was a young British army officer, a younger son of the first Earl Mornington, an Anglo-Irish aristocrat who had estates in County Meath. Arthur was attracted to Kitty, and she to him. But her father, and later her brother Thomas, who succeeded her father as baron and head of the family, disapproved of Arthur as a marriage prospect, believing Kitty could do better. Refused permission to wed Kitty, Arthur promised her that one day, when his prospects had become brighter, he would prove himself more acceptable; when that happened, he said, he would still feel the same toward her.

Years went by. Arthur became Major General Sir Arthur Wellesley, a celebrated military hero in India and a man of means. He was still unmarried, as was Kitty. She, though, was engaged to another army officer, Lowry Cole, the second son of the Earl of Enniskillen. When she learned that her old flame, now famous, was still interested in her (although he had never written to her, nor she to him, all the time he was making a name for himself in India), she broke off her engagement to Cole, causing much anguish to herself as well as to him. To the mutual friend who had informed her of Wellesley's continued interest, Kitty wrote worriedly: "I am very much changed and you know it within these last three years, so much that I doubt whether it would now be in my power to contribute [to] the comfort or happiness of any body who has not been in the habit of loving me for years like my Brother or you or my Mother."[16]

At age thirty-four, Kitty had become thin and worn-looking, her youthful prettiness and vivacity having faded. Warned by friends of her changed appearance, Wellesley, three years older than Kitty, said he did not care about that, that it was her mind he cared for.[17] In April 1806 he sailed for Ireland from England to claim his bride. Edward also sailed for Ireland, with his regiment, in time to attend Kitty's wedding to the man who would soon become one of England's greatest heroes of all time.

To help combat the growing menace of Napoleon's ambitions, England demanded that Denmark surrender its fleet of warships to prevent it from falling into Napoleon's hands. Even though England promised to return the ships when the war with France was over, Denmark refused. In August 1807 England sent an expeditionary force to Copenhagen to seize the Danish fleet. Edward, his brother Hercules, and his new brother-in-law, General Wellesley, were all part of the expedition. Wellesley was placed in command of a division that was to be the reserve force in the attack, but as events unfolded he led his troops against a Danish force that sallied out from Copenhagen's defenses to engage the British invaders. In a battle at the port city of Koge on August 29, Wellesley defeated the Danish defenders, allowing the British to besiege Copenhagen, Wellesley's troops taking positions beside the city's walls. Following a prolonged British bombardment, Copenhagen was surrendered to the British commander, Lieutenant General Sir William Cathcart, on September 6.

The Danish mission accomplished, Edward returned with his regiment to England. Not long afterward, he was off again, to Nova Scotia. His ship, the *Flora,* arrived at Halifax in April 1808. He and his regiment waited there until December before embarking for Barbados, where a ten-thousand-man British army was being assembled for an assault on the French island of Martinique. Edward and his regiment reached Barbados on December 29, and Edward was briefed on the attack plan drawn up by the expedition's commander, Major General George Beckwith. The plan called for a massive, main assault on the island's protective fortress, Fort Royal, from the west. A secondary assault would be launched from the east and would include the Seventh Fusiliers, Edward's regiment. On February 1, 1809, the British attacked, and in the successful assault, Edward was struck by a gunshot in his shoulders.

"The shot passed from the right to the left shoulder, quite at the lower part of the neck!" he wrote, describing the wound to his mother.

"It took leave of me within a hair's breadth of the last"—a reference to his previous neck wound. "Nearly satisfied with self, delighted with my comrades and proud of my leader, [Sir George] Prevost, I am hourly mending."[18]

Edward had again narrowly escaped death on the field of battle.

Returning home, he reached London in August 1809. There he found news concerning his brother-in-law. At Talavera, Spain, on July 27 and 28, Wellesley had won a ferocious battle with a French army twice the size of his own (twenty thousand versus forty thousand), losing some five thousand of his men in the fight but inflicting some seven thousand casualties among the troops commanded by Joseph Bonaparte, Napoleon's brother. "It was the hardest fought battle of modern times," Wellesley reported. "Never was there such a Murderous Battle!" For his achievement, Wellesley was rewarded by being created Baron Douro of Wellesley and Viscount Wellington of Talavera. Edward's brother-in-law was now Lord Wellington.

Edward was torn between his admiration for Wellington and his love for his sister Kitty, whose marriage with Wellington, never on firm ground, was growing increasingly shaky. Friends of the couple may have inferred problems between the two from the very beginning when, after a brief honeymoon, they had returned in a carriage with her sitting inside it and him seated outside. Wellington's brother, the Reverend Gerald Wellesley, who had performed their wedding ceremony, must have had an idea of how Wellington felt toward Kitty; even before the wedding, Wellington had confided to Gerald, "She has grown ugly, by Jove."[19]

Everyone who knew the couple realized they were flagrantly ill matched. He was a stickler for detail and a master of it. She was the opposite. He was carefully organized in his thoughts and habits. She was not. He was a take-charge person. She struggled to handle what she was asked to do. A letter that Wellington wrote to Kitty while he was away and she was supposed to be tending to the affairs of their estate reveals his feelings of frustration with her, providing an intimate peek into the life they uncomfortably shared:

> I enclose a letter from a Bricklayer. I thought you had paid him. Let me know whether you have or not. . . . Let the Gardener [who had been fired] be taken back. . . . I am much concerned that you should have thought of concealing from me any want of money. . . . I don't understand how this want occurred or why it was concealed. . . . I acknowledge that the conclusion I draw from your conduct upon the occasion is that you must be Mad, or you must consider me to be a Brute, & most particularly fond & avaricious of money. Once for all you require no permission to talk to me upon any subject you please; all that I request is that a [fuss] not be made about trifles . . . & that you may not go into tears because I don't think them deserving of an uncommon degree of attention. . . . It is to be hoped that at some time or other I shall be better understood."[20]

Impractical, disorganized, nearsighted Kitty stood in awe of her illustrious husband, making communication between the two of them extremely difficult and rare. Talking to her about his concerns, he confided to a friend, was as useful as talking to a child. When at home, he complained, he had "no creature to speak to"; discussing political or important subjects "was like talking Hebrew to her."[21] Nevertheless, she managed to conceive twice and bear Wellington two sons.

Edward apparently refused to allow his feelings for his sister to color his attitude toward Wellington. When, in August 1809, Edward was sent to Portugal to deliver dispatches to his brother-in-law, he saw the opportunity he sought "to link his fortunes with the Spanish army,"[22] fighting under the leadership of Wellington. That opportunity was to provide the crucial turning point in Edward's military career.

## ∴ 4 ∴

# The Man Who Would Be General

By May 1791 Andy Jackson, needing to attend to his professional duties, had returned to Nashville, having satisfied himself that Rachel was safe and comfortable as a guest in the home of a friend, Abner Green, a wealthy planter who lived with his family in a mansion once the country home of the Spanish commandant at Natchez, Don Manuel Gayoso de Lemos, about twenty miles from Natchez. While back in Nashville, Andy heard welcome news: Lewis Robards had obtained a divorce from Rachel.

What was disturbing about the news, however, particularly to the Donelsons, Rachel's family, were the allegations that Robards had made to support his petition for divorce. They infuriated Andy. Robards claimed that his wife had deserted him and since then had been living in adultery with another man. The other man, of course, was Andy, whose first impulse now was to track down Robards and at pistol point make him retract those allegations.[1] Instead, however, Andy sought out the widow Donelson and requested her permission to marry Rachel, which he received.

Andy eagerly returned to Natchez to wed Rachel. Accounts of what happened next vary. According to one account,[2] the wedding was held in August 1791 in the parlor of Springfield, the stately brick home of Thomas Marston Green Jr., not far from Abner Green's mansion, where Rachel had been staying.[3] Thomas Green's father, a magistrate (or former magistrate), reportedly performed the ceremony.

From Springfield Andy and his bride traveled to a trading post Andy had earlier established on Bayou Pierre, near Natchez. In a nearby log house that stood on a bluff overlooking the broad, brown Mississippi, they began their married life, apparently.[4] Two months later, in October 1791, the newlyweds returned to the Nashville area. Andy bought from John Donelson, Rachel's brother, a plantation called Poplar Grove, situated in a bend of the Cumberland River. The honeymoon over, Andy returned to his work and was soon deep in court matters.

Then, in December 1793, came heart-stopping news. Through his friend John Overton, who had seen a transcript of the court proceedings in Harrodsburgh, Kentucky, Andy learned that Robards's divorce from Rachel had been granted only recently, on September 27, 1793. Reports of an earlier divorce decree were now proved false. Andy and Rachel, it turned out, had been married while she was still married to Robards. What had been granted two years earlier was not a divorce but merely permission by the Virginia legislature, which was necessary in divorce cases not only in Virginia but in Kentucky, which at that time was part of Virginia, to sue for a divorce. The bill that the legislature had approved in 1791 read, in part:

> A jury shall be summoned . . . to inquire into the allegations contained in the declaration; . . . and if the jury . . . shall find in substance that the defendant hath deserted the plaintiff, and that she hath lived in adultery with another man since such desertion . . . thereupon the marriage between the said Lewis Roberts [*sic*] and Rachel shall be totally dissolved.[5]

Andy and Rachel suddenly found themselves in a deeply embarrassing, even disgraceful, position, in part because Andy, a lawyer himself, inexplicably had not bothered to verify the report of Robards's divorce before he married Rachel. Equally inexplicable, if the report had originated with Robards, was the fact that he had put out the false information, since a reading of the bill approved by the Virginia legislature clearly showed that he had merely negotiated the first step of the divorce procedure. A letter written at that time by Robards to Rachel's brother-in-law, Robert Hays, concerning a division of Robards's and Rachel's property further suggested that Robards believed the divorce had occurred in 1791. But whether out of ignorance, misunderstanding, or some other cause, Robards had put off filing for the actual divorce for two years after having been granted official permission to do so.

At first Andy refused to even consider going through another wedding ceremony, despite the advice of his friend and fellow attorney John Overton (who, though still Andy's friend, was Robards's lawyer in Nashville). In the eyes of God and in "the understanding of every person in the country," Andy maintained, he and Rachel had become husband and wife in the ceremony in Natchez.[6] It apparently was true that people in the communities along the Cumberland River believed Rachel to have been divorced in 1791 (as eighteen of them, all prominent citizens, would later state); thus Andy and Rachel were not the only ones who believed they had been free to marry that year. In the view of many of their neighbors, they had married in good faith.

Andy soon backed off from his insistence that one wedding ceremony was sufficient. On January 9, 1794, he posted the then usual marriage bond, and affirmation of it was duly made:

> Know all men by these presents that we, Andrew Jackson, Robert Hays and John Overton, of the County Davidson and Territory of the United States of America South of the River Ohio, are held and firmly bound . . . in the sum of one thousand pounds to be paid . . . if there shall . . . hereafter appear any lawful cause why Andrew Jackson and Rachel Donelson, alias Rachel Roberts should not be joined together in holy matrimony.[7]

On January 17, 1794, a marriage license was issued to Andy and Rachel. The wedding took place the next day, the ceremony performed by Robert Hays, who was the Davidson County justice of the peace. Andy and Rachel's legal union was at last completed, though the controversy surrounding it would go on for years.

Marrying into the Donelson family helped Andy attain the life he had tasted as a youth in Charleston. The social connections provided by the large, respected family and the status gained by having become part of it all worked to his advantage, but he was at the same time making a name and a fortune on his own as a lawyer and landowner. He was acquiring sizable tracts of frontier land, much of it for as little as a penny an acre, which he would later sell at an immense profit. Much of that land was received as payment for legal services, his fee sometimes being paid with as much as a square mile of land. He kept extremely busy in his lucrative private law practice. In the four terms of court held in 1794, between Nashville and Jonesborough, Andy acted as counsel in 228 of the courts' 397 cases, or 57 percent of the total.

In February 1791 the territorial governor, William Blount, aware of Andy's diligence, energy, courage, and success as a prosecutor, had offered Andy an appointment as attorney general of the Mero District, the western part, of the territory; Andy had accepted. Blount, concerned that white settlers keep up their end of a new treaty with the Cherokees, needed a tough enforcer. He wanted the treaty, he instructed Brigadier General James Robertson of the territorial militia, "preserved inviolate and if this can not be done I beg you to make examples of the first violators of it. It will be the duty of the Attorney of the District Mr. Jackson to prosecute on Information all such cases and I have no doubt he will readily do it."[8]

On September 10, 1792, Governor Blount appointed Andy judge advocate, or chief legal officer, of the territorial militia's Davidson County cavalry regiment, commanded by Robert Hays, a militia colonel. It was Andy's first military appointment, made apparently entirely on the strength of his legal abilities. He had, however, previously served with the militia as a private, and within six months of arriving on the Cumberland he had participated in a small, bold expedition to punish a band of Indians that had attacked James Robertson's station near Nashville. That action had resulted in the capture of some of the Indians' weapons and much of their supplies, but most of the Indians themselves escaped. Nevertheless, Andy's conduct was so noticeably vigorous that his comrades praised him as "bold, dashing, fearless and mad upon his enemies."[9]

Indian attacks naturally followed white encroachment on Indian lands in violation of treaties. Armed by the Spanish, who sought to prevent further expansion of the territories held by English-speaking settlers, Cherokee warriors made war on the white settlements. They assaulted Robert Hays's blockhouse and killed two of its defenders. From their base near Chattanooga they raided settlements along the Cumberland River, sometimes joined by Creeks and Chickasaws. Andy participated in several retaliatory attacks on Indians, and on August 29, 1793, he managed to escape death when he and a Lieutenant Telford, reconnoitering around Knoxville, the territorial capital, rode into an Indian ambush. An account of the incident stated that "the Lieutenant was taken and . . . put to death. . . . Mr. Jackson made his escape."[10]

Moved in part by continued Indian depredations and by the federal government's ineffectual policies for dealing with the menace, Governor Blount in 1794 began a campaign to have what was popularly called the Southwest Territory admitted to the Union as the state of Tennessee, so that its leaders could handle the Indian problem as they saw fit, without federal hindrances. Peace with the threatening tribes, Blount wrote in a letter to Brigadier General Robertson, "will never arrive until this Territory becomes a State and is represented in Congress."[11]

Following a census to determine that the territory had enough inhabitants to qualify as a state (sixty thousand were needed; seventy-seven thousand were counted) and a plebiscite in which more than 70 percent of those voting favored statehood, a convention was called to draw up a constitution for the proposed new state. In the election to select delegates to the convention, Andy was one of the five men chosen to represent Davidson County.

Tennessee became a state on June 1, 1796, when, following Congress's approval, President George Washington signed the bill that made it the sixteenth state of the United States of America. Elected to represent it in the United States Congress were two political figures from east Tennessee, the former territorial governor, William Blount, and William Cocke, from Hawkins County. The new state was entitled also to have one member of the House of Representatives. Blount, one of Tennessee's two most powerful political leaders (the other being the famed Indian fighter and Revolutionary War hero John Sevier, who was elected Tennessee's first governor), decided that Andrew Jackson was the man for the job. Because the two senators were both from east Tennessee, having a west Tennessean, like Andy, as the state's third member of Congress made political sense. Furthermore, Andy met Blount's other requirements for a candidate. He would be a voice for frontiersmen, taking their position in the matter of the ongoing struggle with Indians. He was also loyal to Blount's political faction and could be depended on to support it. In addition, he was electable.[12] With Blount's support, Andy was elected in the fall of 1796 with only token opposition. At age twenty-nine he would become a member of the United States Congress, the first United States representative from the state of Tennessee.

He was also interested in another election. Tennessee's militia followed the popular militia custom of electing its commanding officers, up to the grades of regimental commanders. The militia's field-grade officers (major and above) elected their brigadier generals, each of whom commanded one of the state's three military districts. The brigadier generals and the other field-grade officers together elected the militia's overall commander, who held the rank of major general. Andy decided he would seek that position, believing that the experience he had accumulated in fighting Indians over the past few years, plus his status as a judge advocate and his natural leadership abilities, would place the position within his grasp.

Tennessee's new governor, John Sevier, had his own candidate, George Conway, whom he wanted to see elected major general, and he used his considerable influence to Conway's advantage. The election was held in November 1796. Conway won. From that losing experience, Andy determinedly set out to prepare for the next time an election of militia commander would be held.

On December 5, 1796, Andy claimed his seat in the House of Representatives in Philadelphia. Within the month, Congressman Jackson seized the opportunity to champion Tennessee militiamen and right the wrong he believed had been committed against them by President

Washington and his secretary of war, Henry Knox. At issue was a petition by Hugh Lawson White, a member of the Tennessee militia who was seeking compensation for his services in a militia campaign against Cherokees three years earlier. Secretary Knox claimed that the campaign was, contrary to law, offensive, not defensive, and that it had been undertaken without presidential authority and in violation of orders from the War Department. Knox and Washington had denied the petition. The congressional Committee of Claims, which stated that although settlers in Tennessee had been harassed and provoked by the Cherokees' repeated murders and thefts, the militia campaign was of doubtful necessity and justice.

Jackson leaped to the defense of the militia. Taking the floor of the House of Representatives, he argued that the campaign, which had been led by John Sevier, most certainly was just and necessary. It was high time, he declared, for the people of Tennessee, through their militia, to take action "when it was seen that war was waged on the State, that the knife and the tomahawk were held over the heads of women and children, that peaceable citizens were murdered." He disputed Secretary Knox's findings, asserting that from June through October 1793 about twelve hundred Indians had attacked the militia, "carried their station and threatened to carry the Seat of Government."[13] The action of the militia was therefore, he insisted, completely defensive and the petitioner's request should be granted. He then offered a resolution to the House: "Resolved, that General Sevier's expedition into the Cherokee Nation, in the year 1793 was a just and necessary measure, and that provision ought to be made by law for paying the expenses involved."[14]

The House declined to take further action that day and adjourned with the matter unresolved. The next day Congressman Jackson again took the floor. This time he attacked the proposition that the militiamen had acted without proper authorization, persuasively putting forth an important principle of military conduct. He argued that the militiamen had been ordered out by a superior officer and that they were therefore bound to obey. Any "contrary doctrine would strike at the very root of subordination," he contended. "It would be saying to soldiers, 'Before you obey the command of your superior officer, you have the right to inquire into the legality of the service upon which you are about to be employed, and, until you are satisfied, you may refuse to take the field.'"[15] Such a doctrine, he asserted, would effectively undermine all military authority. Sevier and his militiamen, he argued, had been required to obey their orders to wage the campaign against the Cherokees, and they had acted with "full confidence that the United States would pay them, believing that they had appointed such officers as would not call them into the field without proper authority."[16]

Convinced of the rightness of the principle set forth in his argument, Jackson now demanded compensation not for White alone but for every man who had participated in the campaign, all of whom were as deserving as the petitioner. Following a long debate, the House decided to name a committee to consider the matter further; Jackson was appointed its chairman.

After a month of deliberation in which Jackson dramatically elaborated on the events that caused the campaign to be undertaken, the special committee issued a report that recommended full payment for the whole militia. The report was approved by the House Ways and Means Committee, and the necessary funds—totaling $22,816—were approved for inclusion in the federal appropriations for 1797. Tennessee's militiamen were going to be paid after all. Their vigorous, insistent representative had won justice for them. They would not forget him.

In 1797 William Blount, the former territorial governor and one of Tennessee's recently elected senators, was expelled from the United States Senate for his part in a British plan to oust the Spanish from Florida, Blount seeing in the plan an opportunity to prevent the Spanish from controlling the Mississippi River, a Tennessee lifeline of commerce. It fell to the Tennessee legislature to elect Blount's replacement in the Senate. Jackson agreed to have his name placed in nomination, and he won the election, receiving twenty votes to his opponent's thirteen. Back to Philadelphia he would go, although not altogether happy about it.

Rachel, left behind in Nashville, hated his being gone and perhaps resented his willingness to leave. Her feelings doubtless affected Andy's attitude. He wrote to his brother-in-law, Robert Hays, that the "situation in which I left her—Bathed in Tears—fills me with woe. Indeed Sir, It has given me more pain than any Event in my life."[17]

Besides bearing the disquieting displeasure of his wife, Jackson was heavily burdened with financial troubles. His Tennessee land speculations, involving many thousands of acres, and his expanding mercantile business, which stretched from the Nashville area northward into Kentucky and southward to Natchez, had enmeshed him in an intricate scheme of finance that had collapsed when his debtor defaulted and his creditors demanded payment. He painstakingly maneuvered into new financial arrangements, not knowing whether they would succeed or whether he would escape debtor's prison. The matter would remain worrisomely unresolved for years.

In addition to these concerns, there were the requirements of the job of senator hanging over his head. One of his biographers described Jackson as "little suited to the formal methods of that body [the Senate]. . . . He was, in fact, fitted neither by talents nor inclination for a legislative body."[18] Ever a man of action, Jackson was bored and put off by the details of debate. He was uncomfortable and obviously misplaced in his role as senator. After one session of the Senate, Jackson begged off of further attendance and in April 1798 returned home to Nashville and to Rachel. Immediately after his arrival there, he resigned his seat in the Senate, having served less than one year of his six-year term.

He then set out to obtain a judgeship on the state superior court. As a justice on that court, he would be paid $600 a year, just $150 a year less than the governor's salary. The money was not especially important to Jackson, however. He was more interested in the prestige and power of the office and the opportunities it afforded to make himself known throughout Tennessee as he followed the job from court to court around the state. The position was one that the Tennessee legislature filled, and with the support of the Blount political faction, Jackson was elected without opposition in December 1780.

For the next six years he presided at court sessions mostly in Nashville, Knoxville, and Jonesborough, earning a reputation, despite his limited knowledge of the law, as a fearless, fair, and swift dispenser of justice, running his court with complete authority and with no tolerance for disrespect of the law or of himself. In the course of his travels through the state, Jackson made and maintained contacts with members of the militia, capitalizing on his position and his reputation, always with his eye on the major general's job. In 1802 George Conway, who had bested Jackson earlier to become the militia's commander, died, throwing the job open once more. Jackson would run for the position again, this time with more support from militia leaders around the state. But this time, he soon learned, he would have to face a more formidable opponent.

John Sevier, whose generalship in the Revolutionary War and in the continuing struggle with the Indians was legendary, was going to seek to regain the command that he had formerly held. He had served three consecutive terms as Tennessee's governor, the constitutional limit, and now he wanted his old job back. He was astonished that Andrew Jackson, whom he called a "poor, pitiful, pettyfogging lawyer," with only meager military experience, had the audacity to contest him for the position.

The election was held on February 5, 1802. The results: for Brigadier General James Winchester, three votes; for John Sevier, seventeen votes; for Andrew Jackson, seventeen votes. In the event of a tie, the law provided that the governor would cast the deciding vote. The new governor, who had succeeded Sevier, was Archibald Roane; like Jackson, he was a member of the Blount political faction. He was also a friend of Jackson. Governor Roane cast his vote for his friend and political ally. Fourteen months later, on April 1, 1803, the governor signed Jackson's commission.

It was official then. Andrew Jackson, at age thirty-five, had become Major General Andrew Jackson, an event that would profoundly affect the course of the history of the United States of America.

∴ 5 ∴

# The Napoleonic Menace

NAPOLEON Bonaparte, the man whose wars would spread across Europe and produce violent repercussions in the New World, was nine years old when he went off to study war at the provincial French military academy at Brienne. His parents were not especially interested in his having a military career. No Bonaparte had ever been a career soldier. But Napoleon's father, Carlo, a lawyer and nobleman with financial problems, could not afford the kind of professional education he wanted for his sons, and so he sent them to the two kinds of schools where the government would pay to educate them. Giuseppe, the older boy, would go to the seminary at Aix to study for the priesthood. Napoleon would learn to be a soldier.

After graduating from Brienne, Napoleon became a cadet at the Ecole Militaire in Paris at age fifteen. His best subjects were mathematics and geography; his poorest were German, drawing, and dancing. His intention was to seek service in the French navy, rather than the army, believing the navy offered more adventure and action. Because of his naval interest and his proficiency at math, he was placed in the artillery class at the Ecole Militaire; he did so well that he was allowed to graduate in one year instead of the usual two. There were no openings for him in the navy then, and so in September 1785, two weeks after his sixteenth birthday, he was commissioned a second lieutenant of artillery in the French army. King Louis XVI himself signed the commission.

As a garrison officer, Napoleon had a lot of time on his hands, much of which he spent reading. According to one of his biographers,[1] he was most influenced by a French translation of John Barrow's multivolume book *A New and Impartial History of England, from the Invasion of Julius*

*Caesar to the Signing of Preliminaries of Peace, 1762*. Napoleon had a habit of making notes on what he was reading, and he made more notes on Barrow's work than on anything else he read.[2]

Napoleon's interest was particularly drawn to Barrow's account of England's Alfred the Great, who in the ninth century instituted reforms that included a civil code that combined Christian teachings with a strong monarchy, and to the provisions of the Magna Carta, the constitution signed into law by England's King John in 1215 and from which the right of Englishmen to trial by jury and to habeas corpus were later derived. Constitutions that provided reform were a subject on which Napoleon's thoughts fastened. He began forming new ideas about government.

At that time, France, Europe's most populous and formerly most prosperous nation, was tormented by a government that was nearly bankrupt, rising taxes that fell heaviest on the poorest citizens, inflation that deepened the division between haves and have-nots, widespread fear of hunger, and a raging wildfire of democratic ideas. An increasingly restive population of peasants and bourgeoisie demanded a new deal in a new system. Revolution was inevitable.

In March 1789 Lieutenant Bonaparte was stationed with the Sixty-fourth Regiment in Auxonne, about 175 miles southeast of Paris, when townspeople in nearby Seurre, afraid their food was being taken from them, rioted and seized a bargeload of wheat. The regiment, Napoleon included, was ordered in to quell the disturbance. Napoleon thus got his first taste of action.

In Paris four months later, on July 14, 1789, an armed mob stormed and captured the Bastille, the prison-fortress that was the nation's most notorious symbol of tyranny. The French Revolution had come. Many months of near anarchy would follow. By spring of 1792 the bloody, chaotic upheaval in France had set off a hostile reaction in neighboring countries. Fearful that revolution might sweep across their borders, Austria's emperor and Prussia's king declared war on the French people and sent troops into France, vowing to restore the regime of the powerless Louis XVI. In Paris the Assembly, the nation's revolutionary government, was in near panic, threatened by advancing foreign armies and harried by Jacobin radicals who pressed for an end to the monarchy.

In September 1792 the revolutionary government abolished the monarchy, and on January 21, 1793, the deposed king, Louis XVI, went to the guillotine. On October 16, 1793, his infamous wife, Marie Antoinette, daughter of the Austrian emperor, was likewise beheaded.

Napoleon, meanwhile, not only had managed to survive two minor military disasters but had been promoted to captain. By then he had seen enough of civil war, and he wrote to the French War Office, asking that he be posted to the Army of the Rhine, where he could fight France's invading foreign enemies instead of his own countrymen. He partly got his wish when he was ordered to take command of the artillery in the siege of Toulon, on France's Mediterranean coast, which had rebelled against the revolutionary government and had allowed English and Spanish ships into its port and English and Spanish troops, some eighteen thousand of them, into the city, their intention being to undo the revolution.

After two changes of command in the besieging army, Napoleon, with a new promotion, to major, found himself under a commanding general who was receptive to his ideas. Napoleon had built up the besiegers' artillery from a few men and five guns to sixty-four officers, sixteen hundred men, and 194 pieces of artillery, and he had a plan to take the city by using his artillery to attack the enemy fleet, anchored in the harbor. To do so required capturing a nearly impregnable English-occupied fort that stood protectively on the high ground south of the city, guarding the harbor.

His plan was approved by the new commanding general, Jacques Coquille Dugommier, and on December 17, 1793, Napoleon's artillery opened fire on the fort, pounding its defenses, attempting to silence its guns and breach its walls. That evening, in high winds and heavy rain, Dugommier led five thousand French troops in a bayonet assault on the fort while Napoleon stood commanding a reserve of two thousand, his artillery continuing to hammer the fort's massive walls. Twice repelled by the English defenders, Dugommier ordered Napoleon to attack with the reserve.

His horse having been shot beneath him, Napoleon led his troops on foot, their muskets slung over their shoulders, their swords gripped in their teeth as they scrambled over the parapets and wormed their way through gunports, forcing their way into the fort, where they fought with bayonet, sword, and pike. About three o'clock the next morning, after two hours of fierce hand-to-hand combat, the fort fell.

Later that day, December 18, as Napoleon had predicted in his battle plan, the lesser forts of the city were abandoned by their defenders. Napoleon's artillery then began an intense bombardment of the enemy ships. On the evening of the eighteenth, under cover of darkness, the English ships, commanded by Admiral Samuel Hood and with the troops of England and Spain aboard, sailed out of Toulon harbor and escaped into the Mediterranean Sea. The following day, the French army entered and occupied Toulon.

The counterrevolutionary rebellion in the south of France had been quashed, and a dangerous enemy force had been expelled from French soil. The revolution had been saved, for now. Napoleon had played a major role in the victory, suffering a severe stab wound in his left thigh in the process. His conduct drew high praise from his commanding officer, Dugommier. "I have no words to describe Buonaparte's merit," Dugommier wrote to the minister of war. "Much technical skill, an equal degree of intelligence and too much gallantry. There you have a poor sketch of this rare officer."[3] Napoleon's achievement was quickly rewarded. On December 22 he was promoted to brigadier general, at age twenty-four.

By the end of the summer of 1794, Napoleon had survived two near misses in the reckless political purges of the army, one of which had placed him under house arrest and in danger of being sent to the guillotine. He was then on inactive duty, living in a run-down rooming house in a poor section of Paris. Finally cleared of any word or deed subversive to the revolutionary government, the so-called Committee of Public

Safety, in the spring of 1795 Napoleon was offered a new command, in the infantry. He begged off the assignment, which he considered a demotion, by requesting and receiving sick leave.

The country, particularly Paris, was sharply divided between royalists, who sought restoration of the monarchy under the beheaded king's brother, and Constitutionalists, who were determined to preserve the Revolution. On the night of October 4, 1795 (or 12 Vendemiaire, according to the revised calendar and renamed months that the revolutionists had devised), Napoleon, on his way to a theater, witnessed National Guardsmen calling for volunteers to arm themselves and march on the Tuileries, the former royal palace in Paris, where the Convention, the newest revolutionary government, was meeting to write another new constitution. From the theater Napoleon made his way to the Tuileries, entered, and took a seat in the public gallery while the Convention was meeting.

The Convention had named one of its members, Paul Barras, a former army officer, as commander in chief of the Army of the Interior in response to the threat of the royalists and anarchists bent on overthrowing the revolutionary government. Around midnight Napoleon met with Barras, and Barras, a successful politician but not much of a soldier, asked Napoleon to help him. The Revolution needed saving again, this time urgently and desperately. A force estimated at twenty-five to thirty thousand armed men was about to overwhelm the Convention and seize control of the government.

Agreeing to serve under Barras to confront the threat, Napoleon immediately asked, "Where are the guns?" By six o'clock the next morning, October 5, 1795, Napoleon had gathered forty artillery pieces and some eight thousand troops, regulars and militia, and had positioned them in the streets around the Tuileries. He ordered the guns loaded with case shot, small projectiles contained in a case, a particularly lethal antipersonnel ammunition.

In a steady rain the army waited all morning and into the afternoon for the rebel force to appear. About three o'clock in the afternoon, to the sound of drums, shouts, and musket fire, the rebel force launched its assault, advancing behind blazing muskets, with fixed bayonets, bursting through the barricades on the Rue Saint Honore, then into the Rue Neuve Saint Roch while meeting heavy small-arms fire from government troops, who fell back under the force of superior numbers.

Barras, commanding on horseback while Napoleon stood on foot, ordered two eight-pounders to open fire. Their case shot sliced down the advancing horde but failed to stop it until after many murderous salvos. The rebels then withdrew from the Rue Neuve Saint Roch to try another street leading to the Tuileries. There six other of Napoleon's guns blasted them with case shot. In a matter of minutes the attack was ended, and the rebels took flight, pursued by government troops.

Once more the Revolution had been saved, again through the efforts of the able General Bonaparte, who was praised before the Convention and cheered by its members.

Three weeks later, on October 27, 1795, a new revolutionary government, the Directory, succeeded the Convention. Under the provisions of the new constitution, Barras, one of the directors, was required to resign his army command, which he did. To replace him as commander of the Army of the Interior, Barras and his fellow directors named Brigadier General Napoleon Bonaparte, promoting him at the same time to the rank of full general. Napoleon was then twenty-six years old.

On March 9, 1796, Napoleon married the woman he called Josephine (born Marie-Josephe-Rose Tascher and called Rose by her friends, she had married the Vicomte Alexandre de Beauharnais, who became a French general, deserted her and their two children, and in 1794 was guillotined by the revolutionists). Two days later Napoleon interrupted his honeymoon to return to combat. He had been ordered to lead a French army across the Alps and into Piedmont, in northwest Italy, and there engage and overcome the allied forces of Austria and Piedmont, which the revolutionary French government saw as a threat. He was then to occupy the Austrian duchy of Milan and force the Austrians to sign a peace agreement favorable to France.

Napoleon first set up a headquarters at Nice, on the French coast, then moved to Albenga, then to Genoa, keeping to the coast. On the morning of April 12, 1796, he sprang his trap. Having lured the Austrian general Argenteau into an attack on the French-held fort of Montenotte, Napoleon suddenly struck Argenteau's front, flank, and rear simultaneously. Napoleon's troops, fighting in a chilling rain, defeated the Austrians, killing or wounding some one thousand and taking some twenty-five hundred prisoners.

Moving swiftly through mountain passes and up and down the slopes of the Alpine foothills, Napoleon's outnumbered forces repeatedly outmaneuvered the Piedmontese and Austrians, winning battles at Millesimo and Dego and defeating a force of six thousand Austrians sent by the Austrian commander, Beaulieu, to support the Piedmontese troops. Next followed the capture of a string of cities—Mondovi, Cherasco, Fossano, Alba—forcing the Piedmont king, Victor Amadeus III, to dispatch two representatives to Napoleon's headquarters in Cherasco to work out a peace agreement. Napoleon dictated the terms of the agreement, and he and the king's representatives signed it as dawn broke on April 28, 1796.

His next objective was the capture of Milan. In a daring move to avoid crossing the Po River at Pavia, an Austrian strongpoint, Napoleon sped his army to Piacenza and sent a nine-hundred-man force across the river to establish a bridgehead before attempting to move the main body of his troops across. In the face of enemy fire from the far side of the river, the advance force, in a flotilla of small boats, made it across the five hundred yards of the Po's breadth, landed, seized the opposite bank, and held it while the rest of Napoleon's army crossed during the next two days.

Pushing headlong toward Milan, Napoleon soon faced another critical river crossing. This time it was the Adda. The river was spanned by a wooden bridge at the town of Lodi, and the Austrian commander, General Beaulieu, had posted some twelve thousand troops and sixteen artillery pieces there to hold the bridge and prevent Napoleon's crossing. The bridge was twelve feet wide and about two hundred yards long. Above it on the far side, the Austrians' guns were mounted in a centuries-old fort and in a tall, massive tower. They opened fire as Napoleon himself moved forward toward the bridge to reconnoiter.

Disregarding the opinions of his generals, Napoleon decided to storm the bridge and, under heavy enemy fire, force his way across. He ordered his cavalry to dash up the river and find a spot where they could ford it, then turn back toward Lodi and hit the Austrians' flank while his infantry assaulted the front of the Austrian line at the far end of the bridge.

His cavalry dispatched, he then turned his attention to his four thousand infantrymen, gathered in formation in Lodi's town square. He somehow had to challenge them into rushing across the bridge in the face of the murderous Austrian fire. On a white horse, he rode slowly up and down the ranks of soldiers, talking to them as they stood looking up at his mounted figure. He told them what had to be done. He told them he was not sure they were up to the task. He said he lacked confidence in them. He said they might act as if they were going to do it, but when the moment came to cross the bridge, they would refuse. He goaded the men, incited them, worked them up into a state of eagerness to prove themselves to him, to prove him wrong about them. Around six o'clock that evening, when he could see that they were now impatient to charge across the bridge, he ordered his band to play "La Marseillaise." To those stirring strains, his troops marched briskly toward and onto the bridge, shouting, "Vive la Republique!" while Napoleon, astride his horse at the entrance to the bridge, urged them onward.

The fire from the Austrian artillery and small arms was devastating. Still the Frenchmen kept coming. Fifty yards from the opposite bank, many of them leaped off the bridge into the river and waded ashore to attack the enemy line. Austrian cavalry quickly splashed into the river to meet them. As Napoleon sat watching the desperate struggle, suddenly his cavalry raced into view, sweeping the Austrians' flank and silencing many of their guns. Napoleon's infantry now poured across the bridge.

By then darkness was creeping over the site, and the Austrians soon turned and ran into the gathering night, leaving behind them 335 dead or wounded comrades, seventeen hundred prisoners, and sixteen artillery pieces. Napoleon had lost some 200 dead. Elated with the results, he later confided, "That evening, for the first time, I no longer considered myself a mere general, but a man called upon to decide the fate of peoples."[4]

Napoleon immediately put his troops on the road to Milan, and four days later, on May 15, 1796, he entered the welcoming city, where he turned his conquering army loose on the population, allowing what one biographer calls "an orgy of destroying, rapine, and killing" to be inflicted upon Milan's helpless citizens.[5]

Pleased with his success, Napoleon wrote to the Directory to report that "The [French] tricolor flies over Milan, Pavia, Como and all the towns of Lombardy."[6] In June 1796 he recrossed the Po River, invaded the Papal States, smashed the papal army of eighteen thousand men, and took Florence and Leghorn, where the English had established a commercial center. Having intimidated all of central Italy and seized booty that included forty million francs, mostly in gold, he returned to Milan in July.

He saw his chance to further devastate the Austrians when, in early 1797, he learned that two Austrian armies, one of twenty-eight thousand men and the other with seventeen thousand, were marching to converge on Mantua and there relieve the Austrian garrison that was encircled and struggling to stay alive on horsemeat. In a surprise nighttime attack, Napoleon's outnumbered troops shattered the twenty-eight-thousand-man Austrian army commanded by General Alvinzi, driving it from the field, forcing it to leave behind some eight thousand men killed, wounded, or captured. Seven thousand more were taken prisoner as they retreated.

Napoleon quickly wheeled and struck the seventeen thousand troops commanded by General Provera, taking most of them prisoner. Mantua then fell, and Austria ceased to be a controlling presence in Italy. With only minimal resistance, Napoleon's army then swept into the papal cities of Bologna, Faenza, Forli, Rimini, Ancona, and Macerta. Napoleon was now in a position to dictate the fate of the pope, sixty-nine-year-old Pius VI. He apparently had no intention of deposing the pope, however, although the Directors, the revolutionary French government, were eager to see the papal government, which opposed the

Revolution, destroyed. "My ambition," Napoleon wrote duplicitously to Pius, "is to be called the savior, not the destroyer of the Holy See."[7] He then set out to dismember the papal empire. He forced the pope to give up three papal states and thirty million francs in gold. "My opinion," Napoleon wrote to the Directors, "is that Rome, once stripped of Bologna, Ferrara, Romagna and thirty millions, can no longer exist."[8]

In March 1797 Napoleon marched four divisions swiftly across the snowy Alps and Dolomites into Austria, catching Vienna surprised and undefended. The Austrian emperor, Francis II, was left little choice but to come to terms with Napoleon. By a preliminary treaty signed on April 18, Francis agreed to give up the duchy of Milan and make peace with France.

In the thirteen months since Napoleon had begun his Italian campaign, he had accomplished all he had set out to do, except for what he held secret in his heart. "What I have done up to this point is nothing," he remarked to the French diplomat André Miot de Melito, who in June visited him at the mansion that was his Italian headquarters. "This is but the beginning of my career."[9]

Miot observed during his visit that Napoleon "was no longer the general of a triumphant Republic, but a conqueror on his own account, imposing his own laws on the vanquished."[10] Confident of his ability to command the loyalty of France's armies, on the battlefield and elsewhere, Napoleon had no fear that he would be reined in by the Directory. "Let the Directory try to take this command from me, and they will see who is master," he told Miot. "The nation must have a chief, a chief rendered illustrious by glory, and not by theories of government, by phrases, by speeches which the people do not understand."[11]

The chief that Napoleon had in mind for France was himself, and the path to achieving such a status was not, he candidly made clear to Miot, through peace. "Peace is not in my best interests. You can see . . . what my position is here, what I can do in Italy. . . . I do not want to leave unless it is to play a role in France similar to the one I have here, and for that the time has not yet come. The pear is not yet ripe."[12]

Nevertheless, after signing the finalized peace treaty with Austria (which ceded Holland and Belgium, among other former Austrian territories, to France) in October 1797, Napoleon returned to Paris on orders from the new French government that had come to power following a coup d'état in September. He arrived in early December, furious that he had been summoned and that the new government had replaced him as commander in Italy. "I can longer obey them," he told Miot. "I have made up my mind, if I cannot be master, then I shall simply leave France."[13]

Napoleon's new orders placed him in command of the inceptive army being assembled on the Channel coast. Its assignment would be the invasion and conquest of England, the only nation with which France was still at war. In February 1798 Napoleon made an extensive tour of the ports and camps of the gathering army of his new command. After careful study and consideration, he recommended against an invasion, explaining to the Directors that the time of year was wrong, that the element of surprise had been lost, and that England's naval power could not then be challenged. It would be several years, he told the Directors, before France would achieve naval superiority.

He further told them that an invasion of England was something France should prepare for and eventually effect, but that Europe was "just a molehill" and that Asia was the place where truly great empires were built. What he had in mind was an invasion of Egypt, at least as a starting point. "In order to destroy England utterly," he declared, "we must get possession of Egypt."[14] Charles-Maurice Talleyrand, the hugely influential French foreign minister, agreed on Egypt's importance as a strategic objective. "Egypt was once a province of the Roman Empire," Talleyrand told his government, "and now must become one of ours."[15]

What Napoleon had in mind, according to one biographer,[16] was actually a global confrontation with England, through an invasion of England and Scotland and simultaneous assaults on British-held India, as well as the conquest of Egypt. He proposed an enormous shipbuilding program to allow France to successfully contest Britain's rule of the waves. As an indication of his ultimate military goal, he ordered the captains of his Egyptian invasion fleet to have the men on their ships each evening sing the revolutionary anthem "March on England."

On the morning of May 19, 1798, Napoleon's armada set sail from five French ports, bound for Egypt. On June 9 Napoleon arrived at Malta and intimidated its garrison of defenders into surrendering the island to him. Managing to dodge England's Mediterranean fleet, commanded by Rear Admiral Horatio Nelson, the armada sighted the Egyptian coast on June 30. At three o'clock the next morning, Napoleon stepped onto Egyptian soil, about eight miles outside Alexandria. By lunchtime, his troops had taken the city, with a loss of only some two hundred men.

From Alexandria, Napoleon marched south. At Giza, in sight of the great pyramids, he met Egypt's defending army. Deftly employing artillery, maneuver, and firepower, Napoleon and his invaders killed, wounded, or captured virtually the entire army of defenders, some twenty-four thousand strong, and suffered only minor losses themselves. Napoleon then took possession of all of lower Egypt, marching into Cairo two days later. By October 1798 he had occupied the entire country.

He had also lost his fleet. Admiral Nelson had been scouring the Mediterranean in a relentless search for Napoleon's ships. On August 1, 1798, he found them, anchored in Abukir Bay, east of Alexandria. Quickly ordering his fleet into action, Nelson engaged the French ships and in a fierce battle destroyed or captured eleven of Napoleon's thirteen warships, leaving Napoleon's invasion army without a lifeline to France and without means of returning to it while Nelson's fleet, uncontested, blockaded Egypt's coast.

Napoleon's attempt to force his way overland, across the Sinai, into Gaza and northward toward Turkey and Syria, was, after early successes, eventually defeated at Acre in May 1799 by a combined English and Turkish force. Napoleon then turned back to Egypt. In Alexandria he learned that a powerful new alliance had been formed against France—including England, Turkey, Austria, and Russia—and that one

Austrian and Russian army had invaded Switzerland and another had marched into Italy and taken back much of what Napoleon had won for France. Furthermore, a combined English and Russian army had landed in French-occupied Holland. To make matters still worse, the revolutionary French government was tottering.

Napoleon decided to abandon his army, some twelve thousand men, in Egypt and head back to France. Taking four small vessels that remained uncaptured by the English, he, with a handful of aides, secretly sailed away on August 23, 1799, and managed to slip through Admiral Nelson's blockade.

He arrived in Paris at dawn on October 16, 1799. By the end of the next day he was already being courted to participate in a conspiracy to unseat the French government. Three and a half weeks later, on November 9 and 10, he and his coconspirators, with the support of his troops, executed a coup d'état and set up a new regime, the Consulate, which was established under the terms of a new constitution. The new governing body was composed of three so-called consuls. Napoleon, the key figure in the coup, was named First Consul, the nation's chief executive, with nearly dictatorial power, including the right to name the two other consuls, who acted mostly as advisers to First Consul Bonaparte. Put to a national vote after Napoleon had assumed the office, the new constitution was overwhelmingly approved by French voters.

Immediately Napoleon began reviving the French economy and instituting social, political, economic, judicial, and religious reforms that were well received by a French population wearied by years of civil turmoil, government abuses, and enervating wars. "I listen to advice from all sides," he said of his governing policy, "but in the end, my head is my only counsel."[17] Louis de Bourrienne, Napoleon's secretary, observing all that was transpiring, came to believe that, as he said, "It was in fact not simply the matter of an absolutist form of government that Bonaparte was now attempting to establish in France, but of a military dictatorship," which was, he felt, "worse yet."[18]

On Christmas Day, 1799, while ostensibly seeking peace with England in a letter written to King George III, Napoleon wrote to his armies proclaiming that they should prepare for a further war that would require them "to invade the enemy states."[19]

On February 19, 1800, in a spectacularly symbolic act, Napoleon marched his government's ministers and legislators, escorted by three thousand troops, to their new home in the Tuileries, the Paris palace of the overthrown Louis XVI. Napoleon, he wished the world to know, was France's new monarch.

On May 5, 1800, with a conscripted army financed by money extorted from Swiss, Dutch, Italian, and Portuguese officials and merchants, and from wealthy French merchants as well, Napoleon marched into northern Italy, won a series of triumphs, and concluded his campaign in the Battle of Marengo, in which he snatched victory from imminent defeat, losing some seven thousand men while the Austrians lost twice that number. Another of Napoleon's armies, commanded by General Jean-Victor Moreau, advancing up the Danube, concluded its Austrian campaign with victory at the Battle of Hohenlinden on December 3, 1800. Following those crushing defeats, the Austrian emperor was forced to come to terms with Napoleon. His representative signed the Peace of Luneville on February 9, 1801, ceding back to France not only northern Italy but also Belgium and the left bank of the Rhine, making that river France's new eastern border.

In early 1802, following the resignation of the hawkish William Pitt as prime minister and his replacement by the more flexible Henry Addington, England agreed to a treaty with Napoleon and, on March 25, 1802, signed the Peace of Amiens. On the same day that Napoleon's legislature ratified the Amiens treaty, May 6, 1803, it also named him, at his insistence, consul for life, instead of for the ten-year term provided by the constitution. In August a constitutional revision allowing the change was approved in a national plebiscite engineered by Napoleon's interior minister, his brother Lucien Bonaparte.

By 1803 Napoleon was making new preparations to invade England. In July he ordered the execution of a plan to assemble more than two thousand boats to ferry one hundred thousand men and three thousand horses across the Channel to England's shores. England responded with the return of William Pitt as prime minister and by strengthening its navy and land forces. English warships began a campaign of bombardment of French vessels and ports along the Channel coast from Boulogne to French-occupied Flushing.

While his invasion preparations were under way, Napoleon decided he would become emperor, the founder of a new French dynasty, his title and powers to be inherited by his progeny. In May 1804 he ordered his legislature to so provide, which it did in another constitutional revision. That revision was approved on November 6, 1804, in another manipulated national plebiscite in which negative votes were discarded and the total reported votes showed that an implausible 99.99 percent had favored the change.[20] At Notre Dame Cathedral in Paris on December 2, 1804, in an enormous and enormously costly spectacle, the intimidated Pope Pius VII conducted the coronation of Napoleon Bonaparte as Emperor Napoleon I.

Repeatedly thwarted by England's bold and vigorous navy, Napoleon at last gave up his English invasion plans following the Battle of Trafalgar on October 21, 1805, in which Admiral Horatio Nelson's twenty-two-ship fleet annihilated a combined French and Spanish fleet of thirty-two warships, without the loss of a single English vessel. England's greatest loss in the battle was Nelson himself, who was one of the casualties.

After the disaster of Trafalgar, Napoleon concentrated his efforts on the land wars that would subdue the continent under his rule. He crushed the combined army of Russia and Austria at the Battle of Austerlitz, in Austria, on December 2, 1805. In 1806 he captured the Kingdom of Naples and installed his brother Joseph (Giuseppe) as king. He turned the republic of Holland into the Kingdom of Holland and made his brother Louis its king. He formed most of the German states into a new entity he called the Confederation of the Rhine and made himself its protector. When Prussia allied itself with Russia to attack the confederation, Napoleon attacked and destroyed the Prussian army in battles at Jena and Auerstadt, in the confederation. He then confronted the Russian army at Friedland, in Prussia, and destroyed it, forcing Czar

Alexander I to make peace. Under the terms of the peace agreement, the Treaty of Tilsit, signed on July 7, 1806, Russia became France's ally and recognized Napoleon's conquests and annexations. Prussia was also forced to cede territory to France in a treaty signed on July 9, 1806. Among the territories Napoleon added to his empire were the Kingdom of Westphalia, of which he appointed his brother Jerome king, and the duchy of Warsaw.

In an attempt to ruin England's economy, Napoleon in 1806 created, through an action called the Berlin Decree, his so-called Continental System, which barred British ships, products, and materials from all ports on the Continent. He later extended the prohibition by forbidding all trade with Britain by France, its allies, and all neutral nations, including the United States. England defiantly retaliated with its so-called orders in council, which prohibited virtually all trade by England with any nation obeying Napoleon's Berlin Decree.

English trade continued clandestinely through Holland, Belgium, Sweden, and Denmark, but in Portugal, English ships, naval as well as merchant, were openly welcomed, infuriating Napoleon. In the fall of 1807 he ordered a French army commanded by General Andoche Junot to march through Spain, which was a French ally, and into Portugal and seize Lisbon and Portugal's royal family and occupy the country. Fiercely determined to isolate and cripple England, Napoleon vowed, "I will no longer tolerate a single English envoy in Europe. I will declare war on any power that has one."[21]

Having been permitted by Spain to cross its frontier on the way to invading Portugal, Napoleon moved his troops into Spanish cities as well, occupying Pamplona, Barcelona, San Sebastian, and Figueras. He sent in 118,000 additional men, and on March 24, 1808, French troops commanded by Marshal Joachim Murat, Napoleon's brother-in-law, entered and seized Madrid. Napoleon then lured the Spanish royal family and Spain's de facto ruler, Manuel de Godoy, to Bayonne, France, near the Spanish border, and there took them prisoner and manipulated the abdication of King Carlos IV. On May 6, 1808, Napoleon proclaimed his brother Joseph Bonaparte the new king of Spain. (To replace Joseph as monarch of Naples, Napoleon appointed his brother-in-law, Murat.)

An outraged Spanish populace rose in rebellion against French rule. In one week in May, Spanish patriots assassinated the French military governors of Badajoz, Cadiz, and Cartagena, and armed resistance quickly broke out in three other provinces. By early June 1808, rebellion had erupted throughout the country. Then, soon realizing their need for assistance in their efforts to drive Napoleon's armies from their land, Spanish rebel leaders turned to the one nation that could help—England.

## ∴ 6 ∴

# The Brother-in-Law

In June 1808 Edward Pakenham's brother-in-law, thirty-nine-year-old Sir Arthur Wellesley, promoted two months earlier to lieutenant general in His Majesty's army, received orders to command an expeditionary force being assembled at Cork, Ireland, and bound for the Spanish colony of Venezuela to assist colonists in the revolution there. The assignment would put him in the same theater of operations as Pakenham, who was then serving in the Caribbean.

Aware of events in the Iberian Peninsula, however, and of Spanish appeals for British help, Wellesley knew there was a good chance that his army would go to war not against the Spanish but *with* the Spanish against Napoleon's troops occupying Spain. Although Britain was officially at war with Spain, the British government's policy, as set forth by its foreign secretary, George Canning, was that "Britain would proceed upon the principle that any nation in Europe which stirs up with a determination to oppose [France] . . . becomes immediately our ally."[1] With its revolt against French rule, Spain now qualified as a new British ally.

Wellesley began reorganizing his army to prepare it for the kind of fighting it would have to do in the extensive, hilly countryside of Spain, and in Portugal as well. He was also training it to deploy and maneuver in ways that he believed would successfully counter the actions of Napoleon's troops. He had been studying the battlefield tactics that Napoleon had been using so effectively as his armies marched unvanquished from one end of Europe to the other. Napoleon's armies, Wellesley concluded, employed "a new system of strategy which has outmaneuvered and overwhelmed all the armies of Europe. . . . They may overwhelm me, but I don't think they will outmaneuver me. First, because I am not afraid of them, as everybody else seems to be. And secondly because if what I hear of their system of maneuvers is true, I think it is a false one against steady troops."[2] Apparently eager to test his countermeasures, Wellesley was training his army in preparation for their use. On July 20, 1808, aboard a fleet of transports and warships, he and his troops set sail for Corunna, in northwestern Spain. When he went ashore at Corunna to confer with the Galician Junta, a rebel body that had appealed to England for help, Wellesley discovered that the rebel leaders did not want British troops, but only arms and money. They suggested Wellesley take his army to Portugal and fight the French there.

Wellesley and his men reached Oporto, in northwestern Portugal, on July 24. There he learned that the French army, commanded by General Androche Junot, had concentrated most of its forces around Lisbon but, except for the rugged area around Oporto, was able to move throughout the country, terrorizing the populace, without serious opposition. On July 25 Wellesley sailed for the mouth of the Tagus River, about fifteen miles southwest of Lisbon, to meet with the British naval commander, Admiral Sir Charles Cotton, whose ships controlled the seas off the coasts of Portugal and Spain. A decision was made to land the entire British force in Portugal, the ten thousand troops who had sailed with Wellesley plus the five thousand troops of General Sir Brent Spencer, which had already been in action with Spanish rebels in Andalusia and which upon Wellesley's arrival had come under his command.

The landing site chosen by Wellesley and Cotton was the mouth of the Mondego River, where a protective fortress had been captured from the French by Portuguese university students and turned over to a force of British marines, who were holding it. Wellesley's troops were ashore by August 5, having suffered some losses of men and matériel in the rough surf. The troops led by Spencer were landed by August 8.

On the morning of August 10, Wellesley's expeditionary force, hampered by insufficient horses to mount all its cavalry and draw all its artillery, moved out on the coastal road and headed south from Figueira, near its landing site, marching toward Lisbon. At the town of Leiria Wellesley rendezvoused with forces commanded by the Portuguese general Bernardino Freire—some six thousand troops for whom Wellesley had supplied muskets and equipment. Freire proved to be mostly a useless ally who pessimistically insisted that the combined armies take a hilly, interior route to avoid marching against the French in open country. Wellesley rejected that idea and continued his march toward Lisbon, leaving Freire and his troops at Leiria, except for a sixteen-hundred-man contingent of light infantry commanded by a British officer in Portuguese service, Colonel Nicholas Trant.

By now Wellesley had been informed from London that he was not to command the expeditionary force after all. Wellesley was the choice of England's secretary of war, Robert Stewart Castlereagh, but Castlereagh now had been overruled by the Duke of York, the king's brother, who had the king's backing and apparently cared for neither Wellesley nor Castlereagh. Wellesley was notified that he was to yield command to Lieutenant General Sir Harry Burrard, a man in his fifties and a member of Parliament with good political connections. Also now assigned to the army in Portugal were Lieutenant General Sir Hew Dalrymple, fifty-seven, governor of Gibraltar, and Lieutenant General Sir John Moore, forty-six, both senior to Wellesley.

None of those three generals had yet arrived, and Wellesley, unwilling to wait for them, resumed his march toward Lisbon. His intelligence revealed that a French force of some six thousand troops under the command of General Henri François Delaborde had taken a position athwart the Lisbon road at Obidos, about fifty miles north of Lisbon; another French force, some nine thousand men commanded by General Loison, was encamped either at Abrantes, about seventy-five miles east of Obidos, or at Tomar, a bit farther east.

On August 14 Wellesley's forces entered the town of Alcobaca, about fifteen miles north of Obidos, and the next day three companies of the British Ninety-fifth Rifles encountered and routed French troops posted at a forward outpost at Brilos, three miles north of Obidos. Delaborde now gave up his position at Obidos and withdrew to the village of Rolica, about twelve miles farther south, moving into a strong defensive position, which the terrain favored.

Wellesley's army spent the night of August 16 at Obidos, and an hour before dawn the next day, they were ready to advance on the French position. Wellesley now put into effect the tactics he believed would prove successful against the French.

Napoleon's standard tactics placed a swarm of skirmishers, called *tirailleurs,* in front of solid columns of infantry to shield the columns and disorganize the fire from the enemy's lines. Napoleon's armies also moved their artillery up beside or in front of the columns of infantry, within two hundred to three hundred yards of the enemy line, to knock out as much of the enemy line as possible with canister or case shot.

Wellesley advanced toward Rolica in three columns and deployed into battle formation at a distance of two miles from Delaborde's lines. At the same time, far ahead and on the right side of the main body of scarlet-coated infantrymen, a flanking force of 1,350 Portuguese light infantry under Colonel Trant hurried through the hills to form one half of a pincer movement while ahead, on the left of the main body (the direction from which General Loison might come with reinforcements) 4,500-man force, including cavalry and artillery, commanded by Major General Sir Ronald Ferguson, also hurried through hills to form the other half of the pincers. Wellesley hoped that Delaborde would concentrate his attack on the British main body, thereby springing a trap that would have Trant's and Ferguson's forces attacking Delaborde's flanks and rear while the main body of Wellesley's army, preceded by Wellesley's skirmishers and supported by artillery, hit the French head-on.

The battle did not go according to Wellesley's plan. Delaborde, a canny veteran commander, did not react with an all-out attack on the British main body, and the trap was not sprung. Instead, Delaborde laid down a heavy fire and then withdrew to a new position. Wellesley's flanking attack was foiled when one of his commanders in the main body, instead of exchanging fire with Delaborde's *tirailleurs,* pressed too far toward the French line and was cut off, taking heavy fire from the French and suffering many casualties. Wellesley then ordered a full frontal assault on the French position, which was at last overrun, forcing a general but orderly retreat by Delaborde's troops.

The Battle of Rolica went down in history as a British victory—not large, but significant because an army of Napoleon had been bested, a rare event, even when outnumbered by the enemy, which it was at Rolica. Wellesley had succeeded in his first test against the French. His casualties were reported at 485. French losses were put at 700.

In the afternoon of August 20, the ship bearing General Burrard, to whom Wellesley was to turn over command of his army, arrived at the mouth of the Maceiro River, about fifteen miles southwest of Rolica. Wellesley was rowed out in a small boat to confer with Burrard, who ordered him to hold up on his plan to march immediately on Lisbon. Burrard wanted to wait for the reinforcements under the command of General Moore, which were expected to arrive at the mouth of the Mondego River soon. Having squelched Wellesley's plans, Burrard told Wellesley that he, Burrard, would stay aboard ship another night to get some letters written. Wellesley bade him good night and was rowed back to shore, then made his way to his command post.

Shortly after midnight Wellesley was informed that a French force was advancing toward his position, which was near the village of Vimiero, moving northward up the road from Torres Vedras. By dawn Wellesley had his entire army ready for action and was himself atop a ridge peering south, surveying the terrain. Around nine o'clock that morning clouds of dust stirred by marching feet could be seen to the east of Wellesley's position. Now he maneuvered to face an imminent attack as the French advanced in three columns.

From his vantage point Wellesley could see that one column was moving directly northward and another was moving northwestward. The third column, apparently the strongest, was advancing from the east toward a flat-topped hill that rises on the south side of the village of Vimiero. The terrain across which the columns were advancing was rolling and partly wooded, and the troops' movements, occluded by the trees, could be best followed by the dust the men were raising as they marched. Wellesley could see that the strongest column would strike first.

As the column neared the hill, it began forming in the classic Napoleonic deployment. It split into two columns four hundred yards apart, with two battalions of infantry in each, one battalion marching behind the other, shielded by *tirailleurs,* supported by artillery that advanced with the columns, cavalry guarding their flanks, all according to Napoleon's tactical formula that had worked so well in so many battles against so many adversaries.

Wellesley countered by placing half of one brigade and part of another about eight hundred yards in front of the hill, forming a strong line of skirmishers, all armed with rifles, which were far more accurate and had greater range than the British army's standard Brown Bess muskets. The hill itself was held by the five remaining battalions of those two brigades, three positioned on or near the crest, two behind them in reserve. Also atop the hill were twelve artillery pieces.

Soon the troops were close enough to engage. The *tirailleurs* ran into the deadly accurate, persistent fire of Wellesley's rifles and instead of disrupting the British main line were forced to get help from their own main column to stop the advance of Wellesley's skirmishers. When at last the stubborn British riflemen gave ground and the French were able to move forward, they were met by a murderous volley of artillery fire that blasted the French ranks with canister shot. At the same time, the British main line devastated the advancing French column with small-arms volleys, one every fifteen seconds. In their formation, the French columns could each bring no more than two hundred of their twelve hundred muskets to bear on the British line, while British infantrymen, posted in a broad line, assaulted the oncoming French troops with every one of their nine hundred muskets, the British flanks gradually bending forward to encircle the French attackers.

With each lethal volley of British fire, the French troops of the left column recoiled until finally they turned, broke, and ran, with Wellesley's redcoats in pursuit. The parallel column on the right took an even worse beating, Wellesley's skirmishers delivering a withering rifle fire that dropped infantry and artillerymen alike, preventing the French artillery from establishing an effective return fire. A unit of Wellesley's infantry wheeled into the flank of the French formation, forcing it to break and flee in hasty retreat also.

The two French columns were regrouping to make another attempt at the Vimiero hill when General Burrard arrived on the scene. He wisely stayed out of the fight and allowed Wellesley to continue in command. Again the French advanced, this time with fresh troops, using the same tactics, again sending a swarm of *tirailleurs* ahead. This time Wellesley's artillery was better positioned to deliver fire on the advancing column, and it devastated the formation's ranks, its howitzers raining deadly shrapnel shells on the attackers. The French artillery again proved ineffective. Three British battalions counterattacked, converging on the embattled Frenchmen from north and south as well as from Vimiero hill on the west. The French column disintegrated under the continuous fire of Wellesley's encompassing infantry.

By eleven o'clock the fighting was virtually over, the victor decided. Wellesley's troops, some 16,500 men, had inflicted a loss of 2,000 men, killed, wounded, captured, or missing, on the French force, which had numbered about 13,000. The British had suffered the loss of 720 of its men. The French army had been driven from the field, losing at least thirteen artillery pieces in the process. Wellesley's countermeasures had worked extremely well.

Wellesley urged Burrard to order the pursuit and destruction of the French, now substantially weakened, demoralized, and disordered. "Sir Harry, now is the time to advance," Wellesley told him forcefully. "The enemy are completely beaten, and we shall be in Lisbon in three days."[3] Burrard, however, with little experience as a field general and unable to recognize the opportunity, refused, saying the army had done enough for one day. Wellesley's protests came to nought.

The next day, August 22, 1808, Burrard turned over command to his senior officer, Sir Hew Dalrymple, who was even less experienced at fighting than was Burrard and as obstinate in refusing to pursue the crippled French force. While Wellesley and his two seniors conferred, trying to decide what to do next, the French general François-Etienne Kellerman, escorted by a squadron of dragoons carrying white flags, rode up to the British command post and proposed an armistice and negotiations for surrender of the French army. Although Burrard and Dalrymple were blind to the defeat of the French, the French commander in chief, General Junot, was not. Believing the British had far greater numbers in Portugal than they did and fearful that he would lose his entire army, Junot was suing for a deal.

The details proposed by Junot included the surrender, intact, of all fortifications and military stores in Portugal, which met British objectives. But Junot's proposals also called for the evacuation of French troops, together with whatever they had looted from the Portuguese, and transportation safely back to France aboard British ships, without any pledge that those troops would not be used against the British in the future. Dalrymple thought it a good deal and told Wellesley to sign the agreement, the so-called Convention of Cintra. According to Wellesley, he had not had much to do with the terms spelled out in the convention. "I beg you will not believe that I had any hand in wording [the agreement]," he wrote to Castlereagh, the British secretary of war. "It was negotiated by the General [Dalrymple] himself in my presence and that of Sir Harry Burrard; and after it had been drawn out by [French General] Kellerman himself, Sir Hew Dalrymple desired me to sign it."[4] And so sign it he did.

Not long after that, Wellesley began to make it known he wanted to return home, that he was, as he said, "sick of all" that was happening in Portugal. "It is quite impossible for me to continue any longer with this army, and I wish therefore that you would allow me to return home," he wrote to Castlereagh.[5] He said he would rather be unemployed than continue to serve under generals of "stupid incapacity."[6]

Allowed to return to London, he arrived on October 4, 1808, to find that the terms of the Convention of Cintra had created a furor. Not only were Dalrymple and Burrard in popular disgrace for having allowed a French withdrawal aboard British ships but he himself, for having signed the agreement, had been tarred by the same brush. The board of inquiry that was formed called all three generals to testify and ended up exonerating all three by voting four to three to approve the Convention.

In the meantime, the thirty-thousand-man British army that Wellesley had left in Portugal had been placed under the command of General Moore and had not fared well. Moore had taken it from Lisbon toward Valladolid, in north-central Spain, but had been forced to retreat when confronted by a French army of superior numbers and commanded by Napoleon himself. For a time Napoleon pursued Moore's army as it fled northwestward, but around Astorga he turned over the pursuing army to Marshal the Duke de Soult, who followed Moore all the way to Corunna. At Corunna, while Moore's troops were embarking aboard transports, Soult's force attacked on January 16, 1809; in that battle, which proved indecisive, Moore was mortally wounded.

Despite Moore's failure and his assertion that Portugal could not be held, Secretary of War Castlereagh and Britain's Tory government decided to continue the fight in the peninsula. Wellesley, now with the confidence of the king, the army, and the nation generally, on April 6, 1809, was appointed to command the British forces there. He quickly set sail for Lisbon, arriving on April 22 with an army of twenty-five thousand British soldiers.

On learning of Wellesley's return to Portugal, the French swiftly moved to check him. Marshal Soult led a twenty-three-thousand-man army down the coast to Oporto, and a second French army, commanded by Marshal Claude Victor, advanced along the Tagus River, toward Lisbon. Wellesley decided to attack before the two French armies could link up. First he would hit Soult. With his British force reinforced by fifteen thousand Portuguese troops commanded by William Carr Beresford, he marched north to a spot on the Douro River opposite Oporto. On May 12, 1809, he crossed the river and struck Soult from the north, taking him by surprise and routing his army, which lost some six thousand men and all its artillery.

Instead of pursuing Soult's shattered force, Wellesley moved swiftly southward to confront Victor's army. On hearing of Soult's defeat, Victor had turned back to the east and marched to Talavera, in central Spain. There he was reinforced by troops sent by King Joseph, Napoleon's brother, swelling Victor's army to forty-six thousand men.

Wellesley's army, as it marched toward Talavera, now included twenty-three thousand British troops and thirty-six thousand Spaniards. On July 27 and 28, 1809, Wellesley attacked the French position and, despite the flight of many of the inexperienced Spaniards, forced Victor and his army from the field, with a loss of seven thousand men and seventeen artillery pieces. Wellesley lost some five thousand men.

For his victory at Talavera, Wellesley was rewarded by the British government with an income of two thousand pounds annually for three years and was created Viscount Wellington (a name chosen by his brother William and taken, William said, from a town of that name in Somerset, England, not far from a community named Welleslie).

In August 1809 Pakenham returned to London from his service in the Caribbean just as news of Talavera reached England. Bursting with pride, Pakenham wrote to his mother, "What a degree of fame that man has arrived at! I still hope it may ultimately produce as much comfort to his family as honour to his country."[7]

Before the end of August, Pakenham was sent from London to deliver official dispatches to Wellesley, Pakenham saw opportunity in the contact that assignment would provide. He was hoping, he let his mother know, that he would be able to link his career with that of his illustrious brother-in-law.

As if responding to Pakenham's wish, Wellesley—now Wellington—appointed Pakenham to his staff, along with two other officers who were related to him by marriage, both having wed nieces of Wellington. In November 1809 Pakenham became Wellington's deputy adjutant general, a job Pakenham was not entirely happy with, calling it "damned clerking business."[8] Nevertheless, Pakenham would use the position to learn more about commanding an army. The job placed him in practically daily contact with Wellington, from whom he would learn much, particularly about tactics and maneuver.

Pakenham arrived at Wellington's headquarters at a time when events were not going well for the British in the peninsula. Napoleon had defeated the Austrians at Wagram in July 1809, had divorced Josephine, and in March 1810 had married Marie Louise, daughter of the Austrian emperor, a marriage that made Austria a nominal ally. Now, no longer having to contend with Austria as an enemy, Napoleon was able to shift some 138,000 troops to Spain. In the face of that hugely increased French strength, Wellington retreated into Portugal.

Pakenham's old outfit, the Seventh Fusiliers, arrived in Portugal from Halifax in July 1810. About that same time, to Pakenham's delight, Wellington relieved him of his staff duties and placed him in command of a brigade that included the Seventh Fusiliers. Now Pakenham was going to see action as a commander under the great Wellington. First would come the Battle of Bussaco, north of Coimbra, Portugal, then a retreat southward to Torres Vedras, north of Lisbon. After that, Wellington, with Pakenham, would resume the offensive against the might of Napoleon.

## ∴ 7 ∴

# The Hero of Salamanca

At Torres Vedras, a village just north of Lisbon, Colonel Sir Edward Pakenham could see the extensive fortifications that Lieutenant General Lord Wellington had ordered built to make of Lisbon a nearly impregnable shelter for his army, a last-ditch refuge that would be needed should Napoleon's armies overwhelm the British and Portuguese forces and the Peninsular War threaten to come to an inglorious end. On high ground on either side of Torres Vedras, stretching diagonally more than twenty miles across the Lisbon peninsula from the River Tagus to the Atlantic Ocean, British engineers and thousands of Portuguese laborers had erected barriers of earthworks and palisades, of gabions and fascines, in front of which they had dug deep trenches. Behind those formidable obstacles, gun emplacements had been constructed to allow defenders to direct artillery fire onto an advancing enemy. Altogether, Pakenham could see, it was a daunting line of defense.

Although thus prepared, and conscious of London's concern for the safety of the British army under his command, Wellington was sure that Napoleon would not commit to the Portuguese front sufficient troops to force a British evacuation. To do so would make French-held areas in Spain, and the French forces that garrisoned them, too vulnerable to the armies of aggressive Spanish rebels. Despite calls for him to abandon Portugal and return his army safely to Britain, Wellington was determined to stay and fight.

The French, led by Marshal Andrea Massena (whose proficiency at warfare was such that he had risen from sergeant to general in less than four years), had marched seventy thousand troops against the allied

British and Portuguese armies, and Wellington, in the face of those superior numbers, had withdrawn from western Spain into western Portugal. Wellington had stopped to make a stand at Almeida, but a catastrophic explosion that blew up a gunpowder magazine had defeated that effort, and Wellington's army had quickly withdrawn from Almeida and continued its retreat down the Mondego River valley.

On September 27, 1810, at Bussaco, in west-central Portugal, Wellington's army had once again halted to face Massena's dogged pursuers. Pakenham was commanding a brigade composed of the Seventh Fusiliers and the Seventy-ninth Foot, some 1,792 men, one of the brigades that Wellington held in reserve. So successful were Wellington's measures to counter the standard Napoleonic tactics employed by Massena, clearly demonstrating the superiority of the firepower of a line over that of a column, that Pakenham's units had not seen action at Bussaco. After some five hours of fierce fighting, Massena had called off the assault on the allies' positions. Of some 65,000 men, Massena had lost 4,600 killed, wounded, or captured, among them more than 300 officers. Four French generals had been wounded; another had been killed. Wellington's forces, about 25,000 British and 25,000 Portuguese troops, had lost 1,252, half of them Portuguese, half British.

The next day, September 28, 1810, threatened by the French cavalry's sweeping flanking movement, Wellington had resumed his retreat toward his prepared defenses at Torres Vedras. Massena had swiftly resumed pursuit.

By October 8, the day that Portugal's annual autumn rains began that year, Wellington's army had begun taking positions behind the lines of Torres Vedras. It was on October 10 that Pakenham first saw the massive system of fortifications—three lines of obstacles, both man-made and natural, laced through hill and valley and plain, bristling with bastions, masonry citadels, hilltop forts, and hundreds of artillery emplacements. The fortifications were manned by 25,000 Portuguese militiamen, 8,000 Spanish troops, and 2,500 British marines and artillerymen, already in place as Pakenham's brigade and the rest of Wellington's retreating troops poured in to take positions behind them.

At each end of the lines the British navy, manning small craft mounted with guns in the Tagus and larger vessels in the Atlantic and the mouth of the Saint Laurenca River, lay protecting against any waterborne flanking movement.

On October 14 Massena got his first look at what Wellington had wrought. He halted his army before the lines of Torres Vedras and with apparent chagrin demanded to know why he had not been warned that such an impassable obstacle barred his approach to Wellington's sanctuary in Lisbon. He apparently got no good answer but was told only that Wellington had erected the defenses, as if that were an explanation.[1] Thwarted but unwilling to assault Wellington's defenses as he had disastrously done at Bussaco, Massena ordered his troops to dig in, establishing a defensive position of their own and hoping either that Napoleon would send reinforcements or that Wellington would come out from the Torres Vedras lines to attack the French position.

Wellington knew there was not enough forage in the area to supply Massena's army, in part because Wellington had ordered the destruction of all food and crops, and supply from the rear was nearly impossible over such a great distance from a French base. Wellington therefore settled in for a long wait, his soldiers as well as the area's civilian population being amply supplied throughout the five hundred square miles of his strategic refuge.

"The Armies have remained close in presence with each other for near a month," Pakenham reported in a letter dated November 9, 1810. "The enemy are employed in seeking provisions, whilst we are occupied in strengthening our position."[2]

Not all was business behind the lines, however. Pakenham also reported that Wellington had staged a grand ball to celebrate the knighting of Sir William C. Beresford, the British officer who commanded Wellington's Portuguese troops. "The facts of a general having invited the officers of his army to an amusement distant from the nearest point from three to four leagues, and an opposing army of fifty thousand strong close to our lines appears like madness, but look at the result," Pakenham wrote. "All Lisbon were invited to meet us. The

Portuguese Officers have been pleased by witnessing the distinction granted to their commander (Beresford) which honour is attributable to their own good conduct! In short, by this simple or apparently mad act of amusement, confidence has been transmitted to the Capital—pride and self-confidence instilled into the National troops of Portugal. Viva!!!"[3]

For more than a month Massena's army remained dug in around the town of Sobral, southeast of Torres Vedras. Then, in November, Massena pulled back about thirty miles to the north, and by December his troops had dug into new positions between Santarem and Rio Maior, there again to wait while each side viewed the other without daring to risk its army in a major assault. During the calm, Wellington's adjutant general, Charles Stewart, went on leave, and Wellington again assigned Pakenham the job of deputy adjutant general to fill in for Stewart. In January 1811, after several weeks in the job, Pakenham gently complained to his brother that "I have taken to the quill as a matter of duty and shall do the best I can, though to my hand I cannot but consider it an unnatural instrument."[4]

After many months of wear, the uniforms of Wellington's troops, as well as those of his officers, were becoming ragged, giving Pakenham a new concern as he fretted at his unenjoyable tasks. "I beg you will have sent out by the first safe opportunity," he wrote to his brother, "cloth for Regimental coat, blue cloth sufficient for facings, cuff and collar-trimmings." He also asked for boots and buttons. "I am in very great distress," he told his brother.[5]

In early March 1811 Massena's army, losing men at the rate of five hundred a week from sickness, starvation, and the depredations of Portuguese peasants retaliating for cruelties committed by French soldiers, finally began withdrawing, headed toward the Portuguese-Spanish border. Wellington set his troops in motion to follow and harry the retreating Frenchmen, withdrawing in two columns. Pakenham joined the pursuit, observing in horror the desolation left behind by Massena's army. "The debased ingenuity of man," he reported, "when converted to human torment could hardly be supposed capable of suggesting the acts of horror actually committed by these fiends of hell; every village and town had been set fire to, all peasants taken have been killed in the most cruel manner, the women, nay, even females from childhood violated."[6]

On April 10, 1811, satisfied that the French menace was now gone from Portugal, Wellington issued a proclamation stating that the enemy, having suffered great losses—an estimated twenty-five thousand troops—had withdrawn across the Agueda River into Spain. The people of Portugal, he declared, were "therefore at liberty to return to their homes."[7] In April Pakenham gave his own report of the situation, writing, "There now remains in Portugal, of one hundred and four invading Battalions, but two as the garrison of Almeida. . . . Half that army commanded by Massena has been sacrificed, viz. . . . 30,000 men; and the remnant are disorganized and to a degree unhealthy."[8]

When, in mid-April, Wellington decided to see for himself what the French were doing at Badajoz, just across the Spanish border, some 165 miles east of Lisbon, he left his army under the temporary command of Sir Brent Spencer, a general known more for his bonhomie than his military ability. Pakenham, apparently reflecting the view shared by his fellow officers, complained to his brother that Spencer was "as good a fellow as possible to meet at a country club, but as to succeeding Wellington, it is quite Dam . . . . . . . n [*sic*] to him. I have so much horse-duty I have quite knocked my animals to pieces."[9]

Wellington ordered a siege of the French garrison at Badajoz, placing General Beresford in command of the allied forces there, then raced back to rejoin his army south of Almeida, which Massena now attempted to reinforce and which was the last position held by the French in Portugal. Massena's troops and Wellington's met in a three-day battle at Fuentes de Onoro, a town just east of Almeida, and despite allied failings that greatly upset Wellington, the French were defeated and forced to abandon Almeida. Pakenham's family biographer, Valerie McNair Scott, refers to the memoirs of Lieutenant William Grattan, who, recounting the battle at Almeida, reported that Pakenham "fought with particular gallantry in this action. . . . [Grattan] paints a vivid picture of him riding through the streets of the town as the French round shot ploughed up the ground about him."[10] The French lost 2,192 men in the fight; the allies lost 1,545.

The news from Albuera, where Beresford had battled to keep his position in his siege of Badajoz, was also mixed. Beresford had managed to hold on to his position but had suffered heavy casualties under bombardment by the artillery of the French marshal Nicolas-Jean de Dieu Soult, losing four thousand men from his army of ten thousand. Dismayed by the heavy losses, Wellington decided to abandon his siege of Badajoz in the face of advancing French reinforcements.

Four days after the battle at Albuera, Pakenham learned what the cost had been to his beloved fusiliers, who had played a prominent role in the fight. Many of his old comrades had fallen; thirty-four officers from the Seventh Fusiliers, Pakenham's own regiment, had been wounded. Eighteen hundred troops had been lost, almost two-thirds of the regiment. Pakenham seemed heartbroken, not only by the losses but by his not having been with his regiment. Wellington had ordered him to stay with General Spencer in the vicinity of Almeida. Having seen the reports of the Albuera battle, Pakenham was highly critical of Beresford and the spin Beresford had put on his report. "In truth," Pakenham wrote to his brother Tom, "there never was an official detail which more completely failed to put the Authorities . . . in possession of both the circumstances and the fact of the affair."[11]

To his brother, Pakenham repeated his desire to "have done with the clerking business and once more get into the line of a soldier commanding a Brigade."[12] On July 25, 1811, he wrote again to his brother, this time with good news, which he credited to his brother-in-law. "I find I am to go to a Brigade," he said. "Wellington though quite the Commander of Forces is positively my brother in all our dealings."[13] In August Pakenham received more good news. He had been promoted to brigadier general, a fact that was taking some getting used to. "I have been obliged to assume some reserve," he wrote to his brother, "to avoid laughing at the constant 'General' commencing and concluding sentences."[14]

He saw brief action in September 1811 when some of his units were ordered to prevent the French from resupplying their garrison at Ciudad Rodrigo. At the end of October, however, he was stricken with what was described as an intestinal obstruction, which nearly became fatal but from which he recovered, at least partly so, within in a matter of weeks. In November he was sent home, apparently to complete his recovery.

Bad news was waiting for him in London. His Majesty's ship *Saldanha,* captained by Pakenham's brother William, had gone down in a gale; its entire crew, including William Pakenham, had been lost.

Edward stayed with his sister Kitty, Lady Wellington, in her home on Harley Street in London and there regained his health and vitality. In January 1812, at age thirty-three, he was promoted to major general. The following spring, pursuing an active social life after recuperating, he fell in love.

She was nineteen-year-old Annabella Milbanke. Gossip had it that she had already rejected several suitors, her expected inheritance perhaps making her unusually choosy. Pakenham—for whatever reason, for Annabella has been described as unimaginative and humorless—was immediately drawn to her, perhaps revealing something of his own personality. He attempted to charm her with tales of Wellington, the nation's most illustrious soldier, hoping no doubt that some of Wellington's glamor might rub off on him. Annabella apparently was not charmed by stories of the great Wellington nor impressed by the things military that Pakenham loved. She found Pakenham's manner a bit too formal and his fondness for military subjects off-putting. She also, perhaps out of jealousy, was stingingly critical of Kitty, Lady Wellington. Annabella at last concluded that, as she said, "General Pakenham's opinions are not founded on the same principles as mine."[15]

And so it probably was not surprising to her confidantes that when Pakenham proposed to her on Saint Patrick's Day, 1812, she turned him down. Part of her explanation was that she had heard "that all the Pakenham family have a strong family tendency to insanity,"[16] a claim unsupported by evidence. Not long after she rejected Pakenham, she dismissed another suitor, it was said, claiming that in his family, too, there was a strong strain of insanity. (In January 1815 she married the sexually ambivalent, clubfooted poet and rake Lord George Gordon Byron, whose notorious affairs included one with his half sister. After giving birth to a daughter in December 1815, Annabella left Byron and moved back in with her parents in January 1816. Byron left the country three months later, never to return.)

Soon after Annabella turned him down, Pakenham shipped out for Portugal once again. On April 1, 1812, Kitty wrote to their brother Hercules, also serving in the Peninsular War, about Edward. "Edward goes to-morrow," she said in the letter. "I am glad he does, though not as strong as we wish him, but he is free from illness and is become so anxious to join you all now that you have been moving, that a longer delay in this country would but vex and irritate his nerves."[17] By the end of April he was back in Lisbon.

He also was back in his sickbed, his fever having recurred. He spent the next several weeks treating his illness with quinine, impatient to return to action. During Pakenham's absence, Wellington's army had taken the fortress of Ciudad Rodrigo, in western Spain, after an eleven-day siege that ended on January 19, 1812, and had turned its attention south to Badajoz, another Spanish fortress city and considered the key to Portugal.

With a force of some 60,000 men, British and Portuguese, Wellington once again laid siege to Badajoz. The first assault against the city's fortifications was launched on the night of April 6, 1812, and was turned back by the French defenders with heavy losses by the allies. Wellington ordered a second assault, which also was repulsed with heavy losses. Five assaults were made on the fortification before attackers finally reached the top of the ramparts with ladders and attacked the defenders at the breaches that had been pounded into the walls by the allies' artillery. The breaches were then stormed, and after days of carnage, Badajoz at last fell to Wellington's forces.

Nearly all of Badajoz's 5,000 French defenders perished in the assaults, only a few cavalrymen escaping. Allied losses totaled 4,760. Among the British casualties was Pakenham's brother Hercules, who was severely wounded in the assault of April 16.

Edward was so eager to return to his units that he took it upon himself to leave Lisbon and rejoin his men in May 1812, during heavy rains. A sudden return of his fever, however, forced him back to bed, and it was not until June that he was well enough to return to active duty. No sooner had he rejoined Wellington's forces than Sir Thomas Picton, commanding general of Wellington's Third Division, still suffering from a severe wound received at Badajoz, asked that Pakenham, an old friend, be his replacement as commander, a request that Wellington approved. Therefore as Wellington turned his army northeast toward Salamanca, Pakenham rode with it as a division commander, a new role and new challenge for him.

Wellington was showing respect for Pakenham's generalship. He told one of his colonels that "my partiality for him [Pakenham] does not lead me astray when I tell you that he is one of the best we have."[18] That assessment was not a solitary one. Another British officer, Sir George Napier, called Pakenham "one of the most candid, generous, honourable, active and intelligent general officers in the service."[19]

Salamanca, one of Spain's most historical cities, stands more than twenty-five hundred feet above sea level on the north bank of the Tormes River in western Spain, on the trade route from Astorga in the northwest to Seville in the southwest. Originally an Iberian settlement, it was sacked by Hannibal in 217 B.C. and rebuilt as a walled city by the Romans beside the arched bridge they erected to span the Tormes River. Occupied by Moors from the eighth to the eleventh century, it was won back and repopulated by Christians after 1087. Among its architectural splendors are the University of Salamanca, Spain's oldest university, founded by King Alfonso IX in 1218; the old Romanesque cathedral, construction of which was begun around 1140; and the "new" cathedral, begun in 1513. In the cloister of Salamanca's Church of Saint Esteban in 1486, Christopher Columbus was examined by the Council of Theologians. Saint Teresa of Avila founded a Carmelite convent in Salamanca in 1570, and a Jesuit seminary, which later became the Pontifical University, operated there from 1617 to 1755.

Before dawn on June 13, 1812, Wellington marched his 48,000 troops on Salamanca, advancing in three columns and meeting little opposition on the way. On June 17, 1812, he rode across the arched Roman bridge into the ancient city, there to receive a wildly enthusiastic welcome by the city's officials and inhabitants. Marshal Marmont's army had quickly withdrawn from the city upon Wellington's approach. The only remaining French force in Salamanca was a garrison that Marmont had left to defend a set of fortifications in the western suburbs of the city, which Wellington immediately besieged. Marmont had moved the bulk of his fifty-thousand-man army to better maneuver against the allies.

Wellington responded by moving all but the besieging Sixth Division north of the city, establishing positions on a set of hills near the village of San Christobal, apparently hoping that Marmont would attack him in an effort to save the besieged French garrison in Salamanca. On the evening of June 20 Marmont began an advance on San Christobal, but over the next two days, although the two armies were within artillery range of each other, only minor action occurred. Several of his generals, including Pakenham, urged an attack on Marmont at that point, but Wellington, who had a reputation for doing things his own way, disregarded their advice and declined to engage.

On the night of June 22, while Wellington delayed an attack on the French position, Marmont shifted his army to the east. Meanwhile, the besieged French garrison in Salamanca, hammered by Wellington's eighteen-pounders and howitzers that rained fiery hotshot onto the fortification, finally had had enough punishment and surrendered on the afternoon of June 27, suffering the loss of 800 men, including 600 taken prisoner. British losses were put at 430. Once the garrison had been subdued, Wellington was able to turn his full attention to Marmont's main force, which was encamped at the village of Huerta, on the Tormes River, about a half day's march from Salamanca.

Marmont refused to wait for Wellington's next move, suddenly shifting part of his strength to the southeast to move against Wellington's supply lines, then shifting again to the north. Wellington countered with a movement toward the north. The two armies were now separated by the Duero River, Marmont on the north bank and Wellington on the south, and stood facing each other between the towns of Toro and Tordesillas, about fifty miles north of Salamanca. There they cautiously eyed each other until July 16, when Marmont suddenly marched west, crossed the Duero, and began a series of maneuvers apparently designed to force the allied army back to Ciudad Rodrigo, to the southwest.

On July 18 Marmont turned south, and Wellington did also, the two armies moving in parallel, within artillery range of each other. At dawn on July 22 both armies were south of Salamanca, in mostly treeless, rolling country, moving southwesterly, toward Ciudad Rodrigo. Marmont's force, moving more swiftly, was beginning to turn the allies' southern flank. Pakenham's Third Division, along with a brigade of 450 Portuguese cavalrymen commanded by the British brigadier general Benjamin D'Urban, had been detached from the main body of Wellington's army. It was moving southward on a route to the west of the main body, apparently to support a retreat if one became necessary, or to act as a reserve in case Wellington decided to attack or was attacked.

Later that day Wellington was able to observe from the height on which he stood that in their rush to block the allies' route and force a fight, the French had overextended their line as it curved toward the west, and Marmont's westernmost element, the infantry division commanded by Brigadier General J. G. B. Thomieres, had advanced too far to be quickly supported by the units to the east of it. It was the sort of mistake Wellington had been waiting for. He quickly swung up into his saddle and sped off toward Aldea Tejada, to the west, in search of Pakenham, so that he could deliver his orders to him in person. Finding him, Wellington galloped up, dismounted, and commanded Pakenham to launch a direct assault on Thomieres's division.

As Pakenham rode off to launch his attack, Wellington turned to the staff officers who had accompanied him. "Did you ever see a man who understood so clearly what he had to do?" he asked, then galloped off to deliver orders to his other division commanders.[20] Captain James Campbell was one who recalled Pakenham's rapid response to his orders. "To me, as Brigade-Major of the right brigade," Campbell wrote, "Sir Edward Pakenham, in his quick, decided manner, pointed out the direction we were to take, and desired me to tell Colonel Wallace, 88th regiment, the officer in temporary command of the brigade, to move on with as much rapidity as possible, but without blowing the men too much."[21]

Campbell then described the action that followed the execution of Pakenham's orders:

> The division was soon under arms, and moved off rapidly in open column, right in front, the 45th regiment leading. . . . We soon descended into a kind of valley, or rather hollow, and having brought up our left shoulders a little, we pushed on at a quick pace, but in excellent order, to the right; the side of the hollow towards the enemy concealing our movements from their sight.
>
> The whole scene was now highly animating. The left brigade, headed by the 5th regiment, was, I saw, marching parallel to the right, so as to be ready to form a second line. The Portuguese [infantry] brigade followed the right, and the whole of the left flank of the columns was covered by a cloud of sharpshooters, composed of light infantry companies, and riflemen of the 5th battalion, 60th regiment.
>
> Having moved a considerable distance in this order, (field officers and adjutants prolonging the line of march) the head of the column, by bringing up the right shoulder, began gradually to ascend the hill, on the top of which we expected to find the enemy still extending to their left. At length, having fairly outflanked the French left, the whole formed line, and with Sir Edward Pakenham in front, hat in hand, the brigades advanced in beautiful style, covered by our sharpshooters, the right of the first line admirably supported by the left brigade.[22]

Pakenham had apparently marched his division in column south to a point where it was even with the advancing line of Thomieres's troops, then faced his column to the left to present a broad front line to the

French, who were taken by surprise. As the troops of the Third Division formed into a line, Pakenham rode along the divisional units, giving a pep talk to each battalion.

Pakenham's troops were now too close for the French to retreat in good order. French artillery apparently were unable to set up and fire, since the advancing British and Portuguese had come upon the French lines so suddenly. What is more, Thomieres's troops were outnumbered by Pakenham's. A vigorous assault by D'Urban's brigade of Portuguese cavalry, protecting Pakenham's right flank, had left Thomieres with but four battalions of infantry to face the charge of twelve allied battalions. Meanwhile, Pakenham's artillery had now set up on a ridge to the north and had commenced firing into the confused mass of French infantry.

Captain Campbell recorded the ensuing action:

> The enemy's skirmishers and ours now set to work, yet we did not wait for their indecisive long shots; but advancing still rapidly and steadily, our right soon came into contact with their left, which had opened a very heavy and destructive fire upon us, and which would have lasted long enough had the brigade been halted to return it, but it was instantly charged and overthrown. It was now evident to us all that Sir Edward Pakenham knew how to handle Picton's division.[23]

Volleys from the nearly eighteen hundred muskets of Lieutenant Colonel Wallace's three infantry battalions in the lead brigade and grapeshot from the division's artillery cut into Thomieres's division as Pakenham's troops advanced, their flanks protected on the right by D'Urban's Portuguese dragoons and on the left by cavalry under the command of Lieutenant Colonel Arentschildt. The leading French battalions took enormous losses, and General Thomieres himself was killed in the onslaught. The French infantry units dissolved in the slaughter and the rearward rush of the survivors, the artillery units leaving their guns behind in their flight. Pakenham's division now began to drive the enemy before it, as ordered.

At the sound of combat coming from the west, the signal that Pakenham's units had struck Thomieres's division, Wellington ordered his other divisions into the battle, attacking Marmont's formation from the north and west in a massive, coordinated assault. Marmont's army was overwhelmed, destroyed as an effective fighting force, only its tattered remnants managing to escape back across the Tormes River and wherever else its fleeing soldiers could find safety. Marmont had lost approximately 30 percent of his army as casualties on the battlefield, and another 30 percent had simply disappeared. Against the allies' losses of fifty-two hundred, French casualties totaled around 13,000. Marshal Marmont had been severely wounded in the battle, and his second-in-command, General Bertrand Clausel, who had taken over for Marmont, was also wounded.

The victory at Salamanca was the greatest British triumph of the Napoleonic Wars and the biggest French defeat in more than ten years. It not only smashed Marmont's army but, more significantly, was, as one chronicler put it, "the beginning of the end of French domination of Spain."[24] It also opened the way for the recapture of Madrid. Wellington, whose fame now spread across the continent, gave Pakenham much of the credit for the battle's success. "I ordered Major Gen. the Hon. E. Pakenham to move forward with the 3d division," Wellington wrote in his report, "to turn the enemy's left on the heights. The attack upon the enemy's left was made in the manner above described, and completely succeeded. Major Gen. the Hon. E. Pakenham formed the 3d division across the enemy's flank, and overthrew everything opposed to him."[25]

In another report, one that was less formal and more candid, Wellington wrote, "I put Pakenham in the 3d Division by General Picton's desire when he was ill, and I am very glad I did so as I must say he made the manoeuvre which led to our success."[26]

For Pakenham, Salamanca was to prove the high point of a career.

## ∴ 8 ∴

# The Approaching Conflict

When James Madison took over as America's secretary of state in May 1801, following Thomas Jefferson's election as president in 1800, he was fifty years old, a mild-mannered, unprepossessing man who habitually dressed in black, five foot six, small-boned, thin, and thin-voiced, all of which made him a conspicuous contrast to his effervescent, fun-loving wife, Dolley, who was tall and buxom, fashionably and colorfully dressed, and sixteen years younger than he. From his appearance and manner, someone who did not know about Madison might mistake him as meek and weak. His words and actions would more faithfully reveal the man he was.

Two years into Jefferson's administration, Britain's war to prevent Napoleon's complete conquest of Europe was consuming the combatant countries and threatening to consume neutrals as well. The United States, against its will and interests, was being drawn into the conflict, which after a less-than-one-year hiatus resulting from the Treaty of Amiens, reignited in 1803.

Not all of the war's effects were bad for the United States. In 1802 President Jefferson had set out to buy the strategic city of New Orleans and west Florida from France. But when Napoleon, strapped for cash to pursue his conquests, offered the entire Louisiana Territory, from the Mississippi River to the Rocky Mountains and from the Gulf of Mexico to Canada, for fifteen million dollars, Jefferson jumped at the opportunity. On April 30, 1803, the date of the sale treaty, the United States doubled its size with the addition of Louisiana to its territory.

Andrew Jackson, meanwhile, realizing that such a vast expanse of real estate, with important cities and trade routes included, would need an administrator, one who could defend it against all claimants, applied for the job of governor of the new acquisition. Jefferson, however, gave the job to William Charles Cole Claiborne, a Jackson friend and the man who had succeeded Jackson as congressman when Jackson was elected to the Senate in 1797. Their paths would cross again.

Propelled solely by its own concerns, which came to include the acquisition of New Orleans, Britain was fast turning the United States into a victim of its war with Napoleon. In response, Secretary of State Madison in May 1803 sent his ace negotiator, James Monroe, to London to work out two big problems foisted upon the Americans by Britain. What Madison had in mind was a treaty designed, as he said, to "put an end to every danger to which the harmony between the two countries is now subjected."[1]

The problem that most outraged the American public was impressment. Britain ruled the seas, which was especially important to do in its efforts to contain Napoleon, but to continue to rule required a large fleet of warships manned by a very large number of crewmen, who mostly served under harsh conditions for poor pay. At the same time, America's merchant fleet was growing and needed more sailors to man its vessels, which offered better conditions and higher pay than did the British navy and merchant marine. British seamen forsook their ships and signed aboard American vessels. Some were deserters from the British navy; many were simply former British subjects who had decided to become Americans and earn a living on American ships. One estimate places the number of British seamen on American vessels at 25 percent of the total number of sailors working on American vessels, or upwards of 12,500 men.[2]

Faced with a dangerous drain on its seagoing manpower, Britain in the 1790s began stopping American ships on the high seas, boarding them, and forcibly removing any seamen believed to be British (their accents were usually a dead giveaway), pressing them into service aboard British naval vessels. Between 1803 and 1812, according to one estimate, some six thousand seamen had been abducted from American ships and forced to serve aboard British vessels.[3]

In the face of American protests, the British government released victims of impressment who could substantiate their claim to be American citizens, but the process of substantiation and release, conducted through the two nations' diplomatic channels, was long and drawn out, often taking years. Meanwhile, the men affected—citizens of the United States—continued their forced service aboard British warships, facing all the hazards of Britain's naval warfare.

The other big problem that Madison and President Jefferson wanted solved had several parts to it but was basically a matter of the rights of neutral nations whose shipping was affected by the principal combatants in the Napoleonic Wars, Britain and France. France had instituted policies designed to injure, if not shut down, Britain's trade with other nations. Britain had retaliated with its own policies designed to counter France's policies and limit neutrals' trade with France. The effect of that conflict was the seizure of American merchant vessels by both Britain and France and the confiscation of cargoes, resulting in huge losses to American merchants, traders, and shipping interests.

In dispatching Monroe to London to negotiate a treaty, Madison and Jefferson felt that American trade, exports as well as imports, was so important to the belligerent countries, especially Britain, that the British government could not fail to respond to American grievances. If Britain nevertheless did fail to meet those grievances, Madison and Jefferson were prepared to impose retaliatory restrictions, to the point of ordering an embargo aimed at shutting off all American trade with the British.

Apparently believing that Monroe could use some assistance in the negotiations, Jefferson and Madison sent Baltimore lawyer William Pinkney to help him persuade British officials. After many months of dickering, the British government finally came up with a treaty proposal, the so-called Monroe-Pinkney Treaty. In the eyes of Madison and President Jefferson, the treaty had a couple of unacceptable faults. It provided that in the event that France attempted to block American trade with Britain, the British reserved the right to retaliate by denying American trade to France, meaning that seizures and confiscations of

American vessels and cargo would recur, in effect nullifying the treaty. On the matter of impressment, the British refused to yield, claiming that impressment was their right. And so impressment was not mentioned in the proposed treaty, which Monroe and Pinkney, on behalf of the American government, on December 31, 1806, nevertheless signed and soon thereafter shipped off to Madison.

The document reached Madison on March 3, 1807; he promptly delivered it to Jefferson, now in his second term, resignedly telling he president that he thought it was about as much as could reasonably be expected from the British, which was a lot less than what Jefferson wanted.

To take effect, the proposed treaty had to be ratified by the United States Senate, but first it had to be submitted to the Senate by the president. Jefferson refused to submit it. Britain's failure to promise to end impressment made the treaty unacceptable to Jefferson and Madison and, Jefferson believed, would make it unacceptable to the Senate as well. The proposed treaty and its provisions simply died on President Jefferson's desk.

In June 1807 American-British relations were strained further. The United States Navy frigate *Chesapeake* was known by British officials to include a number of British subjects in its crew, four of whom they believed to be deserters from the British navy. Frustrated in their attempts to retrieve the deserters by diplomatic means, the British decided on a direct approach. The commander of the British naval squadron stationed at Halifax, Nova Scotia, Sir George Berkeley, ordered his ship captains to apprehend the deserters, using force if necessary.

On June 22, 1807, one of Berkeley's warships, HMS *Leopard,* sailed up to the *Chesapeake* in sight of the Virginia coast and demanded that it allow a party to come aboard and look for deserters. The captain of the *Chesapeake* refused, whereupon the *Leopard* fired three broadsides into the *Chesapeake,* killing three crewmen and wounding eighteen others. Unwilling to suffer further damage, the American captain yielded. A

British party boarded the *Chesapeake* and carried off the four alleged deserters. The *Chesapeake* then headed back to port.

The incident set off expressions of public and official outrage, and President Jefferson ordered all British warships to leave American waters. The British government disavowed the assault on the American warship and offered to pay reparations. It also offered to return three of the four alleged deserters, who were found to be American citizens—the fourth, a British subject, was hanged—and the British navy relieved Berkeley of his command (although it later gave him another one). Settlement of the matter dragged on until 1811, while American anger smoldered.

Some months after the *Chesapeake* affair, the British government came up with new outrages. In his so-called Berlin Decree of November 1806, Napoleon had pronounced the whole of the British Isles under blockade, making vessels attempting to land in a British port subject to seizure. In January 1807 Britain retaliated with a series of decrees, called Orders in Council, intended to control all trade between neutral countries and the Continent. The Orders in Council at first forbade trade between ports on the Continent, which American ships had been carrying on. Then the orders placed under blockade all ports from which British goods were barred, the penalty for violation being seizure. Then they demanded that ships of neutral nations carrying cargo bound for a port on the Continent stop first at a British port and pay a duty on their cargoes. Napoleon responded with his so-called Milan Decree, which made all ships complying with the Orders in Council subject to seizure by the French.

Madison and Jefferson reacted to the Orders in Council with a hard-line countermeasure. Devoutly believing that Britain could be brought to its knees by economic pressure, Jefferson and Madison asked Congress for legislation that would prohibit American ships from trading with Europe. Congress all too hastily complied, passing the Embargo Act on December 22, 1807. The act soon began hurting American interests more than those of Britain. American exports, which totaled $108 million in 1807, dropped to $22 million in 1808,[4] and hundreds of American ships, with their crews, were idled. America's loss was Canada's gain. American farmers desperate for a market for their products soon figured out that they could ship their goods by river and lake into Canada, where they were then turned over for shipment to Britain. Canadians took over much of the export business that had been in the hands of Americans, and Canadian farmers gained an expanded British market for their produce. Britain at the same time developed new markets for its products in South America, no longer having to compete with businesses in the United States.

Far from Madison's expectations, the Embargo Act turned out to be a political and economic disaster, particularly in New England, where the economic injury was so severe that talk of secession began to grow. Members of Congress and others who looked to Jefferson to remedy the situation found him, as his term neared its end, thinking not of solutions to the nation's problems but of retirement to Monticello and the peaceful Virginia countryside. Jefferson seemed content to let his successor handle the mounting troubles of the nation and come to terms with its adversaries across the Atlantic.

After the Electoral College voted in December 1808, the nation learned who the new president would be. The man who would succeed Jefferson, who would now bear the heaviest responsibility for dealing with—and resolving—America's swelling crisis, was James Madison.

Madison was inaugurated as the fourth president of the United States on March 4, 1809, twelve days shy of his fifty-eighth birthday. On that same day the Embargo Act was repealed by a Congress dominated by Madison's own Republican Party. Weeks earlier Congress had rejected a proposal made by Madison and Secretary of the Treasury Albert Gallatin to begin preparations for war and to close the loopholes of the Embargo Act. Now, wishfully thinking there was a better way to see the country through its woes, Congress passed the Non-Intercourse Act. It purportedly prohibited trade with Britain and France and their colonies but allowed trade with all other nations. In fact, however, it permitted a certain amount of trade with Britain and France because once American ships left their harbors, they were free to go wherever they pleased. British and French ships, though, were banned from United States ports.

After a year of the Non-Intercourse Act's failure to affect British and French policies toward neutrals, but still clinging to the notion that the belligerents could be manipulated by economic means, Congress in May 1810 repealed the act and enacted a measure called Macon's Bill No. 2. At the heart of that measure were provisions that reinstituted trade with both Britain and France but that promised to renew sanctions against either country if it revoked its restrictions on trade with neutrals.

In August 1810 Napoleon, perhaps as a ploy, let Madison know that he would rescind the Berlin and Milan decrees with the understanding that the United States would also force Britain to respect its rights as a neutral. In November 1810, under the provisions of Macon's Bill No. 2, Madison reimposed nonintercourse restrictions against the British and told British authorities that they would have to revoke the Orders in Council before trade with the United States could be resumed. They refused.

Relations with Britain continued to worsen. Early in 1811 the United States envoy to England returned home, letting a mere chargé d'affaires run America's diplomatic business in London. Minor British officials were doing the same in Washington. In May another explosive confrontation occurred between American and British warships, this time the American vessel getting the better of it. Aiming to deter further impressment of American seamen, the United States Navy ordered the heavy frigate *President* to patrol the Atlantic coast. On the night of May 16, 1811, the *President* encountered HMS *Little Belt,* a smaller ship, and the two vessels exchanged fire. In the exchange nine crewmen aboard the *Little Belt* were killed, and twenty-three others were wounded. In Britain the incident was called unprovoked aggression, and several British newspapers demanded retaliation. "The blood of our murdered countrymen must be revenged," the *London Courier* declared. "The conduct of America leaves us no alternative."[5] Many Americans, on the other hand, considered the affair a fitting payback for the *Leopard*'s deadly attack on the *Chesapeake*.

In July 1811 a new British minister to the United States, Augustus John Foster, arrived in Washington with new demands to make on President Madison. Threatening retaliation if the United States did not accede, he demanded that the nonintercourse restrictions be lifted, claiming that Napoleon was *not* voiding the Berlin and Milan decrees but was still interfering with the trade of neutrals. He further declared that the Orders in Council would not be rescinded unless Napoleon allowed British goods to be imported to the Continent. In his dealings with Madison's secretary of state, James Monroe, Foster seemed to reflect a British attitude that had become even more contentious. By August 1811, Madison had decided that "Foster seems more disposed to play the diplomatist, than the conciliatory negociator."[6]

The mounting grievances of Americans against Britain were not all about outrages at sea. When, in 1810, new Indian uprisings, led by Tecumseh, a Shawnee, and his brother, known as the Prophet, occurred in what was then the United States' northwest frontier (present-day Indiana), British troublemakers were blamed for providing the Indians with encouragement and supplies. The governor of the Indiana Territory, William Henry Harrison, marshaled an army of a thousand regular troops and militiamen and began a march on the Indians' camp at Prophet's Town, at the confluence of the Wabash and Tippecanoe rivers, not far from present-day Lafayette. Before Harrison's soldiers reached the Indian camp, however, they were taken by surprise in a predawn attack by six hundred or more Indians on November 7, 1811. Although suffering nearly two hundred casualties, Harrison's army defeated the attackers, killing about a hundred and driving off the rest, in what came to be known as the Battle of Tippecanoe. The day after the battle, Harrison's army continued on to Prophet's Town and burned it to the ground.

Indian attacks on white farms and settlements nevertheless continued, and the level of alarm of the white settlers and their representatives remained high. "Most of the Citizens in this Country [Indiana]," Governor Harrison reported, "have abandoned their farms and taken refuge in Such temporary forts as they have been able to construct."[7] Newspapers around the nation saw bloody British hands reaching across the Canadian border to foment the Indian atrocities. Stories of the attacks appeared under headlines that shouted, "Anglo-Savage War," and "Anglo-Indian War."[8] In Massachusetts, the *Lexington Reporter* wrote, "The war on the Wabash is purely British. The scalping knife and tomahawk of British savages is now again devastating our frontiers."[9]

The murderous Indian uprisings, which had been occurring intermittently since the 1760s, had become more frequent, and American public opinion coincided with that expressed in the March 7, 1812, edition of *Niles' Register:* "We have had but one opinion as the cause of the depredations of the Indians; they are instigated and supported by the British in Canada."[10] The public outcry was for the United States to expel the British from Canada. Much of the public also was urging military action in west Florida, where Spain, preoccupied with resistance to Napoleon's takeover and allied with Britain in the Peninsular War, was allowing the British to establish bases, and in east Florida as well, where on Amelia Island, just below the Saint Mary's River, which separated Spanish Florida from the United States, the British were running a smuggling operation to evade the nonintercourse restrictions.

The cause of frontier settlers, demanding expulsion of the British from Canada and Florida and advocating frontier expansion, was being championed by a vigorous group of congressmen, among them Felix Grundy of Tennessee; Henry Clay and Richard M. Johnson of Kentucky; George M. Troup of Georgia; Peter B. Porter of New York; John A. Harper of New Hampshire; and John C. Calhoun, Langdon Cheves, William Lowndes, and David R. Williams of South Carolina. All those men had a frontiersman's lusty spirit and were too young to have known the terrors of the last war with Britain. Their zealotry in espousing war earned them the nickname of War Hawks.

By the autumn of 1811 President Madison had despaired of resolving the conflict by diplomatic or economic means. Unlike some others, such as Alexander Hamilton, who saw in Britain a natural friend whose interests ordinarily coincided with those of the United States but whose current hostile policies were dictated by a desperate need to combat the menace of Napoleon, Madison saw British moves as evidence of a haughty attitude that refused to accept the United States as a free people, a sovereign nation deserving respect among nations.

Madison would agree with Congressman Jonathan Roberts of Pennsylvania, who asserted that Britain's purpose was "to make us subserve her interests as a colonial dependency."[11] He could also agree with John C. Calhoun, who warned, "If we submit, the independence of this nation is lost."[12] "Submission or war were the only remaining alternatives," Congressman William Plumer of New Hampshire put it.[13] Members of Congress from around the nation echoed these remarks, calling for a war that would defend the honor of the United States, humble the British, and establish the sovereignty and integrity of America.

In October 1811 Madison left Montpelier and returned to Washington to prepare the speech that would be presented to Congress at the opening of its session. The nation's Twelfth Congress, in which Madison's pro-war Republican Party held a large majority (75 percent of the House, 82 percent of the Senate) convened on November 4, 1811. The next day Madison sent his speech to the Capitol to be read to the Congress, according to the custom.

The speech was not as bellicose as the war hawks had hoped it would be. The only grievance that it mentioned was the Orders in Council, the odious decrees that impeded American trade. It did, though, ask Congress to begin making specific preparations for war. The Speaker of the House, Henry Clay, referred the president's requests to the House Committee on Foreign Relations, which he had packed with fellow war hawks.

On November 29, 1811, the committee chairman, Peter B. Porter of New York, delivered the committee's report and recommendations. They called for raising an enlarged regular army, authorizing the use of state militias, strengthening the navy, and arming the nation's merchant ships. In his message to Congress, Porter made it clear that what the committee was proposing was war and that only those in favor of declaring war should vote for the resolutions containing the recommendations. Each of the committee's six resolutions was approved by a substantial margin. Congress was acting with unusual togetherness, leading a member of the opposition Federalist Party to remark, "There appears to be a greater degree of unanimity in the national legislature than I have observed on any important question since the conclusion of the Revolutionary War."[14] The Senate was as united as the House, and together, America's legislators enacted a series of measures to prepare the nation for war.

On March 31, 1812, Secretary of State James Monroe reported to the House Committee on Foreign Relations that President Madison believed "that without an accommodation with Great Britain, Congress ought to declare war before adjourning."[15] According to some, Madison was hoping against hope for some solution short of war as he waited for the arrival of the United States sloop *Hornet*, which would soon be returning from France and Britain bearing diplomatic dispatches, the latest reports of America's representatives in Paris and London. According to others, Madison was merely hoping for some new foul British deed, or a contrary French one, intending to use the news to further unite the nation as it commenced war against Britain.

The *Hornet*, overdue, at last arrived in New York on May 19, 1812, and on May 22 the long-awaited dispatches reached Washington. There was nothing in them to deflect Madison from proceeding on the course toward war and nothing to further incite American public opinion. Napoleon had not given any ground, and Britain's Orders in Council, although they continued to be vigorously protested by British industry, remained in effect. Nothing had changed.

The war hawks, their patience exhausted by the want of hopeful news, now looked to Madison for the decisive move. On June 1, 1812, he sent to Congress a message reciting the nation's grievances and asking for a declaration of war against Britain. He also asked for a delay in deciding on possible action against France.

On June 4, 1812, the United States House of Representatives approved the declaration of war by a vote of seventy-nine to forty. On June 17, 1812, the United States Senate approved the declaration, nineteen to thirteen.

On June 18, 1812, President James Madison placed his signature on the declaration. It was official now; the United States would once again make war on its mother country.

On June 23, 1812, the British government suspended its offensive Orders in Council, too late to avoid the war that was coming.

## ∴ 9 ∴

# The Indian Fighter

On May 12, 1812, while Martha Crawley's husband was away from their farm on the Duck River, some forty miles southwest of Nashville, a band of Creek Indians, apparently returning from one of Tecumseh's militant, Indian-solidarity rallies in the north, rode up to the Crawleys' farmhouse, found two of the Crawley children playing in the yard, and killed them both. Martha, inside the house, quickly hid her two younger children in a food cellar beneath the floor. The Indians broke down the door of the house, seized Martha, and dragged her outside. Deciding against killing her, they rode off with her, headed toward the ancient Indian town of Tuckaubatchee, farther south, on the upper end of the Tallapoosa River, which flows from west Georgia into Alabama.

The Indians were part of a group of dissident Creeks called Red Sticks (because their tomahawks were painted red), and they had already raided a number of other farms along the Duck River, murdering the settler families and stealing horses. Their attacks set off a wave of reaction among Tennesseeans, many of whom faced the same possible fate that had befallen the Crawleys and the murdered other families along the Duck River. Feelings of outrage and hostility toward the Creeks swept through the people of the state.

Andrew Jackson, major general of the militias, perhaps knew some of the murdered settlers, since he owned a claim to property along the Duck River. He was out of the state when the murders occurred, but on his return to Nashville, he immediately raised his voice against the Creeks and called for swift justice. "They must be punished and our frontier protected," he declared in a letter to Governor Willie Blount, "and as I have no doubt but they are urged on by British agents and tools, the sooner they can be attacked, the less will be their resistance, and the fewer will be the nations or tribes that we will have to war with."

In tough terms Jackson insisted that the Tennesseans march into Creek territory and "demand the perpetrators, at the Point of Bayonet—if refused—that we make reprisals—and lay their Towns in ashes." He urged Governor Blount to give him the necessary provisions and arms, promising that he would lead 2,500 volunteers against the Creeks and show them what "retributive justice" means.[1]

Next he wrote to George Colbert, half-breed chief of the Chickasaws, and forcefully remonstrated with him for allowing the party of Creek murderers to pass through Chickasaw territory, along with the horses they had stolen and the white woman they had abducted. "Creeks have killed our women and children," Jackson said. "We have sent to demand the murderers, if they are not given up, the whole Creek nation shall be covered with blood, fire shall consume their Towns and villages: and their lands shall be divided among the whites."

"I am your friend and the friend of your nation," Jackson told Colbert, but he warned that his friendship and the friendship of the United States would end if Colbert continued to allow Creeks to use the Chickasaw territory as an escape passage. For their co-operation Jackson vowed to protect the Chickasaws from the Creeks if "the Creeks dare to touch you for your friendship to us."

He also delivered another warning: if Colbert allowed the Creeks to carry any more scalps or stolen horses through Chickasaw territory, "your Father the President" will learn of it and know that the Chickasaws have violated their treaty with the United States and have taken the enemy "by the hand."

Jackson concluded by demanding that Colbert give him the names of those in the band of Creek murderers, the names of the towns where they lived, and the name of the place where the woman prisoner was being held. Jackson told him that he, Colbert, claimed to be the friend of whites. "Now," Jackson demanded, "prove it to me."[2]

After two months, with nothing having been done to apprehend the Creek murderers, Jackson went public with his protest and appeal. He wrote an editorial that ran in the *Democratic Clarion* on July 8, 1812. "No vengeance has yet been taken: no atonement has yet been made," he said and called for that vengeance and atonement to be imposed on the Creeks. "Citizens, hold yourselves in readiness," he exhorted. "It may be but a short time before the question is put to you: Are you ready to follow your general to the heart of the Creek nation."[3]

There was still no action by the governor, no army-sized posse commissioned to hunt down the killers and inflict punishment on them. What the government failed to do, however, was done to some degree by the Creeks themselves. Creek chief Big Warrior dispatched a party of loyal warriors to capture the offenders. Eight of the band of Red Sticks were caught and executed. Martha Crawley was rescued from Tuckaubatchee by Tandy Walker, who for a long time had lived among the Creeks and had become a friend of another Creek chief, Oceocheemotla, to whom Walker appealed for the woman's release. Walker reported that he found Mrs. Crawley "very feeble," and that her mind had been "impaired by suffering." She also had suffered injuries to her legs and feet. She was taken to the home of George Gaines and his wife and left in the care of Mrs. Gaines. After a week, she recovered to the point that her "mind appeared to be restored."[4]

Jackson would have to wait for the vengeance he sought. In the meantime, Governor Blount notified Jackson that President Madison's administration, preparing to wage war against Great Britain following Congress's approval, had sent him seventy blank commissions for volunteer officers and Blount had written in Jackson's name on one of them. Jackson was now a major general of United States Volunteers. Furthermore, Jackson was ordered by the governor to gather an army of volunteers and take it to New Orleans, where he would receive orders from President Madison concerning the mission of Jackson's army.

On a frigid day, January 7, 1813, General Jackson assembled his troops and sailed from Nashville, traveling down the Ohio River and the Mississippi to Natchez, where his army disembarked and halted, on orders from the commanding general in New Orleans, Major General James Wilkinson. After several weeks of waiting for new orders, Jackson on March 15, 1813, received an astonishing message. President Madison's secretary of war, John Armstrong, ordered Jackson to dismiss his army and hand over to General Wilkinson "all articles of public property" that it possessed. (Jackson suspected Wilkinson of manipulating Armstrong to thwart Jackson, but the cause of the order was more likely that Madison's administration, unknown to Jackson, had decided against a campaign in east Florida and Jackson's troops were no longer needed.)[5]

Jackson could hardly believe such orders. There he was, with more than 2,000 troops, 150 of them sick, 56 of them seriously so. They were nearly five hundred overland miles from home, the men without enough money to buy transportation or food. He was furious. Secretary Armstrong, Jackson complained to Felix Grundy, his congressman, "must have been drunk when he wrote [the orders] or so proud of his appointment as to have lost all feelings of humanity and duty."[6] Armstrong had been in the job just two days when he issued the orders.

It did not take Jackson long to decide to disregard the orders, and he wrote a message of protest to Armstrong, telling him so: "These brave men . . . deserve a better fate and return from their government. . . . They followed me to the field; I shall carefully march them back to their homes."[7] To pay the costs of the return march, northeastward up the Natchez Trace to Nashville, Jackson would spend his own money. Not satisfied to tell only Armstrong what he thought, he also wrote to President Madison, saying that he considered the part of Armstrong's orders that directed him to give up his tents and other equipment to Wilkinson to be a mistake, and therefore he would disregard it.[8]

With only eleven wagons to transport the sick, Jackson gave up his own horses (three of them) to sick soldiers and ordered his officers to do the same; then, like the men he commanded, he walked back to Nashville. During that long march home, Jackson's soldiers more than ever came to admire his toughness and his concern for them. According to one of his biographers, it was during that march that his troops gave him the nickname "Old Hickory," in recognition of his tenacity and endurance.[9]

Averaging about seventeen miles a day, Jackson's army reached Nashville within a month, and there Jackson was hailed as a hero for leading his men home. "Long will their General live in the memory of his volunteers of West Tennessee for his benevolent, humane, and fatherly treatment to his soldiers," the *Nashville Whig* editorialized. "We believe there is not a man belonging to the detachment but what loves him."[10]

Within a matter of months, Jackson was enmeshed in another, almost deadly, controversy. Lieutenant Colonel William Carroll was Jackson's brigade inspector, a man apparently not easy to like and made less so by the nature of his job in the volunteer army. One of his enemies was a lieutenant named Littleton Johnson, and as soon as the volunteers were mustered out of the army in May 1813, Johnson challenged Carroll to a duel. Carroll declined, saying Johnson was not a gentleman. The friend of Johnson who had delivered the message (Jesse Benton, brother of Jackson's aide-de-camp, Colonel Thomas Hart Benton) then himself challenged Carroll.

Carroll accepted the challenge and asked Jackson to be his second, which Jackson agreed to do. The two duelists met and faced off. Upon the command to fire, Jesse Benton twisted and dropped into a squatting position. As he did, Carroll's shot caught him in the buttocks. It was a humiliation that neither he nor his brother, Thomas, could abide without redress.

Thomas's anger fell most heavily on Jackson, who, he felt, should have been wise enough to come between Carroll and Jesse and prevent the duel, instead of participating in it. He wrote an angry letter to Jackson, denouncing what he had done, and Jackson replied with a letter telling Thomas, more or less, that he needed to get his facts straight. Thomas fired back with another letter, accusing Jackson of conducting the duel in a "savage, unequal, unfair, and base manner."[11] Unwilling to let go and attempt to make peace (Thomas and his family had been friends of Jackson), Jackson resented Thomas's attitude and his words, which he was repeating in public, and swore that he would horsewhip Thomas the next time he saw him.

The morning of September 4, 1813, was the next time. According to one of the two most detailed accounts,[12] the Benton brothers had ridden into Nashville the previous day and had taken rooms not at their usual inn, but at the City Hotel, apparently to avoid running into Jackson. Later, Jackson and his good friend John Coffee also arrived in town. Around nine o'clock in the morning on September 4, Jackson, carrying his riding whip, as he usually did, set out with Coffee for the post office, a few doors down from the City Hotel.

The accounts differ on exactly what occurred next. Apparently the Benton brothers were standing on the walk in front of the hotel, and as Jackson and Coffee approached, Jesse stepped into the hotel barroom while Thomas remained standing in front of the door that opened into a hallway leading to the rear of the hotel, where there was a porch that overlooked the Cumberland River. Jackson, with whip in hand, walked toward Thomas and told him, "Now, you damned rascal, I'm going to punish you. Defend yourself."[13]

Thomas reached his hand into his breast pocket, as if to draw a pistol. As he did so, Jackson swiftly took a pistol from a back pocket and pointed it at Thomas, who instantly drew back a couple of steps. Jackson stepped toward him and held his pistol to Thomas's heart. Thomas continued to back up, through the hallway, nearing the rear porch as Jackson kept coming toward him.

Suddenly, behind Jackson and evidently unseen by him, Jesse entered the hallway, raised his pistol, which was loaded with two balls and a slug, and fired. The slug hit Jackson in the left shoulder and shattered it. One of the balls struck him in the upper left arm and lodged near the bone. The other ball crashed harmlessly into a wooden partition in the hallway.

Jackson immediately crumpled and fell, blood gushing from his wounds. Coffee rushed up and saw Jackson prostrate and bleeding; believing it was Thomas who had shot him, Coffee rushed at Thomas with his pistol and fired. The shot missed, however, and Coffee brandished the weapon to pistol-whip him. Before Coffee could strike him, Thomas backed onto the top step of a stairway and plunged to the bottom of the stairs. Coffee then turned to his fallen friend.

Bleeding profusely, Jackson was carried to a room in the Nashville Inn. Nashville's physicians were summoned to treat him; taking a look at his wounds, all but one of them recommended amputation of the arm. Still conscious despite the trauma and the enormous loss of blood, Jackson refused amputation. The doctors dressed his wounds, using the home remedies of Indians and frontiersmen—poultices of slippery elm and other medicinal plants, according to the account. No attempt was made to remove the ball lodged in his upper left arm.

The Benton brothers, meanwhile, celebrated outside the hotel where the shooting had occurred and in the public square, railing against Jackson and congratulating themselves for having shot him down. A short time later, however,[14] before Jackson's friends had time to come after him, Thomas rode out of Nashville, headed for the safety of his home in Franklin, Tennessee. Presumably, Jesse did likewise.

Jackson was unable to rise from his bed for two weeks or more, but soon after, he began showing signs of recovery. He was at home at the Hermitage in late September 1813 when he received an order from Governor Blount, directing him to call out the militia to meet a new Indian crisis. His wounds still healing, Jackson responded immediately to the governor's order. On September 24, 1813, he issued a general order summoning his troops and telling them, "The health of your general is restored. He will command in person."[15]

On October 7, 1813, Jackson, looking haggard, his left arm in a sling, assumed command over the twenty-five-hundred-man army assembled at Fayetteville, in south Tennessee. Brigadier General John Coffee, commanding the militia cavalry, had already marshaled his men and moved into Creek country. On October 11 Jackson's troops moved out, marching thirty-two miles in nine hours and the next day meeting up with Coffee's cavalry at Ditto's Landing on the Tennessee River, just south of the frontier settlement of Huntsville (Alabama). That was where Creek country began.

The cause of these actions by Tennessee's governor and its militia commander had occurred on August 30. At a fortified settlement known as Fort Mims (its owner was settler Samuel Mims), about forty miles north of Mobile, in what was then Mississippi Territory and is now Alabama, William Weatherford (who called himself Red Eagle and was more Caucasian than Indian) led a horde of a thousand Red Sticks in a savage massacre. They slaughtered more than 250 white settlers, Negro slaves, soldiers, and friendly Indians and so-called mixed bloods, most of them having left their homes to seek protection within Mims's fort, which was garrisoned by federal troops.[16]

When news of the massacre reached the nation's capital, President Madison quickly realized the dangers of a widespread Indian uprising coming at a time when the nation was already engaged in war with Britain. Intending to quash the Red Stick threat before it could spread to other tribes, he ordered four armies—one from east Tennessee, one from west Tennessee, one from Georgia, and one from the Mississippi Territory—to march into Creek territory from different directions and converge at the confluence of the Coosa and Tallapoosa rivers, just north of present-day Montgomery, Alabama, at the heart of the Creek nation.

Jackson, commanding the west Tennessee army, planned to march straight south. As he went, he would hack out of the wilderness a road to provide a supply route for his army and an access passage for new settlers to move into lands that he would force the Creeks to vacate. The road would stretch all the way to Mobile, the port city on the gulf. As his army pushed southward, it would also confront and destroy the Red Sticks, wreaking vengeance and eliminating the possibility of future outrages like the murders of the Duck River settlers, the abduction of Martha Crawley, and the slaughter at Fort Mims.

Hampered by an infuriatingly inefficient supply system, by which private suppliers contracted with the army to provide food for the soldiers in the field, Jackson and his troops would be facing battles with hunger as well as with the Creek enemy. As a preliminary step to launching his campaign against the Creeks, Jackson had his troops construct a fortified base—Fort Deposit—on the south side of the Tennessee River, there to store his supplies. At the same time, he sent another detachment of troops into the wilderness with axes to cut a road over the Raccoon Mountains to the Coosa River, some fifty miles southeast of Fort Deposit.

Jackson knew exactly where he wanted to go. Even while still in bed recovering from his wounds, he had dispatched spies into Creek country to gather intelligence about the Red Sticks' numbers and their locations. From that intelligence he formed a plan to move to the Coosa River, then march southwestward from the Ten Islands on the Coosa, sweeping through Red Stick villages and destroying them and wiping out Red Stick warriors in battle. He would then drive through the wilderness to Mobile.

Three days after beginning the push to the Coosa, Jackson's troops arrived at their destination and began cutting down trees to form a stockade and erect a fortification to serve as Jackson's advance base, which he called Fort Strother. Once the fortification was built, Jackson would rest his troops, then launch his campaign to eliminate the Red Sticks.

Thirteen miles east of Fort Strother lay the Creek village of Tallushatchee, where two hundred Red Stick warriors were encamped. Jackson ordered an attack on them, the opening battle of his campaign. On the morning of November 3, Coffee's cavalry assaulted and overwhelmed the Red Sticks. "We shot them like dogs," one of the battle's best-known participants, Davy Crockett, reported.[17] Not one of the Red Stick warriors escaped. Eighty-four women and children were taken prisoner. Coffee's casualties were five killed and forty-one wounded. "We have retaliated for Fort Mims," Jackson announced triumphantly in a letter to Governor Blount on November 4.[18]

Among the Creek children who survived the attack was a young boy (sources differ on his age, from nine months to three years) whose mother lay dead, still clutching her child. The Indian women wanted the boy killed, too, since he no longer had a family to take care of him. Jackson, however, personally fed him and, his sympathy perhaps stirred by memories of his own boyhood as an orphan, ordered him removed to Huntsville, where he would be cared for at Jackson's expense. Later Jackson had Major William White take the boy, named Lyncoya, to the Hermitage, to be raised in the Jackson household as a member of the family. "I want him well taken care of," Jackson said. "He may have been given to me for some Valuable purpose."[19]

Jackson's army now was running low on provisions, and Jackson sent urgent messages to the commander of the east Tennessee army, Major General John Cocke, and to the commander of Cocke's forward units, Brigadier General James White, to hurry to his aid. In the meantime, while White indifferently stalled and dallied at Turkey Town, a friendly Cherokee village twenty-five miles to the north of Jackson's position, Jackson was forced to meet a new Red Stick threat.

Warned that a force of Red Sticks was massing to attack the friendly Indian town of Talladega, about thirty miles south of Fort Strother, Jackson, within hours, set out with his army at one o'clock on the morning of November 8, 1813. By sundown that day he and his troops had come within six miles of the Red Sticks' position. There they halted, exhausted by the swift march through the roadless wilderness. While his soldiers rested, Jackson battled a severe case of dysentery and received intelligence reports on the Red Sticks' strength and positions and the lay of the land around Talladega.

Around midnight Jackson received word that General White, on whom Jackson was depending to protect Fort Strother in his absence, had been ordered by General Cocke to a new position, and so he would not be going to Fort Strother. Some two hundred sick troops and all the supplies stored at the fort were now in jeopardy. Jackson decided on a prompt assault on the Red Sticks gathered before Talladega.

At four o'clock in the morning on November 9, Jackson ordered his army roused, and at the dawn's first light it began to advance. A half mile from the town, the sun now well above the treetops, Jackson deployed his troops in a crescent-shaped formation, the two points of it nearest the town. Then he ordered three mounted companies to ride toward the town to draw the Red Stick warriors from their concealed positions and into the open.

From a tree-lined creek a volley of hostile fire suddenly erupted as the cavalrymen approached. Within moments an army of painted Red Stick warriors, yelling and whooping, burst from the creek bank and charged the troopers, who quickly wheeled and galloped back into the curve of the crescent of Jackson's infantry, into the trap. As soon as the Red Sticks were within range of the infantry's rifles, the mounted troopers turned away and sped from the line of fire.

Though staggered by the volleys of rifle and musket fire, the warriors surged forward. Now the points of the crescent closed, encircling them. More than 1,000 Red Sticks (according to Jackson's estimate) were contained in the ring of Jackson's troops, who were now firing on the Indians at point-blank range. The slaughter might have continued until the last Red Stick warrior had been felled, but a hole opened on the right side of Jackson's formation, and seeing the chance of escape, the Red Sticks rushed through it. They ran for the mountains, three miles away, pursued all the way by Jackson's troops. The pursuit was broken off once the Red Sticks reached the wooded mountains' slopes and crannies.

Three hundred of Red Eagle's warriors lay dead within the crescent. Others had been shot and killed as they fled; uncounted others had been wounded. Jackson's casualties totaled fifteen dead and eighty-five wounded; two of the wounded later died of their wounds. A heavy loss had been inflicted on the Red Sticks, but Jackson had failed to eliminate them and the threat they presented.

Without food and unrelieved by Cocke's army, Jackson decided that he had no choice but to return to Fort Strother rather than pursue the escaped Red Sticks. Two days after the battle at Talladega, Jackson and his hungry soldiers returned to the fort, where they were further disappointed to learn that no new supplies had reached the fort and there was little left to eat. The troops, near the point of starvation, were growing restive and increasingly angry. Jackson, whose wounds from the fight with the Benton brothers were still not completely healed, was nearly disabled with dysentery.

Roughly a third of Jackson's men—one of his army's three brigades—were militia. Facing starvation and the end of their enlistments, they were determined to return to their homes regardless of their commander's orders. As they marched off, Jackson placed a detachment of his volunteers across their route to block them. Unwilling to risk being fired on, the militiamen turned back to the fort. The following day a large number of volunteers decided they would decamp for home. Jackson ordered the militiamen to bar their way just as the volunteers had done to the militia the day before, with a similar result.

With matters at Fort Strother threatening to get out of hand, Jackson summoned his field-grade officers[20] and, promising that supplies would soon arrive from Fort Deposit, appealed for fortitude. "If supplies do not arrive in two days," he told them, "we will all march back together."[21] He ordered each brigade to hold a meeting of all its officers to decide what their units would do. Brigadier General Isaac Roberts's militia brigade decided to stay another three or four days, until it could be learned whether the promised food was indeed on the way. Brigadier General William Hall's brigade of volunteers decided to march off immediately. Brigadier General John Coffee's cavalry brigade voted to stick with Jackson as long as they were needed.[22]

The two days that Jackson had promised would bring them food passed. Three, then four, days passed. Still, nothing arrived. Jackson then called for volunteers to guard Fort Strother while he and the rest of the able-bodied of his army trudged off to Fort Deposit in search of food. One hundred nine men volunteered.

On November 18, 1813, Jackson and his starving troops set out for Fort Deposit. The plan was to find the long-expected provisions, satisfy their hunger, then march back to Fort Strother to continue the campaign against the Creeks. In the unhappy event they did not find the food, the troops would proceed to Tennessee. The column had marched only about twelve miles when, to Jackson's great relief, it met the supply detail coming toward it with nine wagonloads of flour and driving a herd of 150 head of beef cattle. Jackson ordered the troops to slaughter the cattle and feed themselves on beef and bread until they were filled, an order they promptly obeyed.

Satiated, the troops were then ordered by their officers to prepare to march back to Fort Strother. Many refused. Instead, they began plodding off to the north, toward home. Informed of the mutiny, Jackson and members of Coffee's staff and other officers from Coffee's command rode up ahead and blocked the path of the mutineers, threatening to open fire on them if they continued to advance. The troops decided against a showdown and returned to their units.

A little later, however, General Hall's entire brigade of volunteers was at the point of mutiny, one company having already started home. Jackson quickly grabbed up a musket and, mounted, backed his horse into the path of the deserters. With his left arm still in a sling and able to use only his right arm, he rested the barrel of the musket on his mount's neck and pointed it at the men in the advancing mutineers' first rank. General Coffee and Major John Reid quickly rode up beside Jackson as the mutineers halted.

"You say you will march," Jackson declared to the rebellious troops. "I say by the Eternal God you shall not march while a cartridge can sound fire!"[23]

After a few tense moments, the mutineers decided not to defy their commander and returned to camp. (The musket that Jackson had seized to threaten them was later found to be inoperative.)

On December 2, 1813, Jackson's recalcitrant army marched back into Fort Strother. Whatever hopes Jackson had of resuming operations against the Creeks, though, were shattered by the volunteers' insistence that their enlistments would be up on December 10 and that they were then going to leave and head back home. They had volunteered to serve one year, beginning December 10, 1812. They had gone with Jackson to Natchez, had returned to Tennessee with him, and were recalled by him in September 1813. Despite the fact that they saw no service for a period of months, they insisted that their enlistment was for one year only, and that year would end on December 10, 1813.

The reinforcements that Jackson had thought he would receive from General Cocke's troops also proved elusive. One of Cocke's regiments was scheduled to be released in December, and two other of his regiments were to be released in January. Besides that, the term of service of Jackson's militiamen also was about to expire; within a month General Roberts and his militia brigade would march back to Tennessee, too. Most of Coffee's cavalrymen, also volunteers, were about to return home as well. Jackson's army of Indian fighters was evaporating.

In addition to that bad news, Governor Blount had by now given up on the mission of Jackson's army, and he wrote to Jackson advising him to abandon Fort Strother and head for home. Infuriated and unwilling to wait until his anger cooled, Jackson at half past midnight on the morning of December 29, 1813, penned a stinging response to the governor's letter. He reminded Blount that he, the governor, had "bawled aloud for permission to exterminate the Creeks." He reminded him that the Tennessee legislature had promised the Madison administration that it would keep thirty-five hundred troops in the field until the extermination had been accomplished. Now, Jackson wrote:

> Are you my Dear friend sitting with yr. arms folded, . . . Recommending me to retrograde to please the whims of the populace. . . . Let me tell you it imperiously lies upon both you and me to do our duty regardless of consequences or the opinion of these fireside patriots, those fawning sycophants or cowardly poltroons who after their boasted ardor would rush home or remain at those fireside[s] and let thousands fall victims to my retrograde. . . .
>
> Arouse from yr. lethargy—despise fawning smiles or snarling frowns—with energy exercise yr. functions—the campaign must rapidly progress or . . . yr. country will be ruined. Call out the full quota-execute the orders of the Secy of War, arrest the officer who omits his duty, . . . and let popularity perish for the present. . . . Save Mobile—save the [Mississippi] Territory—save yr. frontier from becoming drenched in blood. . . . What retrograde under these circumstances? I will perish first.[24]

The rebuke must have hit home. On January 14, 1814, some 850 new recruits arrived at Fort Strother, sent by Governor Blount. By then, Jackson's army had shrunk to one regiment. Impatient to get on with the war on the Creeks, Jackson hastily ordered his newly strengthened army, now composed of more than 1,000 men, to march against the Red Sticks at Tohopeka, their fortified camp in a horseshoe bend of the Tallapoosa River.

Having advanced to within three miles of Tohopeka (or Horseshoe Bend, as it was later called), on January 21 Jackson halted his troops at Emuckfaw Creek, north of the Tallapoosa. At dawn the next morning Jackson's army came under attack by Red Sticks who had sallied out from their Horseshoe Bend fort and opened fire from concealment behind trees and underbrush. After some time, Jackson's men managed to drive them off and narrowly escape disaster. After that close call, Jackson decided to postpone his plan to assault Tohopeka and return to Fort Strother instead.

The Red Sticks decided to follow him, waiting for a chance to strike again. At Enatachopco Creek they got their chance. As soon as Jackson's artillery entered the stream, following the advance column and a flanking column, the Red Sticks began firing on the exposed troops.

Jackson immediately responded. He ordered his rear guard to turn and face the Indian assault, then ordered the two columns that had already crossed the creek to turn and recross it and advance on both flanks of the Red Sticks' position. As they did, however, the rear guard, made up of the new recruits, panicked in the face of the Red Stick assault, broke, and fled for cover. Remarkably, Jackson managed to rally them, and as the bulk of his army splashed across the Enatachopco and presented an imposing front to the Red Sticks, Jackson's troops let loose an intensive fire on the enemy and eventually drove them off. Left behind on the ground where they fell were some two hundred Red Sticks. Jackson's losses amounted to twenty killed and seventy-five wounded, many of whom later died of their wounds.

Back at Fort Strother, Jackson put his new troops through a rigorous training program and exercised tough discipline. By now he had won the admiration of his commander, Major General Pinckney, whom Jackson had asked for a regiment of regular army troops to stabilize his forces. Impressed by Jackson's energy, methods, and results in the Creek campaign thus far, Pinckney approved the request and sent Jackson the regular army's Thirty-ninth Infantry Regiment. Further reinforced by additional Tennessee militia sent by Governor Blount, Jackson's army by early March had swelled to more than five thousand men. Jackson was now ready to do battle again.

On March 14, 1814, he led his army out of Fort Strother, headed once more for the Red Sticks' fort at Horseshoe Bend on the Tallapoosa. That bend in the river was such that it made a virtual peninsula of the land within it, an area of about a hundred acres, much of it covered by small trees and brush. Across the neck of the peninsula, some 350 yards wide, had been erected a zigzag wall five to eight feet high, fashioned of pine logs and tree trunks stacked like cordwood, with two rows of loopholes and an opening that permitted ingress and egress. The land rose sharply from the banks of the curving river to form a bluff, which protected the fort from a river-borne attack. Inside, as reported by Jackson's spies, were one thousand Red Stick warriors, gathered from several hostile Creek settlements and commanded by Chief Great Warrior (also known as Menewa). Also inside were an estimated three hundred women and children. Along the banks of the river lay a fleet of canoes that was intended to allow the Red Sticks to escape in case their defenses were breached and overrun.

Jackson and his army arrived at Horseshoe Bend around ten o'clock on the morning of March 27, 1814. After surveying the Creeks' fortification, Jackson ordered a detail of Coffee's artillery to swim the river and carry off the canoes, trapping the warriors inside their fortification. He then proceeded to have his troops surround the peninsula, assembling a thousand-man force to storm the protective wall at his command. Some seven hundred troopers of Coffee's cavalry, along with about 500 friendly Cherokees and one hundred friendly Creeks, crossed the Tallapoosa and reached the far bank to complete Horseshoe Bend's encirclement.

At ten thirty Jackson's two artillery pieces, a six-pounder and a three-pounder, opened fire on the fortification, but with little effect, the shot proving practically harmless against the soft pine logs of the rampart. For two hours Jackson's troops peppered the compound with small-arms fire, putting at hazard any warrior who dared show himself atop the wall or defiantly ventured outside it. The friendly Cherokees and Creeks on the river, apparently without orders from Jackson, leaped into the captured canoes, made their way back across the river, set fire to the compound's structures near the riverbank, then scaled the bluffs and attacked the Red Sticks from the rear.

Jackson quickly seized that opportunity to storm the wall. Braving the deadly volleys of the defenders, Jackson's infantry dashed to the wall, the Thirty-ninth Regiment reaching it first and immediately shoving their rifles through the loopholes and firing point-blank at the defending warriors. Major Lemuel P. Montgomery of the Thirty-ninth lifted himself to the top of the wall and ordered his men to follow. A shot struck him in the head, killing him. Ensign Sam Houston instantly assumed command atop the wall and yelled for his men to clamber over it. He was struck by an arrow in the thigh, but, indifferent to the wound, he leaped down into the Creek compound, followed by his troops.

Jackson's infantry soon was pouring over the wall, the battle within the compound suddenly growing fierce and desperate, then turning into a slaughter as the Red Stick warriors were mercilessly shot down. Those who sought to hide were flushed out and shot. The rest of the compound's buildings were set afire. Coffee's troopers along the river shot warriors who ran for their canoes. The killing continued until nightfall. During the night, the Red Sticks' chief, Great Warrior, severely wounded, managed to crawl to the river, find a canoe, and escape, one of the very few who did.

The next morning, March 28, the killing began again, Jackson's troops having found warriors who had hidden themselves along the bluffs above the river. When it was at last over, Jackson ordered a body count. Inside the compound the Creeks' dead totaled 557. An estimated

300 other Red Sticks died in the river, their bodies unrecovered. According to Jackson, altogether some 850 hostile Indians had been killed; only 20 or so had escaped.

Jackson's casualties were put at 26 soldiers killed and 107 wounded. In addition, 23 friendly Creeks and Cherokees had been killed and 47 wounded.

Jackson expressed two regrets over the battle. One was that several women and children had been killed by accident. The other was that William Weatherford, Red Eagle, the Red Sticks' charismatic chieftain, had been away from Horseshoe Bend at the time of Jackson's attack and was still at large. Otherwise, the victory at Horseshoe Bend had been enormously successful, perhaps ending the Creek menace once and for all, Jackson believed.

From Horseshoe Bend Jackson swept down the Tallapoosa River, burning hostile Creek villages as he went, a task at which he was joined by the Georgia army of Colonel Homer Milton. By the end of April 1814, all the armies engaged in the Indian wars had converged on Fort Jackson (the former French Fort Toulouse) southwest of Horseshoe Bend, where the Coosa and Tallapoosa rivers flowed together to form the Alabama River. Into Fort Jackson, war-weary, starving Indians, singly and in groups, began streaming in search of peace and food.

According to one account,[25] one of those who came to Fort Jackson was a tall, light-complexioned Indian who found his way to Jackson's tent and introduced himself: "I am Bill Weatherford." Sources vary on what Jackson's astonished reply was, but Weatherford went on to tell him, "I am come to give myself up. I can oppose you no longer. I have done you much injury. I should have done you more . . . [but] my warriors are killed. . . . I am in your power. Dispose of me as you please."[26]

The Red Stick menace was now over, though Jackson, profoundly impressed with Weatherford, let him go free despite the demands of many that he be executed for his crimes against white settlers.

Jackson's accomplishments did not go unnoticed in Washington. He had been recommended by General Pinckney for appointment to the regular United States Army, and in early May 1814, not long after news of the Horseshoe Bend battle reached the nation's capital, an opening occurred in the regular army for a brigadier general. President Madison offered the position to Jackson. While he was still thinking about it, another message came to him from Washington. Major General William Henry Harrison, hero of the Battle of Tippecanoe, had resigned from the army, and Jackson was now offered the rank of major general, replacing Harrison.

The May 31, 1814, issue of the *National Intelligencer*, a Washington newspaper, succinctly reported the event, monumentally significant in Jackson's career and in the unfolding history of the nation: "Andrew Jackson, of Tennessee, is appointed major-general in the army of the United States, *vice* William Henry Harrison, resigned."[27]

Jackson's command would be the Seventh Military District, composed of Louisiana, Tennessee, the Mississippi Territory, and most of the Creek Nation.

# ∴ 10 ∴

# The Fortunes of America's War

ALTHOUGH General Jackson's war with hostile Indians was being won, the nation's war with Britain was not going well, and like many others, President Madison now realized why. The country had been, and still was, unprepared to fight a war, particularly against one of the world's most powerful nations. Worse, America's military leadership, practically to a man, was either incompetent or otherwise not up to the job of waging war.

One of the members of Congress who had urged the nation to war, George M. Troup of Georgia, soon concluded, "In the wretched, deplorably wretched condition of the War Department, it was impossible either to begin the war or to conduct it. . . . No man in the country is equal to one-half the duties which devolve on the present Secretary."[1] The secretary of war was William Eustis, judged by Senator William H. Crawford of Pennsylvania to be "a dead weight in our hand. . . . His unfitness is apparent to everybody but himself."[2]

"Our executive officers are most incompetent men," was the judgment of Congressman John C. Calhoun of South Carolina.[3] Winfield Scott, who in 1812 was a lieutenant colonel in the army and would later rise to prominence, observed that "the old officers had, very generally, sunk into either sloth, ignorance, or the habits of intemperate drinking."[4] Most officers, he said, were "imbeciles and ignoramuses."[5] The new officers were mostly political appointees, inexperienced in military matters, completely innocent of the practice of war. Among the army's enlisted men inexperience was widespread, morale was poor, breaches of discipline were frequent, and desertions were common. And although Congress had authorized an army of thirty-six thousand men to fight the war, at the outset of the conflict the U.S. Army amounted to no more than twelve thousand, including the men just recently recruited.

The consequences of fielding so inadequate a force to fight a demanding war became quickly and appallingly apparent to President Madison and the Congress. The army's first offensive mission, begun even before war was declared, was the invasion and conquest of Canada, a longtime goal of expansion-minded Americans. The plan was to send a main force by way of Lake Champlain to capture Montreal while at the same time a three-pointed second force moved into Canada from Detroit, Niagara, and Sacket's Harbor, New York, on Lake Ontario.

In command of the force that was to invade Canada from Detroit was fifty-nine-year-old Brigadier General William Hull, a native of Connecticut who had served in the Revolutionary War and later had become governor of the Michigan Territory, the job from which President Madison, desperate for general officers, had recruited him to lead an army. On May 25, 1812, Hull arrived in Dayton, Ohio, to assume command of his troops, which comprised three regiments of militia. From Dayton he marched to Urbana, Ohio, reaching it on June 10, and there his force was joined by the regulars of the Fourth Infantry Regiment. He now had an army of about two thousand troops, headed for Detroit.

News of America's declaration of war reached Montreal on June 24, six days after President Madison had signed it. Canada's governor, Lieutenant General Sir George Prevost, immediately initiated his plans to defend Canada from an expected American invasion. Prevost gave his military commander in western Canada, Major General Sir Isaac Brock, a free hand to handle western Canada's defense as he saw fit while Prevost concentrated on defense in the east.

Hull's army was advancing northward only by hacking out a roadway in the wilderness, through forests and across swamps, and progress was agonizingly slow and laborious. When he reached the Maumee River, which empties into Lake Erie at present-day Toledo, on June 30, 1812, Hull decided he would make the journey easier for his troops by loading his baggage, some equipment, including his troops' entrenching tools, and some medical and other supplies aboard the schooner *Cuyahoga,* which he chartered for that purpose, and having everything shipped up to Detroit. Included with his baggage was a trunk that contained official correspondence and other documents concerning his mission. Hull had not yet learned of the declaration of war, but he knew from his orders that conflict was near, and he also knew that British ships controlled Lake Erie.

On July 2, the same day Hull learned that war had been declared, the British brig *General Hunter* captured the *Cuyahoga* as it passed Fort Malden, the British fortification overlooking the Detroit River, guarding the passage between Lake Erie and Lake Saint Clair. The seized cargo, including Hull's trunk that contained the classified documents, was turned over to the British commander, General Brock. "Till I received these letters," Brock later reported, "I had no idea General Hull was advancing with so large a force."[6] From those documents Brock learned not only the size of Hull's force but everything else he needed to know about Hull's army and plans.

Hull arrived in Detroit on July 5. One week later he led a force of twelve hundred men across the Detroit River and occupied the Canadian village of Sandwich, fifteen miles from the British outpost at Amherstburg, below Fort Malden. Having been alerted by the captured documents to Hull's plan, Brock had strengthened and prepared Amherstburg and Fort Malden for the American attack, although the British forces were still substantially outnumbered. Hull now fell into a fit of anxiety, worried about the possibility of his supply and communications lines being severed. On July 14 he called his senior officers to a council of war and then went along with its recommendation that they wait until heavy guns could be brought to them from Detroit. After a three-week delay, the guns arrived, but Hull dithered again, despite his war council's advice to attack immediately. Believing that the Amherstburg garrison was about to be heavily reinforced by Brock, Hull on August 8 gave up the planned attack and withdrew back across the river.

On August 13 Brock arrived at Amherstburg with a force of 50 regular troops and 250 Canadian militia, and with a six-pounder artillery piece. When joined with the Fort Malden and Amherstburg garrisons, he had an army of 300 regulars and 400 militiamen, which he quickly organized into a fighting force of three brigades. With admirable audacity, Brock on August 15 sent his aide across the river to Detroit to demand Hull's surrender.

Detroit at that time was a town of about eight hundred, with a protective fort that enclosed about two acres with an embankment, a dry ditch, and two rows of obstructive pickets. In case of attack, the nearest help, other than the widely scattered settlers of the territory, was two hundred miles away, and the only road out ran for sixty miles along the shore of Lake Erie, flanked by British warships on one side and hostile Indians on the other. Defending Detroit required tenacity and courage. Hull had neither.

On August 16 Brock took his three brigades across the Detroit River and there, reinforced by six hundred Indians led by Tecumseh, laid siege to Detroit. That same day, without having fired a shot, Hull surrendered. His sixteen hundred militiamen were paroled by Brock and sent home. Hull and almost six hundred regular troops were sent as prisoners of war to Montreal for internment. Twenty-five hundred muskets, thirty-three artillery pieces, the brig *Adams,* and the fort's military stores were seized by the British. That done, Brock issued a proclamation declaring that the territory of Michigan now belonged to the British. (Two years later, following his parole by the British, Hull was court-martialed and found guilty of cowardice. He was sentenced to be hanged, but because of his "revolutionary services and his advanced age,"[7] the court recommended clemency. President Madison approved the verdict and the recommendation.)

Bad news was coming from other parts of the northwestern frontier. On General Brock's orders, the British captain Charles Roberts, commandant of the garrison at Fort Saint Joseph, Canada's westernmost military outpost, on July 26, 1812, had set out to attack Fort Michilimackinac, the American fortification that guarded the strategic passage between Lake Michigan and Lake Huron. Whoever controlled that passage controlled the rich northwestern fur trade and the allegiance of the Indians whose livelihood depended on that trade.

Comprising Captain Roberts's force were forty-five soldiers of the Tenth Royal Veterans, a group of fur traders numbering fewer than two hundred, and about four hundred Indians. They traveled by ship and by canoe fifty miles to Michilimackinac, which they reached early in the morning of July 27. Roberts positioned his six-pounder artillery piece on a hill overlooking the fort and sent word demanding the garrison's surrender. Lieutenant Porter Hanks, commanding the fort's sixty-one-man garrison, wished to avoid its massacre and quickly surrendered.

On August 15, the day before General Hull surrendered Detroit, a force of four hundred Potawotamie Indians attacked Fort Dearborn, at Chicago, catching the garrison in the process of evacuating the fort on orders from Hull. The Indians massacred twenty-six regular soldiers, twelve militiamen, two women, and twelve children. The next morning they set the fort afire. When it burned, the United States' authority on the northwest frontier was extinguished. American expansion had been not merely halted but thrown back.

In the northeast, too, the plan for the conquest and annexation of Canada had hit snags. The American commander in the northeast, and the overall commander in the campaign to capture Canada, was sixty-one-year-old Major General Henry Dearborn, a Revolutionary War veteran who had served as secretary of war under President Thomas Jefferson. Instead of timing his attacks to coincide with Hull's, thereby forcing the British commander Prevost to spread his forces across the broad expanse of the Canadian frontier, Dearborn had set up a headquarters at Albany, New York, and then found some inexplicable reason to go to Boston, where he occupied himself for two months, ostensibly strengthening the nation's coastal defenses. He struggled to decide whether he should remain in Boston or return to his troops in Albany and commence the campaign's main thrust against Montreal.

Meanwhile, the planned invasion of Canada from Niagara, New York, was limping forward. The War Department, apparently in a politically motivated move, had let the governor of New York, Daniel D. Tompkins, choose a New Yorker to command the expedition to be launched from Niagara. Tompkins picked Major General Stephen Van Rensselear, a wealthy, forty-eight-year-old Federalist political leader who was devoid of military experience except for his recent appointment as commander of New York's militia. To assist him he would have a relative at his side, Colonel Solomon Van Rensselear, whose Revolutionary War service apparently qualified him as a military adviser.

Also evidently meant to assist General Van Rensselear was Brigadier General Alexander Smyth, a regular army officer who arrived at Niagara in late September. Smyth, whose army service had begun four years earlier and who had no combat experience, haughtily refused to take orders from a militia general. And so when Van Rensselear drew up a plan to cross the Niagara River and attack the British position at Queenston while Smyth led an attack on Fort George, six miles north of Queenston, Smyth declined to cooperate.

Van Rensselear's army totaled some 6,000 troops. It faced a British force estimated at 1,600 and commanded by General Brock, who had swiftly shifted eastward following his success against Hull at Detroit. Despite Smyth's refusal, General Van Rensselear, on the advice of Solomon Van Rensselear and reportedly fearful of public criticism if he failed to act, decided to go ahead with the plan anyway. On the morning of October 11, 1812, he attempted to embark his invasion force in boats to be rowed across the river but was completely thwarted by a heavy rainstorm, ineptness, and the loss of the oars, bafflingly loaded aboard a boat and carried downriver by an American officer.

Before dawn two days later, on October 13, under cover of a heavy artillery bombardment, Van Rensselear launched another attack. Battling a strong current, a vanguard of some 600 troops managed to make the Canadian side of the river, but were pinned down on the bank by a murderous fire from British troops positioned on the heights above. Solomon Van Rensselear, commanding the assault force, was hit six times by enemy fire. Captain John E. Wool took charge of the troops around him and, having discovered an unguarded footpath that climbed up the heights, led a company of the Thirteenth Infantry Regiment to the top and drove off a force of defenders commanded by General Brock. Brock then regrouped and tried to retake the heights, but he was killed in the attempt. In the heavy exchange of gunfire, Captain Wool was hit also but only wounded.

By now the American vanguard had been strengthened by the arrival of reinforcements commanded by twenty-six-year-old Lieutenant Colonel Winfield Scott. Some thirteen hundred American troops had crossed the river and were now under the command of Brigadier General William Wadsworth, who had succeeded the wounded Colonel Solomon Van Rensselear.

British reinforcements were also arriving, having come hurriedly from Fort George (which they would have been unable to do if Smyth had attacked Fort George as planned). General Van Rensselear now ordered his militiamen to cross the river and to strengthen the American force as it met the British reinforcements. The militiamen, however, refused to cross the river into Canada, claiming their service commitment did not include fighting outside the United States. Van Rensselear tried his best, according to his statements, to rally the militiamen and urge them across the river, but in vain.

Without the militia to reinforce them, the American troops were unable to withstand a British counterattack and were driven from the heights of Queenston. In the end, the Americans on the Canadian side of the river were forced to surrender, and 958 of them were taken prisoner. American casualties totaled more than 300 killed or wounded, three times the number of casualties suffered by the British.

The entire expedition had turned into a disaster, and Stephen Van Rensselear took the blame for it. He asked to be relieved of his duties, and his request was swiftly granted.

The War Department then named the insubordinate Brigadier General Smyth to succeed Van Rensselear as commander of the force facing the British in northwestern New York. Smyth developed a plan to attack Fort Erie, the British stronghold at the south end of the Niagara River, at its entrance from Lake Erie.

In the early morning of November 28, 1812, Smyth sent a contingent across the Niagara River about two and a half miles below Fort Erie and a second contingent across near Frenchman's Creek, above the fort. Both contingents were forced back to the American side of the river by a strong British counterattack. By noon, Smyth still had not been able to embark his main force, apparently because his Pennsylvania militia troops, like their New York counterparts, refused to cross into Canada. Smyth's senior officers, meeting in a council of war, voted to abandon the plan.

Two days later Smyth tried again, managing to marshal some fifteen hundred troops to launch a new assault. A new council of war, however, voted again to kill the whole idea, and this time Smyth caved in and gave up. He asked General Dearborn for a leave to visit his family in Virginia; when permission was granted, he slipped quietly away, never to return to duty. His name disappeared from army rolls.

Meanwhile, General Dearborn was having troubles of his own. In charge of the main assault on Canada, with the capture of Montreal as its objective, Dearborn—whose soldiers nicknamed him "Granny"—had at his command an army estimated at six to eight thousand men. But he had dallied for so long in marching on Montreal that the War Department finally, in exasperation, had bluntly ordered him to "go to Albany or the Lake [Champlain]!" and had insistently told him, "The blow must be struck."[8]

Dearborn then had led his army from Albany to Plattsburgh, New York, on Lake Champlain. His advance unit had crossed the border and entered Canada on the morning of November 20, 1812. Some members of the advance party had skirmished in the predawn darkness with British troops but had also fired on their own men. One account reports that the Americans captured a British blockhouse during the foray,[9] but the engagement proved inconsequential as once again militia troops refused to cross into Canada, and the small gain had to be surrendered. Thwarted by his militia troops' refusal, Dearborn then had withdrawn his entire army, his militiamen departing for home and his regulars going into winter quarters, done for the season, for now having given up on the grand scheme to conquer Canada, which was one of the war's major aims.

Only the United States Navy could claim any success in the war thus far. In 1812 it alone saved the nation from total humiliation at the hands of the enemy. At the outset of the war, the navy's fleet amounted to seventeen ships, including seven frigates, a corvette converted from a frigate, and nine smaller vessels. The officers and men of the navy were experienced at their jobs, many of them having seen action in the undeclared naval war with France in 1798 through 1800 (the so-called Quasi-War) and in the battles with Barbary pirates in the Tripoli War, which lasted from 1801 to 1805. Not a few seamen in America's navy were veterans of the British navy. By and large, the crews of America's warships were professional sailors, skilled, disciplined, and possessed of high morale.

In September 1812 Captain Isaac Chauncey, a forty-year-old navy veteran, had been given command of the United States naval forces on Lake Erie and Lake Ontario and had been ordered to do his best to gain control of the lakes, which Chauncey saw as the key to controlling Canada. He promptly completed preparations for challenging the British naval force and took over the brig *Oneida,* which mounted eighteen guns. He purchased for the navy five merchant schooners, which he then armed and converted into gunboats, building a somewhat respectable fleet with which he hoped to command the waters of Lake Ontario.

To put an American fleet on Lake Erie, where the navy had no ships, Chauncey had dispatched Lieutenant Jesse D. Elliott to Buffalo, New York, to acquire vessels, including two brigs to be built for the navy, and had had ninety sailors sent to man whatever vessels Elliott could buy. On October 8, 1812, still without a warship, Elliott had seized an opportunity to capture two British warships, the *Caledonia* and the *Detroit* (the ship, formerly named the *Adams,* which General Hull had surrendered), as they lay anchored off Fort Erie. He put a force of sailors into two small boats and had them row for two hours to pull alongside the British vessels, which they seized after fighting their way aboard. Without a strong enough wind to let them sail the ships into Lake Erie, Elliott ordered the cables cut to allow them to drift downstream, away from the fort. The *Caledonia* escaped and was beached safely under the protection of American artillery near Black Rock, New York. The *Detroit,* however, was lost when it ran aground within range of British artillery and was destroyed, though the American sailors were able to remove and save most of its guns. With courage and resourcefulness, Elliott's sailors had acquired the first vessel of the Lake Erie fleet.

Soon thereafter, winter weather halted further action on Lake Erie until the coming of spring. On Lake Ontario, though, Commodore Chauncey continued his operations in the *Oneida,* driving some British ships into the haven of Kingston harbor and capturing a number of others. By November 13, 1812, he felt confident enough to report that the United States Navy was in control of Lake Ontario.

Not long after that, he concluded his search for an officer to take command of the Lake Erie fleet that was being built or bought. He heard that twenty-seven-year-old Commodore Oliver Hazard Perry, then commanding a flotilla of gunboats based at Newport, Rhode Island, wanted more action than was available at his present station. Chauncey wrote to him, telling him, "You are the very person that I want for a particular service, in which you may gain reputation for Yourself and honour for your country."[10] Perry signed on, and Chauncey left Lake Erie to Perry's enterprising care while Chauncey concentrated his efforts on Lake Ontario.

America's navy was making itself respectable not only on the Great Lakes but also on the high seas. The *Constitution,* the American frigate that would become known admiringly as Old Ironsides, was in Annapolis receiving a new crew when the war started in June 1812. On July 12, commanded by Captain Isaac Hull (nephew of the disgraced General Hull), the *Constitution,* with its new crew of 450 officers and men, sailed from Chesapeake Bay into the Atlantic, heading northward. On July 17, at two o'clock in the afternoon, Captain Hull spied four ships to the north of him, heading westward in a light wind, moving toward the coast. Two hours later he spotted a fifth ship, northeast of him. He had run up against the British squadron commanded by Captain Philip Bowes Vere Broke, who quickly gave chase to the *Constitution.*

In the light wind the *Constitution* was unable to take advantage of its greater speed to outrun the enemy, and Hull shifted several guns to the stern of his ship to hold the enemy vessels at bay while he maneuvered to elude them. As darkness fell, the wind died, and Hull put out small boats to tow the ship by rowing, as the British also were forced to do. Finding himself in shallow water, Hull had the ship kedged forward, a laborious process in which relatively small anchors are dropped from a small boat, and then their attached cables are hauled in by the crew, pulling the ship up to the anchors. The anchors are again hauled up into the small boat, which its crew rows ahead as the cables are let out, and the anchors are again dropped, and the whole process is repeated. By that heroic procedure and by outstanding seamanship (which British officers came to admire), Hull, doggedly determined that his ship would not be captured, managed to escape, finally taking advantage of a squall to slip away after three days of pursuit. On July 26 he sailed into the safety of Boston harbor.

On August 2, on his own initiative, Hull took his ship out to sea again. He sailed up the coast toward Newfoundland and captured and burned two British brigs in the Gulf of Saint Lawrence. On August 15 he recaptured an American brig taken earlier by the British, then turned southward. On the night of August 18 he learned from an American privateer that a British frigate was sailing in waters farther south. The next afternoon the *Constitution* came upon the British frigate *Guerriere,* commanded by Captain James Richard Dacres and part of the five-ship squadron that had pursued the *Constitution* the month before. With the wind aft of her, the *Constitution* quickly bore down on the *Guerriere.* At about five o'clock the engagement began with the *Guerriere* opening fire. The *Constitution,* carrying fifty-four guns, maneuvered and returned fire. The *Guerriere,* carrying forty-nine guns,[11] maneuvered and fired again, first a starboard broadside, then, after turning about, a port broadside. For nearly an hour the two ships blazed away at each other in a furious exchange, neither inflicting serious damage on the other, many of the shots passing harmlessly through the rigging.

About six o'clock the *Guerriere* veered, and the *Constitution* closed on the British vessel's port beam and unleashed a new cannonade. The *Guerriere* replied, and the furious exchange resumed. The British were now getting the worst of it. The *Constitution*'s guns shot away the *Guerriere*'s mizzenmast, which fell and severely damaged the starboard side, then dangled over the side, trailing in the water. Hull then turned the *Constitution* about and delivered a punishing fire with its starboard guns, carrying away the *Guerriere*'s main yard, then turned again and raked its bow.

The sea was too rough for the crew of either ship to board the other, but the crews delivered fierce musket fire on each other, each suffering casualties. Under the continuing cannonades the *Guerriere*'s mainmast and foremast were both shot away, leaving the vessel dead in the water. It was now a defenseless wreck, its main-deck guns having rolled into the ocean.

The *Constitution* had also suffered damage in the pounding, and at six thirty it disengaged and stood off from the *Guerriere* for several minutes while its rigging and spars were hurriedly repaired. About seven o'clock, two hours after it had fired the first shot, the *Guerriere* struck its colors and surrendered. Fifteen of the *Guerriere*'s crew had been killed; the remaining 267 were taken prisoner, except for 10 crewmen who were found to be impressed American sailors. They had refused to participate in the battle against their countrymen and had been permitted by Captain Dacres to go below to avoid the fight. The *Constitution* had lost six seamen and a marine officer (Lieutenant William S. Bush) killed, and seven others had been wounded. After its crew was removed from the ship, the *Guerriere,* too badly damaged to be towed into port as a prize, was set afire and blew up shortly after.

It was during the battle with the *Guerriere* that the *Constitution* became known as Old Ironsides, as its stout hull shed shot as if the ship were plated with iron. The victory was significant, providing morale-boosting evidence that America's ships could hold their own against His

Majesty's vaunted navy. Other evidence was provided on October 15, 1812, when the frigate *United States,* commanded by Captain Stephen Decatur, defeated and captured the British frigate *Macedonian* in an engagement about six hundred miles west of the Canary Islands. A crew from the *United States* then sailed the captured vessel into Newport harbor. On December 29, 1812, the *Constitution,* under the command of Captain William Bainbridge, encountered the British frigate *Java* off the coast of Brazil and with superior firepower and gunnery shot away *Java*'s masts, forcing the immobilized vessel to surrender. The surviving crew members and passengers were taken aboard Old Ironsides as prisoners, and the crippled British ship was then sunk.

By the end of 1812 the American navy had defeated or captured three British frigates, two sloops, a brig, a transport, and some fifty merchant ships, while losing but three of its own vessels. American privateers, privately owned armed vessels operating under contract with the government, had exacted an even greater toll on British shipping, capturing some 450 merchant vessels. The operations of American privateers, mostly off the coast of Canada and in the West Indies, played such havoc with British commercial shipping that it could be safely carried on only under escort by British warships, which captured or destroyed 150 privateers during the first eight months of the war.

The American army, meanwhile, still struggled vainly for any sort of success. An effort to recapture Detroit ended in a new disaster in January 1813. The new commander that President Madison had appointed for the northwest, thirty-nine-year-old Brigadier General William Henry Harrison, had assembled an army of sixty-five hundred men by the end of December 1812 and ordered it forward from a point below the Maumee River in northwestern Ohio. The left wing of the army, about twelve hundred men, moved out through two feet of snow and on January 10, 1813, managed to reach the Maumee, where the wing's commander, Brigadier General James Winchester, established a fortified camp on the north side of the river.

Into the camp came a message from the settlers at Frenchtown (present-day Monroe, Michigan), on the Raisin River, about thirty-five miles northeast of Winchester's position, roughly midway between the Maumee and Detroit. The Frenchtown settlement was occupied by a garrison of Canadian militiamen and Indians, and the American settlers were hoping that an American army would oust the garrison and return the settlement to them. Apparently without giving it much thought, Winchester divided his force and sent half, under the command of Colonel William Lewis, to attack the enemy at Frenchtown. It was a big mistake.

At nearby Fort Malden, Ontario, where a British force under Colonel Henry Procter was posted, the dividing of Winchester's army was quickly noticed. Colonel Lewis's American troops captured Frenchtown on January 18, and on January 21 Procter took a British force of about twelve hundred men, half of them Indians, across the frozen Detroit River, pulling a number of three-pounder artillery pieces along with them, headed for Frenchtown.

By then, General Winchester had realized his mistake and had hurried to reinforce Colonel Lewis with three hundred troops. They made little difference in the outcome. The British force outflanked and overwhelmed the Americans, hacking many of them to death and taking many others prisoner, including General Winchester, who then surrendered the entire American force. Colonel Procter quickly withdrew his regulars back to Fort Malden, taking with him his prisoners, whose numbers were about equal to his own troops, and leaving the wounded Americans behind to be cared for by American surgeons. As soon as Procter and his regulars pulled out, his Indians, drunk with plundered whiskey, scalped most of the thirty wounded American soldiers and burned the rest of them alive. When General Harrison learned of the disaster, he called off the planned campaign, deciding to wait until spring before making another try at regaining Detroit.

Little was undertaken by the army until April 1813, when a new campaign was launched against Canada in the east. The objective this time was York (later renamed Toronto), the capital city of the province of Ontario. Situated on the northwestern shore of Lake Ontario, York was a town of fewer than a thousand inhabitants, containing some government buildings as well as residences and commercial and military buildings. In the War Department's new plan, York was to be a stepping-stone to the strategic forts on the Niagara River and to a renewed thrust into the northwestern frontier.

On April 24, 1813, a force of 1,800 troops was embarked at Sackets Harbor, New York, ferried across Lake Ontario through stormy seas, and landed just west of York. Though the town was only lightly defended, the Americans suffered some three hundred casualties, including those killed or wounded when a magazine exploded. The outnumbered British defenders quickly withdrew after their telling show of resistance. When the British fled, American troops overran the town. They captured the navy schooner *Duke of Gloucester* and burned a British naval vessel that was under construction and nearly finished. They looted the inhabitants' abandoned houses and then, most memorably—for the British anyway—they set the government buildings, as well as the military buildings, on fire and burned them to the ground.

Seven days after they had landed, the Americans reboarded their vessels on May 1, 1813, and sailed off to the next objective, Fort George, on the Niagara River. The attack on Fort George was delayed by bad weather, and it was not until May 27 that an American force attacked and drove off the defenders and captured the fort. The overall plan then stalled as the British won battles at Stoney Creek, Ontario, and Beaver Dams, Ontario, in June 1813.

The struggle for control of the lakes then passed again to the able hands of the United States Navy. General Procter, in command of British forces in the northwest, could not maintain his posts along the Detroit River without supplies from the east. His Indian warriors and their families, an estimated fourteen thousand people, were dependent on those supplies for subsistence, as were his regular troops. With Perry's vessels contending for control of Lake Erie, the supply of Procter's army became unreliable. Captain Robert Barclay, commanding His Majesty's Lake Erie squadron, received the assignment to eliminate the threat from Perry and secure Procter's supply line.

Major General Andrew Jackson.
*Courtesy of the Library of Congress.*

A bird's-eye view of New Orleans.
*Courtesy of the Library of Congress.*

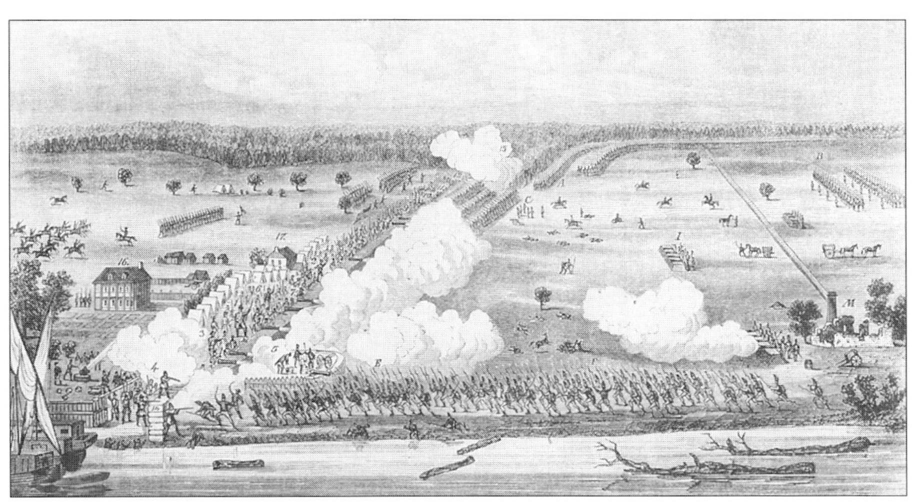

Drawing of the Battle of New Orleans, by Major Lacarriere Latour, Jackson's chief engineer.
*Courtesy of the New England Publishing Associates.*

Brigadier General John Coffee,
Jackson's longtime friend and comrade-in-arms.
*Courtesy of the Library of Congress.*

Commodore Daniel Patterson, commander of United States naval forces at the Battle of New Orleans.

*John Wesley Jarvis (American, 1780–1840). Commodore Daniel Todd Patterson (1786–1839), ca. 1815. Oil on canvas, 36 x 28 inches. Chrysler Museum of Art,Norfolk, Virginia. Museum purchase 65.34.6.*

Major General Sir Edward Pakenham. *Courtesy of the National Portrait Gallery, London.*

Admiral Sir Alexander Cochrane, commander of British naval forces at the Battle of New Orleans and chief planner of the attempt to capture the city. *Courtesy of the Library of Congress.*

Major General Sir John Lambert, who took command of the shattered British army following the death of General Pakenham. *Courtesy of the National Portrait Gallery, London.*

Artist's depiction of the fatal wounding of General Pakenham.
*Courtesy of the Library of Congress.*

General Jackson's wife, Rachel.
*Courtesy of the Library of Congress.*

John Sevier, governor of Tennessee and Jackson's political adversary.
*Courtesy of the Library of Congress.*

Urged on by Canada's governor, General Prevost, Barclay sailed out from Amherstburg, on the Canadian side of the Detroit River, on the morning of September 9, 1813, with the intention of sweeping Perry and his interfering ships off of Lake Erie. At daylight on the morning of September 10, Barclay's six vessels were sighted by Commodore Perry's nine-ship squadron, and by noon the two squadrons had engaged, the British commencing the action by opening fire with their long guns. The American vessels, each previously assigned the British ship that would be its target, closed in to take advantage of their superiority of firepower at short range.

Perry's flagship, the brig *Lawrence,* in the furious exchange of fire, suffered heavy damage and casualties. With half the *Lawrence*'s crew killed or wounded and all but one gun disabled, Perry, miraculously unharmed, with his thirteen-year-old brother and four crewmen climbed into one of the ship's small boats and rowed to the twenty-gun American brig *Niagara,* where he assumed command and continued to direct the battle. The largest of the British ships, the nineteen-gun *Detroit,* where Barclay commanded, was battered and broken, its masts and rigging shot away and many of its crew dead or wounded. Barclay himself, who had lost an arm at the Battle of Trafalgar, had suffered two new wounds and had been forced to retire below deck. His next in command had been mortally wounded. By three o'clock that afternoon the *Detroit* had struck its colors and surrendered, as had the *Queen Charlotte,* the second-largest vessel of Barclay's squadron. Two other British vessels, the schooner *Chippewa* and the sloop *Little Belt,* attempted to withdraw and escape but were captured. By evening, the battle was over. The Americans' victory was complete.

Perry then dispatched to General William Henry Harrison the message that has been remembered by Americans ever since: "We have met the enemy and they are ours." President Madison rewarded Perry by promoting him to captain. The British presence on Lake Erie eliminated, his supply and communications lines severed, General Procter had no choice but to abandon Fort Malden and Amherstburg, the British posts on the Detroit River, and withdraw eastward.

On September 27, 1813, transported by Perry's quickly repaired vessels, General Harrison and his army took over Fort Malden. Three days later they recaptured Detroit. On October 5 they caught up with Procter's army at Moravian Town on the Thames River and crushed it. The British lost more than 600 killed, wounded, or captured. Among the killed was the Indian chieftain Tecumseh. Among the 246 who managed to escape was General Procter. American casualties amounted to seven killed and twenty-two wounded.

The secretary of war, John Armstrong, now once again tried to have the army execute the grand plan to capture Montreal. The attempt, led by General James Wilkinson and General Wade Hampton, failed when Wilkinson's force was battered by stiff British resistance in the battle at Chrysler's farm in November, and Hampton gave up the campaign and withdrew his troops to winter quarters. The British then launched their own offensive, which concluded with the Americans' loss of control of the Niagara River and, as a consequence, loss of a chance to gain Canada.

Along the Atlantic coastline the British, alarmed by the American navy's successes, beefed up their fleet and instituted a blockade of the nation's seaports, bottling up the navy's vessels in harbors from New England southward. One British squadron patrolled off the eastern edge of Long Island Sound, and another cruised off Sandy Hook, New Jersey. His Majesty's frigates and sloops continually patrolled the coasts of the Carolinas and Georgia, and a large naval force blocked all access to and from Chesapeake Bay. By the spring of 1814 the British blockade had all but shut down America's maritime commerce and stymied the American navy on the eastern seaboard.

Still worse for Americans, the war in Europe had finally ended. Napoleon's army had been shattered in the Battle of Leipzig in October 1813; on March 31, 1814, allied armies marched into Paris; on April 10, 1814, after a string of victories, Wellington had invaded France and ended the Peninsular War. On April 11, 1814, Napoleon abdicated. On May 4, 1814, Napoleon arrived on Elba to begin his exile. No longer having to contend with the Napoleonic menace, Britain was free to shift more of its troops from the Continent to the United States.

By May 26, 1814, the British government had decided to move four divisions from the European theater to America. Three of the divisions were to reinforce General Prevost's army in its defense of Canada and launch an offensive into Maine and possibly down Lake Champlain and the Hudson River valley. The fourth division, commanded by Major General Robert Ross, one of Wellington's generals now free for other assignments, was given no specific objectives but was ordered to join the British fleet that was operating off America's Atlantic coast. The fleet was commanded by Vice Admiral Sir Alexander Cochrane—arrogant, crusty, and scornful of Americans.

Ross's official mission was to create along the eastern coast diversions that would pull American troops away from Canada. Cochrane's official mission was to transport and assist Ross in the accomplishment of his mission. Cochrane, however, had taken upon himself an additional mission, partly in response to General Prevost's urging that he retaliate for the Americans' depredations in Canada, particularly in York, where government buildings were burned, and partly owing to his own animus toward Americans. That additional mission was to chastise the enemy. To pursue it, Cochrane ordered his squadron commanders "to destroy and lay waste such towns and cities upon the coast as you may find assailable" and "spare merely the lives of the unarmed inhabitants of the United States."[12]

On August 15, 1814, the transports carrying General Ross and his army of four regiments (the Fourth, Forty-eighth, Eighty-fifth, and Twenty-first) arrived at Tangier Island in Chesapeake Bay. There, where the British had established a fortified base the year before, Ross's force joined that of Admiral Cochrane, commanding a fleet of a twenty warships and a number of transports. Cochrane's battalion of marines increased Ross's force to some four thousand men.

On August 22 the British force reached the Patuxent River, where an overmatched flotilla of American gunboats commanded by Commodore Joshua Barney had sought haven from Cochrane's warships. Seeing the advance of the British land force and the approach of British ships, Barney set fire to his gunboats and withdrew his sailors to safety.

Ross then marched his force, organized into three brigades, to Upper Marlboro, Maryland, about sixteen miles southeast of the city of Washington, the nation's capital. It met no resistance, not even sighting a defender, as it pressed steadily northward. On August 23 Ross turned westward, on the road to Washington.

News of the British army's menacing advance had reached Washington on the morning of August 19. The city was virtually defenseless, largely because of the ineptitude of Secretary of War John Armstrong, who assumed Washington would not be a British objective, and the incompetence of Brigadier General William H. Winder, whom President Madison had appointed to establish the city's defenses. Winder had been in the job since July 5 but had done practically nothing to organize a defense or construct fortifications to resist a British attack.

At the last minute a force of about 7,000 defenders—regular troops, militia, volunteers, and Commodore Barney's sailors and marines—was hastily assembled. Contingents of it, including infantry, cavalry, and artillery, were formed into a defense at a place called the Wood Yard, about five miles west and a little south of Upper Marlboro. Ross's army passed that position on a road to the north of it, in full view of the Americans, including General Winder, who stood or sat idly by watching the enemy pass. Winder never even considered attacking the British column.

Winder then withdrew his forward force to Old Fields, where the road to Washington forked, about five miles northwest of the Wood Yard. As Ross's army approached Old Fields, Winder, without firing a shot, quickly ordered a retreat to Washington by the shortest route possible.

Ross would not take the shortest route, since doing so would mean crossing the broad eastern branch of the Potomac River, on the city's east side, and making his troops vulnerable to American fire as they marched across the bridges. If the bridges were destroyed in advance of his approach, a crossing would be virtually impossible. Thus, when he reached Old Fields, he took the route that led to Bladensburg, about five miles above Washington, where the river was narrow, fordable, and also spanned by a bridge.

A poorly organized American force raced to Bladensburg to form a line and make a stand, but in vain. Ross's infantry dashed through the river and flanked the defenders, routing them, though suffering heavy casualties in the process. By four o'clock that afternoon, Wednesday, August 23, the battle had ended, the American defenders scattered. At six o'clock the British resumed their march on Washington. At eight o'clock, halted by darkness, they made camp just outside the city but within a quarter mile of the Capitol.

Ross shared with Rear Admiral George Cockburn, commander of one of Cochrane's squadrons, a penchant for burning buildings, which they had done in the towns along Chesapeake Bay, and now he sent a detail into the city to set fire to the Capitol. By the ghastly light of the flames consuming the magnificent structure, General Ross and another detail of troops marched to the White House, from which the president's wife and its other occupants had earlier in the day hastily fled. The White House furniture was gathered into the drawing room and set ablaze, and the entire house soon was burning furiously. The arsonists moved on to the United States Treasury building, ransacked it (without finding any money), and burned it.

The next morning, August 25, 1814, the invaders destroyed the Navy Yard, with the help of a disastrous, accidental explosion. They burned the building that housed the State Department, the War Department, and the Navy Department. The British work of wasting the United States government buildings was not ended until a ferocious thunderstorm and tornado struck the city that afternoon, the storm's heavy rain probably saving the rest of the city from the spreading flames of the blazing buildings. Ross then made plans to steal away.

While his curfew kept Washington's residents in their houses, Ross's troops quietly withdrew from the city and from their encampment. Twenty-four hours after arriving on their mission of devastation, they marched through the night to Bladensburg, then back to Upper Marlboro, leaving behind them the ruined structures of official Washington, now but charred, crushed symbols of the threatened new nation.

## ∴ 11 ∴

# The British Offensive

GENERAL Ross's orders forbade him from undertaking "any extended operation at a distance from the coast,"[1] and he had been instructed not to try to hold on to any captured territory. His attacks along the coast were to be hit-and-run raids. And so after he had burned Washington as an act of terrorism and vengeance, he had promptly forsaken it and set off to render similar treatment to another American city, this one of more strategic importance.

From Upper Marlboro Ross marched south to Nottingham, Maryland, where his walking wounded were placed aboard a British warship, the more seriously wounded having been left in the care of Americans at the hospital in Bladensburg. From Nottingham he quickly marched to Benedict, on the Patuxent River, which he reached on the evening of August 29, 1814, and where on the next day he embarked his diminished army onto transports that lay waiting to evacuate it.

While Ross's army marched, Captain James Gordon, commanding the British frigate *Seahorse,* had sailed up the Potomac, leading a squadron that included six other vessels, and reached Arlington, Virginia, on August 28. Defenseless, Arlington's officials immediately surrendered the town to the invaders, who hauled aboard their ships great quantities of tobacco and every other valuable commodity they could loot from the town's warehouses. They then made their way back down the river, suffering damage and casualties from American fire along the banks of the lower river, but finally completing their escape on September 6.

On the night that Ross and his troops left Washington, Thursday, August 25, President Madison was safe in Virginia, some sixteen miles upriver from the smoldering remains of the White House he had abandoned. His secretary of war, John Armstrong, and his secretary of the treasury, George W. Campbell, were in Frederick, Maryland, forty-five miles from Washington. The secretary of state, James Monroe, and the man Madison had put in charge of the defense of Washington, Brigadier General William Winder, were at Montgomery Court House, Maryland, about twenty miles from the capital. With Winder was the remainder of his army.

On the morning of Saturday, August 27, Madison sent word to his scattered cabinet members to join him in Washington. Armstrong arrived in Washington on August 29 and was promptly greeted with a request from the president. Madison wanted the ineffectual war secretary to disappear from the government, and Armstrong obligingly resigned. Monroe, who had urged Armstrong's dismissal, had also urged the president to appoint him, temporarily at least, as Armstrong's successor, while keeping his post as secretary of state as well. The president concurred. With a keen eye for spotting incompetents, Monroe also persuaded the president to appoint him commander of the Washington military district, in charge of the capital's defenses, displacing the inept General Winder.

General Winder, meanwhile, was on the march. Hearing that Ross's troops had moved to Bladensburg after their departure from Washington, Winder, with rare perspicacity, decided Ross must be headed for Baltimore. Winder resolved to pursue him. En route, Winder left his army and galloped off alone toward Baltimore, putting Monroe (before he had been named to replace Winder) and Brigadier General Tobias Stansbury of the Maryland militia in charge, with instructions to continue the advance toward Baltimore. Not yet convinced of his own inability, Winder intended to rush into town and take over the job of defending Baltimore.

The citizens of Baltimore (the nation's third-largest city, with a population of about forty-five thousand) were not waiting for help from Washington. Led by their mayor, they had built an imposing line of redoubts around the city, connected by entrenchments. Along the line they had constructed artillery emplacements, now mounted with guns manned by sailors and commanded by United States Navy officers. Behind and within the city's newly raised fortifications were upwards of twelve thousand troops. Guarding Baltimore's harbor, which opens into the Patapsco River and then into Chesapeake Bay, was Fort McHenry, garrisoned by a force of army regulars, sailors, and volunteers totaling some 1,000 men.

When Brigadier General Winder arrived in Baltimore to take command, he quickly learned that the militia's Major General Samuel Smith, a United States senator, was already in command and was not about to yield his authority, especially not to a subordinate officer with a poor military record. Winder, who had been a lawyer in Baltimore, appealed his case to President Madison and to his cousin, Levin Winder, the governor of Maryland. Neither appeal helped, and he eventually acquiesced.

Baltimore was indeed the British objective. Admiral Cochrane was particularly eager to destroy the city and punish its citizens for harboring an estimated 127 privateers who used Baltimore as a base for their attacks on British commercial vessels. Some five hundred British ships had been captured or destroyed by privateers operating out of Baltimore, which the British considered a detestable pirates' nest. In Washington the British had restrained themselves and burned only government buildings, leaving private property untouched, but Cochrane felt no such restraint about Baltimore. "This town," he wrote to Viscount Melville, first lord of the Admiralty, "ought to be laid in ashes."[2] The wrathful admiral was bothered that General Ross seemed not so passionately vengeful as himself but hoped he would become so. "When he [Ross] is better acquainted with the American character," Cochrane wrote, "he will possibly see as I do that like Spaniels they must be treated with great severity before you even make them tractable."[3]

On September 11, 1814, Cochrane's fleet anchored near the mouth of the Patapsco River, twelve miles below Baltimore. At daylight on September 12 Ross's troops were put ashore at North Point, fourteen miles from the city, where the road they would take would not require them to cross water to march onto their objective. By eight o'clock that morning they were on the move, the light brigade, including the Eighty-fifth Regiment, leading the advance. Behind it was the second brigade, including the Forty-fourth Regiment, and guarding the rear was the third brigade, including the Twenty-first Regiment. Altogether, Ross's reinforced army now amounted to an estimated five thousand troops.[4] As the long, scarlet-coated column advanced, Cochrane moved his warships closer to Fort McHenry.

When news of the redcoats' approach reached Baltimore on September 11, General Smith ordered a militia brigade under Brigadier General John Stricker to move out and impede the British advance. That same evening, Stricker marched his troops about seven miles toward North Point to confront the invaders. The next morning, September 12, he arrayed his men across the road in a defensive formation of three lines, spaced three hundred yards apart, in open fields, with little cover or concealment. He then sent a detachment of cavalry and infantry forward from his lines to a distance of a mile or two, where they soon caught sight of the advancing redcoats and fell back. Stricker then ordered forward four hundred men as skirmishers. They moved out and opened fire on the British advance units but were soon driven back.

As the British advance units moved forward, General Ross and Admiral Cockburn rode together on the road with them. Guessing that more serious resistance lay ahead, Ross turned his mount around and started making his way back to order his light infantry forward. As he moved down the road, a sniper fired from nearby woods and hit Ross in the chest. He crumpled and fell from his horse onto the roadway, where he lay alone until he was discovered by infantrymen rushing toward the sound of the gunfire. He was carried in a cart back to the water's edge, where the transports lay waiting, but he died on the way.

Command of the British troops now passed to Colonel Arthur Brooke. Though Stricker's militiamen had so far been unsuccessful in checking the British advance, Brooke proceeded cautiously. When he observed the American lines spread across the road in front of him, he brought up his entire army and deployed it in a formal order of battle. The Americans, outnumbered, outflanked, and eventually routed, inflicted dauntingly heavy casualties on the invaders in the engagement. The British lost 46 killed and 273 wounded. The Americans lost 24 killed and 139 wounded.

They had been routed by veterans of Wellington's army, but Stricker's untested militiamen had so delayed the British advance that Colonel Brooke decided to halt for the day and bivouac in the open fields his troops had just won. His men spent the night in a soaking rain.

The next morning, September 13, Brooke resumed the march toward Baltimore. By then the Americans had erected obstructions across the path of the invaders, and Brooke's army was forced to progress slowly. It was evening before the British troops came within sight of Baltimore's tallest buildings. About a mile and a half from the city, Brooke ordered his army halted while a reconnaissance of Baltimore's defenses could be made. He was now considering attacking the American line at night, when its artillery would be handicapped by darkness. The assault would be supported by the guns of Admiral Cochrane's warships, which had been pouring mortar rounds, shot, explosive shells, and rockets on Fort McHenry all day and continued to do so, intending to silence its guns and permit Cochrane's smaller vessels to sail past the fort and give close support to Brooke's assault. Cochrane's larger warships had to stand off and pound Fort McHenry from a distance, since the harbor's mouth was blocked by the hulks of twenty-four ships that the defenders had scuttled and sunk. Deep-draft vessels could not get past them.

Sometime after midnight of September 13–14, Brooke received the bad news from Cochrane. A coordinated attack on the Baltimore lines would not be possible. Cochrane's ships, imperiled by the unvanquished guns of Fort McHenry, as well as shore batteries and American gunboats, could not get close enough to help. They had done all they could and all they were going to do. With that message in hand, about three o'clock in the morning on September 14, Brooke gave up any idea of an assault. "Under these circumstances," he reported, "it was agreed between the Vice-admiral and myself that the capture of the town would not have been a sufficient equivalent to the loss which might probably be sustained in storming the heights."[5]

Cochrane's ships had rained an estimated eighteen hundred to two thousand artillery shells, upwards of 700 rockets, and tons of cannon shot on Fort McHenry, all with little effect. The fort suffered four men killed and 24 wounded. Its guns had not been silenced and remained a threat to Cochrane's vessels. What was more, the huge American flag, measuring forty-two feet by thirty feet, with stars two feet across from point to point, and stripes (eight red and seven white) two feet wide, was still flying, triumphantly, above the battered battlements.

In the dawn's early light on September 14, the flag was seen by an American civilian aboard one of Cochrane's ships. He was a thirty-five-year-old Georgetown lawyer named Francis Scott Key, who under a flag of truce on September 7 had sailed out to petition the British commanders for the release of a captured, elderly American physician from Upper Marlboro. Key was so moved by the sight of the flag that morning that he quickly took from his pocket an envelope and composed on it a poem to memorialize the event. Set to music, the poem became the United States' national anthem in 1931.

By noon of September 14, Colonel Brooke and his retreating army had reached and passed the scene of the battle fought two days earlier. The next day, the army reembarked aboard Admiral Cochrane's transports, and as soon as the wind was with them, Cochrane's entire fleet sailed down to the lower Chesapeake, the intended raid on Baltimore totally thwarted and now abandoned.

On September 19 Cochrane left his transports lying in the Chesapeake and sailed for Halifax, Nova Scotia, there to make preparations for a new campaign. After more than three weeks of bobbing on the bay, the transports on October 14 sailed for Jamaica with the British expeditionary force, there to await the new campaign being planned.

The British offensive of 1814 so far had not been a complete success, though in London the temporary capture of Washington and the burning of its government buildings had been mostly cheered as a worthy accomplishment. In July a British force had overrun American defenses and taken over a large part of northern Maine. The British occupied the town of Machias, an Atlantic port, and had gained control of about one hundred miles of the Maine coast. They had established a virtual base on Nantucket, off the coast of Massachusetts, which the island's inhabitants had been forced to yield or face starvation caused by the choke-hold blockade by British ships.

The drive to capture Lake Champlain and move down the Hudson River valley, however, had been blunted by a spectacularly heroic American victory over a British naval squadron in Plattsburgh Bay on September 11. Following the battle, the American commander, thirty-year-old Lieutenant Thomas Macdonough, dispatched a message to navy headquarters reporting that "the Almighty has been pleased to Grant us a signal Victory on Lake Champlain in the Capture of one Frigate, one Brig and two sloops of war of the enemy."[6]

General Sir George Prevost, the Canadian governor, had led an army of ten thousand men across the United States border on August 31 and begun a march down the west side of Lake Champlain, his objective being the town of Plattsburgh, which was defended by an American force of thirty-four hundred men, many of them new recruits, commanded by General Alexander Macomb. Attempts by Macomb to impede the enemy's advance were swept aside by Prevost's overwhelming numbers. The invaders pushed on to the Saranac River, below and to the west of Plattsburgh, but their attempt to flank the formidable American fortifications at Plattsburgh failed. When Prevost learned of the disastrous defeat of the British navy in Plattsburgh Bay, he, like Colonel Brooke, decided that storming the American defensive works would be suicidal without the support of the British vessels' guns. On September 12 he began a retreat back to Canada.

Elsewhere on the Canadian frontier, engagements between American and British forces were inconclusive. An American force had seized Fort Erie and beaten back a British attempt to retake it, but on November 5 the Americans blew up the fort and abandoned the site. British forces, despite their reinforcement by veterans of the Napoleonic Wars, in July were also repulsed in battles at Chippewa and Lundy's Lane, along the Niagara River. Both of those engagements were British responses to American offensives. Both ended in a draw.

When he sailed for Halifax from the Chesapeake, Admiral Cochrane did not know about the British naval defeat on Lake Champlain or about General Prevost's abandonment of the drive on Plattsburgh. Not a good loser, he doubtless would have been even more soreheaded than he had been over the failure at Baltimore. He tried to spin that defeat into something palatable to his men and to the British public by calling the unsuccessful attack merely a "demonstration and reconnaissance, which it was deemed advisable to make upon the city of Baltimore."[7] Glossing over the refusal of Colonel Brooke to make an assault on Baltimore's defenses and his subsequent retreat, Cochrane wrote in his official report, "The primary object of our movement had already been fully accomplished,"[8] apparently referring to the burning of Washington. In a private letter to the first lord of the Admiralty, Lord Melville, however, Cochrane complained that the whole Baltimore operation was "contrary to my opinion, but extremely urged by the General [Ross], to which I reluctantly consented but to preserve unanimity between the two services."[9] He said that he "extremely regretted" the entire operation and said Ross should have gone ashore on the opposite side of the harbor and attacked the city from the west.

Soon emerging from his snit, Cochrane quickly interested himself in a new project. "Give me but 6,000 men including a rifle and cavalry regiment," he told Melville, "and I will engage to master every town south of Philadelphia and keep the whole coast in such a state of alarm as soon to bring the most obstinate upon their marrow bones."[10]

On the same day, September 17, 1814, that he wrote that letter to Melville, he received a dispatch from London informing him that 7,000 troops were being sent to him and they were to rendezvous with his fleet in Jamaica on November 20. Months earlier, Cochrane had submitted a long report to Lord Bathurst, Britain's secretary of war, concerning the possibilities for taking the war to the coast of the Gulf of Mexico. Cochrane stated he had no doubt that three thousand British troops landed at Mobile, where they would be joined by Indians, aided by disaffected French and Spaniards, would drive the Americans entirely out of Louisiana and the Floridas. Now the British government was going to act on Cochrane's suggestion. He had been notified in a dispatch dated August 10 that Ross was being instructed to implement Cochrane's proposal for a campaign on the gulf coast.

Orders had been sent to Ross on the same date. On September 6 Ross was sent detailed instructions about the campaign, including the units and commanders that would be assigned to him to execute the plan. His two paramount objectives—and the purposes of the whole expedition—were also spelled out. First, he was "to obtain command of the embouchure [mouth] of the Mississippi, so as to deprive the back settlements of America of their communication with the sea." Second, he was "to occupy some important and valuable possession, by the restoration of which the conditions of peace might be improved, or which we might be entitled to exact the cession of, as the price of peace."[11]

The British government's aim was to make a major move against the lower United States, enlisting all whom they might to help them secure a stranglehold, perhaps permanent, on the Mississippi, its territory, and its commerce. With the "favor and co-operation" of the inhabitants of the gulf coast region, Ross was told in his orders, "we may expect to rescue the whole province of Louisiana from the United States."[12]

If Ross were to find in the people of the region "a general and decided disposition to withdraw from their recent connection with the United States, either with the view of establishing themselves as an independent people or of returning under the dominion of the Spanish Crown, you will give them every support in your power; you will furnish them with arms and clothing, and assist in forming and disciplining the several levies."[13] Partial dismemberment of the United States was thus a hoped-for result of the campaign that Ross and Cochrane were to conduct.

Now Ross was dead, and a new commanding general would have to be found to take his place. But Cochrane, ever active, had already begun to implement the plan. In May 1814 he sent a boatload of arms to Indians along the Apalachicola River in Florida. An Indian trader, George Woodbine, was commissioned a brevet captain of marines with the task of distributing the arms to the Indians and training them to use bayonets. With the acquiescence of Spanish officials, on August 14 a hundred-man British force moved into Pensacola, the prime port on the gulf coast, and recruited Indians and Negro slaves to bolster their force, commanded by Major Edward Nicolls.

Quick to stir anti-American feelings and extend the British presence westward into Louisiana, Nicolls on August 29 issued a proclamation exhorting the "natives of Louisiana . . . to assist in liberating from a faithless and imbecile government, your paternal soil."[14] To further that aim he led an expedition to seize Mobile, which the United States, claiming it was part of the Louisiana Purchase, had captured from the Spanish in 1813. Nicolls's expedition was defeated when his land force was unable to take Mobile's protective fort, Fort Bowyer, which stood on a peninsula jutting into Mobile Bay, and the bay's waters proved too shallow for the British vessels to navigate.

Up until the summer of 1814, the primary purpose of British operations on the gulf coast had been to divert American attention and strength from Canada and the Great Lakes. Now the British offensive had a new objective—the storied city of New Orleans. The strategy was to capture New Orleans, believed to be an easy feat, and to forever deny to the United States the city and the commerce of the midcontinent that New Orleans controlled, or else to make America pay dearly for its return by exacting a prohibitive price at the peace negotiations taking place in Ghent, Belgium.

The American negotiators, the so-called United States peace commissioners, were John Quincy Adams (the group's chairman), James Bayard, Henry Clay, Albert Gallatin, and Jonathan Russell. They had, nearly to the point of British exasperation, shown themselves to be not merely resistant to British demands but boldly insistent on America's demands, though the war was not going at all well for the United

States, and their bargaining chips made a meager stack. News of the burning of Washington had only slightly affected their steadfastness, bolstered as they were by public opinion on the Continent, where the burning was widely denounced as barbarism and sympathy was on America's side. Stung by severe condemnation from across the Channel, the British government eventually decided that terrorizing Americans was not good policy and ordered Admiral Cochrane to halt his angry campaign of retribution and terror.

Word of the failure at Baltimore and the death of Ross, followed by news of Britain's humiliating naval loss at Plattsburgh, set off a shock wave of consternation in Britain. Government and public alike were rocked by the horrifyingly adverse turn of events. In Ghent, Britain's negotiators, on instructions from London, beat a hasty retreat from their demands for the concession of American territory and now settled for *uti possidetis,* which meant each side would keep the territory that it presently held.

The Duke of Wellington, whose successes against Napoleon had made him Britain's leading authority on military matters, commented on the peace terms that the government was pressing on the Americans. He told Lord Liverpool, the prime minister:

> I confess that I think you have no right from the state of the war to demand any concessions of territory from America. . . . You have not been able to carry it into the enemy's territory, notwithstanding your military successes, and now undoubted military superiority, and have not even cleared your own territory of the enemy on the point of attack.
>
> Then if this reasoning is true, why stipulate for the *uti possidetis?* You can get no territory; indeed the state of your military operations, however creditable, does not entitle you to demand any.[15]

The capture of New Orleans could change all that. With British troops occupying New Orleans and British naval vessels in command of the lower Mississippi River, the British government would place itself in an unassailably strong bargaining position. British officials were apparently so certain that their forces would take New Orleans that they were not bothering to keep their intentions secret. Word passed from government officers to British newspapers that an expedition was being organized to seize New Orleans, and the British press so informed the public, now eager for good news from America.

## ∴ 12 ∴

# The Jewel of the Mississippi

JEAN Baptiste Le Moyne—whose title was Sieur de Bienville and who was known simply as Bienville—had seen the site on his first trip to the Louisiana Territory in 1799. It was a place where he might plant a city on the lower Mississippi, not too far from the river's mouth, a site that would provide a deepwater port and where a new city built upon it would command the river.

The eighth of eleven sons of a French Canadian fur trader and pioneer named Charles Le Moyne, Bienville had come to Louisiana with one of his older brothers, Pierre Le Moyne, known by his title, Sieur d'Iberville. Iberville had distinguished himself as a French naval officer in battles in Hudson Bay and in the North Atlantic during the war with England that ended in 1697 (King William's War); Bienville, who had joined the French navy at age twelve, had served with Iberville in those actions.

After the war, using his influential contacts in Paris, the energetic and enterprising Iberville had managed to gain support for his plan to create a French colony near the mouth of the Mississippi. On the strength of the river's having been explored to its mouth by René-Robert Cavelier de La Salle in 1682, France had already laid claim to the Mississippi and the vast expanse of America that it drained, from the Allegheny Mountains to the Rockies.

Bankrolled by Louis de Phelypeaux, the Comte de Pontchartrain, for whom the lake was later named, Iberville, accompanied by Bienville, had sailed from France in October 1698, bound for Louisiana, the territory that La Salle had claimed and named for his king, Louis XIV. Sailing with the Le Moyne brothers in two French frigates and two transports were a company of French marines and some two hundred settlers—men, women, and children—who were to populate the colony. After several stops along the gulf coast, Iberville and Bienville landed at Ship Island, where the settlers built huts to house themselves in a temporary settlement from which to explore until they could find the mouth of the Mississippi, not an easy task. On Monday, March 2, 1699, after probing the many inlets and streams emptying into the gulf, the brothers at last found the Mississippi.

The day following their discovery was Fat Tuesday, the last day before Lent, and as the bold pioneers began their voyage up the great muddy river, they came upon a wide stream about twelve miles upriver. They gave it a commemorative name—Bayou Mardi Gras.

They made it up the river as far as a bluff on which the local Indians had erected a red ceremonial pole that drew the attention of the Frenchmen. Iberville called that place Baton Rouge—red pole.

The Indians at Baton Rouge proved a friendly bunch, volunteering to help Iberville and Bienville find their way back to Ship Island by an alternate—and presumably quicker—route. Placing remarkable trust in the Indians, Iberville and Bienville followed them in small boats down the Amite River, roughly paralleling the Mississippi some twenty miles to the east, and into a lake, which Iberville named Lake Maurepas, after Count Pontchartain's son. They continued through Pass Manchac into a much larger lake, which Iberville named Lake Pontchartrain, then through the Rigolets pass into Lake Borgne, a bay of the gulf, and on to Ship Island, off the present-day Mississippi gulf coast.

Apparently finding no site to his liking on the Mississippi River, Iberville contented himself with building settlements on the gulf coast. In March 1699 he established colonies at Biloxi, which became the capital of the Louisiana Territory, and at Ocean Springs, Mississippi. He then sailed back to France, leaving Bienville second in command of the colonies, under a French army officer named Sauvole, and allowing Bienville time to explore further. By 1700, when Iberville returned to Louisiana, the colonists, their numbers swelled with new immigrants from France and Canada, had built a protective fort on the Mississippi some seventy miles above its mouth (Fort Boulaye) and another fort on Biloxi Bay (Fort Maurepas).

In 1701, following the death of Sauvole, Bienville, then twenty-one years old, became commandant of the colonies. In 1702, while his brother was occupied elsewhere in the territory, Bienville built a fort on the Mobile River, some twenty-five miles above present-day Mobile. He then moved the Louisiana Territory's capital from Biloxi to the new settlement, Fort Louis de la Mobile. ("Mobile" is a French corruption of "Maubilian," meaning "canoe paddler," which was the name of a local tribe of Indians.)[1]

When Iberville died of yellow fever in Havana in 1706, Bienville became acting governor of the Louisiana Territory. With his new authority, he began making grants of land. His first grant, made in 1708, went to an old friend from Canada, Louis Juchereau de Saint Denys, who had come to Louisiana with the Le Moyne brothers in 1699, when he was twenty-three years old. Saint Denys was given a tract on the west side of Bayou Saint John, which Bienville named for his patron saint and which flows northward into Lake Pontchartrain, through the present city of New Orleans. Bienville also made grants along Bayou Saint John to Antoine Rivard de LaVigne, Baptiste Portier, and four others whose names are now obscured in the records of the French colonial government in Mobile.

The Bayou Saint John area had captured Bienville's imagination. Between the bayou (which streams past present-day City Park in New Orleans) and the Mississippi River there was a portage (along present-day Esplanade Avenue) that Indians in the area used to gain access to Lake Pontchartrain and that provided a shortcut to the gulf. The portage was only a rough trail through a cypress swamp teeming with snakes and alligators, passing an Indian village called Tchoutchouma along the way, but Bienville could see possibilities for this area where the river, because of the huge bend in it, came closest to the lake.

The attempts to settle and exploit the territory, however, were not producing the sort of prosperous return that was expected in France. In 1712, King Louis XIV, disappointed by the lack of profits, transferred control of Louisiana to Antoine Crozat, a rich French banker who quickly replaced Bienville as governor. Bienville's idea of a French city in that giant curve of the Mississippi now looked as if it would exist only in his head.

To replace Bienville as governor, Crozat in 1713 appointed Antoine de la Mothe Cadillac, the man who had founded Detroit. Cadillac proved a poor choice. His harsh attitude toward the Indians of the lower Mississippi led to an uprising by the Natchez Indians against the French settlers in 1716, a conflict that Bienville was called upon to help quell. A year later, in 1717, Crozat decided he had had enough of Louisiana, which continued to drain investment money from him and had yet to produce a profit. The operation of the territory was taken over by an organization then called the Company of the West and later known as the Company of the Indies.

The president of the company was a brilliant financial schemer, gambler, and con man named John Law, a Scot who, following the death of King Louis XIV, had inveigled the French regent, Philip, the dissolute Duke of Orleans, into accepting him and his scheme for solving the problem of France's insolvency. The plan called for the establishment of an investor-owned private bank that would be backed by the revenues of the government of France. It also called for the development of Louisiana on a grander, more aggressive, more imaginative scale than anyone else had so far contrived.

Law wanted to build a city in Louisiana that would be a port of deposit, a transshipment point, for produce and goods coming down the Mississippi and destined for markets in Europe and America's East Coast. He had some definite ideas about what the city should include—a church, an administrative building, a governor's residence, a set of barracks, a jail, and a general store, among other things. Furthermore, he wanted it to attract settlers and developers to Louisiana. To help him get what he wanted, he reappointed Bienville, now thirty-seven years old, as governor. He also recruited a couple of engineers to design the city, Pierre LeBlond de LaTour and Adrien de Pauger.

The site of the city that Law envisioned was left to Bienville to choose, but the city's name was dictated by Law. He did not want a name that would mean nothing to the prospective immigrants he intended to recruit, an Indian name like Biloxi or Mobile. He wanted a name that would make his proposed city sound like a royal French colony. He came up with a name that he considered just right, one that had the desired sound and that also honored the man who had put Law in power, France's regent, the Duke of Orleans. The city would be called, Law declared, la Nouvelle Orleans—the New Orleans.

Set in motion by Law, Bienville quickly returned to his old idea of founding a city in that huge crescent made by the course of the Mississippi, that swampy spot between the river and Lake Pontchartrain. He had to argue with Law and the engineers for the site, but with persistence, he got his way.

Construction began on April 16, 1718.[2] Employing a labor force made up largely of convicts sent over from France, Bienville ordered trees felled, underbrush hacked away, huts and sheds erected for storage and shelter. In June 1718 Bienville wrote in his diary: "We are working at New Orleans with as much zeal as the shortage of men will permit. I have myself conveyed over the spot to select the place where it will be best to locate the settlement. . . . All the ground of the site, except the borders, which are drowned by floods, is very good, and everything will grow there."[3]

In 1721 a hurricane swept through the area and carried away all that had been built. Work started over again. The next year, another strong hurricane demolished the new structures. Work had to begin once more.

The job of designing New Orleans went to Adrien de Pauger, who laid the city out in a parallelogram, with a grid of streets forming sixty-six squares and rectangles within it. It was bounded on the south by the river and on the north by a defensive rampart, later surmounted by three fortifications, one at each end and one in the center of the rampart. The east and west sides of the city were also protected by ramparts. The city's design included a levee along the river and canals that would divert the river's overflow away from New Orleans and into the swamps above and below it.

De Pauger made the focal point of the city a large square, the Place d'Armes, that fronted on the river. The square was to be a parade ground and commons, lined with a church and government buildings across the street from the square's north side and facing the river.

Law launched a mammoth promotional program to attract people to the colony. He had posters put up and handbills distributed throughout France, Germany, and Switzerland, promising free land, provisions, and transportation to all who would sign up to immigrate to Louisiana. Law's promotional material claimed that the soil in Louisiana would yield two crops a year and was so rich that it needed no cultivation. Also promised was the opportunity to find gold, silver, diamonds, and pearls in this exotic land where the climate was so salutary that the inhabitants suffered neither disease nor old age.

Law was not going to wait for volunteers to populate the colony, however. He would coerce some. Vagrants, prostitutes, convicts, and the wretched poor were taken from the streets of Paris and from jail cells and shipped, under guard, to Louisiana. One account of the forced immigration details the methods used:

> The company [Company of the Indies] even kept a whole regiment of archers which cleaned Paris of its rabble and adventurers, and received for this a fixed salary and 100 livres a head. . . . Five thousand people are said to have disappeared from Paris in April, 1721 alone. . . .
>
> Prisoners were set free in Paris in September, 1721 . . . under the condition they would marry prostitutes and go with them to Louisiana. The newly married couples were chained together and thus dragged to the port of embarkation.[4]

By the end of 1720, John Law's bubble had burst, his financial scheme exposed as unworkable and his own fortunes in ruins. He fled from

Paris as a fugitive on December 10, 1720, taking temporary refuge in Belgium, then moving to Vienna, where he died six years later.

Despite the high-handed measures to populate Louisiana, New Orleans was growing slowly. A census taken in 1721 showed that the city had a population of 470, including 277 whites, 172 black slaves, and 21 Indians.

Even so, in 1722 New Orleans became the new capital of the Louisiana Territory, at Bienville's insistence. In February 1724 Bienville was ordered back to France, his supervisors on the Company of the Indies' Superior Council having become displeased with him. His successor as governor, Etienne de Perier, stayed on the job until 1731, when the Company of the Indies, having now abandoned the hope of a profit from Louisiana, gave it back to the government of France, which in 1732 made Bienville, at age fifty-two, governor of Louisiana for the third time. By then the population of the entire territory was around seven thousand. Bienville remained governor until May 1743, when he retired and left New Orleans to live in Paris.

France, which since 1689 had been fighting with England over the two countries' American colonies, relinquished its New World empire in 1763 when it signed the Treaty of Paris, ending the French and Indian War and ceding to England all of Canada and all of the Louisiana Territory east of the Mississippi River, excluding New Orleans, and ceding to Spain all of the Louisiana Territory west of the Mississippi. To unload an unprofitable property, France had given New Orleans to Spain a year earlier, in 1762.

Under Spanish rule, New Orleans began to prosper. Trade flourished as English-speaking pioneers streamed westward to settle along the tributaries of the Mississippi, making of New Orleans a trading and shipping center for their produce and goods. French Canadians from Acadia (who came to be known as Cajuns, a corruption of "Acadiens"), displaced by the British, also were arriving in large numbers, settling along the Mississippi River and along the bayous Teche, Lafourche, and Vermilion.

Louisiana's Spanish governor, Esteban Miro, welcomed the new French settlers, some sixteen hundred of whom were provided free passage to New Orleans by the Spanish government, which also gave them grants of land to farm. "The enthusiasm, industry and loyalty of these new colonists," Miro wrote, "will boost the prosperity of our province"[5]—words that proved to be an accurate forecast.

Two devastating fires—one in 1788 that started at a church altar and spread destruction to nearly half the city's buildings, and another in 1794 that razed more than two hundred houses and stores—allowed the city's Spanish administration to build better, safer, more attractive buildings on the ashes of the French structures, giving New Orleans the architectural charm for which the present-day French Quarter, the original city, has become famous.

Following the second blaze, the Spanish administration enacted new building codes to reduce the risk of future fires spreading throughout the city. The codes required all two-story houses to be constructed of brick or made with timber frames that were covered with cement, with brick filling the spaces within the timber frame. The new structures were required to have flat roofs made of tile and brick.

The new houses were built right up to the sidewalk, with courtyards, or patios, as the Spanish called them, in the center of the structure, hidden from the street. Many such patios contained elaborate gardens with flowing fountains, picturesque little Edens of escape for their owners.

Another outstanding architectural feature of the Spanish-style structures was their use of ornamental wrought iron and cast iron to form railings, fences, and decorative detail, all of which provided a light, lacy contrast to the solid, sturdy structures they adorned. The Spanish also constructed a building around the open-air market near the riverfront, which came to be known as the French Market, though the French had precious little to do with the founding, housing, or running of it.

The rebuilding of Saint Louis Cathedral, on the north side of the Place d'Armes (which became the Plaza during the Spanish administration), was begun in 1789, after the cathedral was razed by the 1788 fire. The work was done through the generosity of Don Andres Almonester y Roxas, who also donated money for the rebuilding of the Cabildo and the construction of the Presbytere, the two structures that flank the cathedral. Almonester also donated the funds to rebuild Charity Hospital after a hurricane destroyed it in 1779.

In 1800, with a new but fleeting vision of a French empire in America, Napoleon manipulated King Charles IV of Spain to return Louisiana to France, but he did so secretly. Two years later, in 1802, the Spanish administration in Louisiana, still exercising authority, revoked the right of deposit that permitted American shippers to transfer their goods in New Orleans without paying fees to do so. Responding to the outcry of farmers and businessmen in what was then the American West, President Thomas Jefferson determined to do his best to acquire the strategic city that Bienville had founded within the giant crescent of the Mississippi River.

By 1803 Napoleon had changed his mind about Louisiana, and he needed money. When he learned the United States was interested in acquiring New Orleans, he told the American representative, Robert Livingston, that he would sell the entire Louisiana Territory—827,987 square miles that would one day be divided to form all or parts of twelve states besides Louisiana—to the United States for $15 million, less than three cents an acre. Jefferson quickly accepted the offer, and the deal was consummated on May 2, 1803, although the treaty was dated April 30, 1803.

In a tardy ceremony on November 30, 1803, the flag of Spain was lowered from its staff in the Plaza and was replaced by the French flag. Appointed by the new French administration as mayor of New Orleans was Etienne Bore, the French-speaking native New Orleanian who had developed a method for granulating sugar and made a fortune growing and processing sugarcane on his plantation some six miles above the city (where Audubon Park is today). Three weeks later, on December 20, 1803, the French flag was lowered in the Place d'Armes and replaced by the Stars and Stripes of the United States of America.

Following the United States' acquisition of Louisiana, New Orleans experienced steady growth. In 1803 the population was about 8,000; by 1814, when the British launched their campaign to capture the city, its population had increased to about 18,000.

The people of New Orleans were a disparate group, a collection of Creoles—descendants of French or Spanish settlers, born and raised in New Orleans or thereabouts—who constituted the largest segment of the population; new arrivals transplanted from the Northeast and from America's western frontier; new immigrants from Europe; Cajuns; black slaves, free blacks (free persons of color, or *gens de coleur libres,* as they were called), many of whom had fled Santo Domingo following the murderous slave uprising of 1791; plus an assortment of Indians, particularly Choctaws, who were the area's first inhabitants.

One account described the people of New Orleans in 1803 as "fiery Creoles, plain, upstanding Acadians, yellow sirens from Santo Domingo, staid and energetic men from the German Coast [a German settlement in Louisiana] speaking perfect French, haughty Castilian soldiers, dirty Indians, Negroes of every shade and hue, and the human trash—ex–galley slaves and adventurers."[6] Another account of a few years later told readers, "Here in half an hour you can see and speak to Frenchmen, Spaniards, Danes, Swedes, Germans, Englishmen, Portuguese, Hollanders, Mexicans, Kentuckians, Tennesseans, Ohioans, Pennsylvanians, New Yorkers, New Englanders and a motley group of Indians, quadroons, Africans, etc."[7]

The people of New Orleans were mostly Catholics, devout in their observance of the church's ceremonies and celebrations. But although an atmosphere of Catholicism pervaded the city, its government and the public at large showed a remarkable tolerance for the sins of the flesh. Brothels flourished openly, and more or less permanent liaisons between white men, particularly those who were affluent, and light-skinned mulatto girls—quadroons, who were typically one-quarter black and three-quarters white—were accepted in polite society as part of the New Orleans way of life. Gambling houses and saloons also thrived, contributing their attractions to help make the city a magnet for the restless, the rowdy, and the reckless.

New Orleans now was the largest American city west of the Appalachian Mountains, and by 1814 it had become as prosperous as it was lively and diverse. It was the river, of course, that brought new residents, visitors, and the profits of commerce to the city. Flatboats, which brought goods down to New Orleans from the upper reaches of the Mississippi and its major tributaries, and tall-masted sailing ships, which carried the exports of Louisiana and the midcontinent across the Atlantic, lined the wharves along the city's riverfront. The first steamboat to arrive in New Orleans was named *New Orleans.* It was owned by a syndicate headed by Robert Livingston, who had negotiated the Louisiana Purchase, and Robert Fulton, the inventor and engineer who developed steamboats into a commercial success. The *New Orleans* had begun its voyage in Pittsburgh, where it was built, and landed along the levee in New Orleans on January 10, 1812.

In 1814, though, the city's ordinarily bustling wharves were practically bare of vessels of any type, the war having brought most shipping to a standstill. Unwilling to risk seizure of their cargoes by British or French warships, shippers who had been exporting from New Orleans simply stored their goods in the warehouses along the wharves and on the levee, waiting for the cessation of hostilities and the resumption of normal trade. Consequently, New Orleans's riverfront was piled high with a wealth of baled cotton and barrels of sugar and other commodities.

Residents of the city had to contend with the lingering peril of deadly yellow fever, the cause of which was unknown in 1814 but was widely believed to be noxious vapors rising from the fetid swamps, or else something in the drinking water. Both Latrobe and his son became victims of the disease. The twenty-one-year-old wife of Governor Claiborne, Claiborne's young daughter, and his secretary all died in the yellow fever epidemic of 1804, one of many that periodically assaulted the city. In 1809 Claiborne's new wife, also twenty-one, also died of yellow fever. Claiborne, perhaps thinking the disease was caused by water pollution or by a polluted atmosphere, complained to President James Madison about the garbage and refuse that were habitually thrown into the river by New Orleans residents.

In 1814 there was only one cemetery in New Orleans (Saint Louis No. 1), which was rapidly approaching its capacity. It had been built in 1783 and was divided into two sections, one for the burial of Catholics, the other as the last resting place for Protestants. Because of the city's high water table, the dead were most often interred above ground, in the tombs that Latrobe described. Those buried in the ground were placed in coffins that had holes in them so they would not float to the surface during heavy rains or other flooding.

Such was the city that Bienville had planted along the banks of the broad, brown Mississippi, and which by 1814 had expanded to the point that it needed two suburbs, one above the original city (the Faubourg Sainte Marie) and one below it (the Faubourg Marigny) to accommodate its burgeoning population and its brisk economy. In 1814 New Orleans was rich from commerce and strategically placed to command the vital Mississippi River. Its importance was described by one British army officer:

> Whatever nation . . . chances to possess this place [New Orleans] possesses in reality the command of a greater extent of country than is included within the boundary line of the whole United States; since from every direction are goods, the produce of East, West, North, and South America, sent down by the Mississippi to the Gulf. But were New Orleans properly supplied with fortifications, it is evident that no vessels could pass without the leave of its governor; and therefore is it that I consider that city as of greater importance to the American government than any other within the compass of their territories.[8]

New Orleans, the jewel of the Mississippi, had become the key to the fulfillment of Britain's new aspirations in North America. It was now the prize the British coveted above all others in the New World.

# ∴ 13 ∴

# Jackson Takes Command

GENERAL Jackson was not thinking of New Orleans. In May 1814 he was ordered to relieve General Thomas Pinckney as the United States commissioner charged with writing and signing a peace treaty with the Creek Indians. Pinckney was considered by many on the frontier as being too lenient. Jackson would not be lenient. As he traveled from Nashville, his mind was on a settlement that he would dictate and that would punish the Creeks for their violence against settlers and discourage them from further aggression.

He reached Fort Jackson in the Mississippi Territory on July 10, 1814, and immediately called a meeting of Creek chiefs, to be held on August 1. At the gathering, Jackson presented his case to support his demand for the cession of Indian lands to the United States, which amounted to some twenty-two million acres, more than half the area of the Creek Nation. Jackson told the chiefs that they had permitted the militant Tecumseh to come among them and so arouse the Creek braves that they had gone out and taken the lives of white settlers. Chiefs friendly to the United States, Jackson argued, should have apprehended Tecumseh, held him as a prisoner, and sent him to "their Great Father the President; or have cut his throat."[1] Since they had not done either, Jackson declared, the entire Creek nation was at fault in the conflict, and all must pay the price.

Besides the cession of land, Jackson demanded that the Creeks end their relations with the British—and with the Spanish—and that they agree to the right of the United States to cut roads through Creek territory and to establish military and trading posts wherever the government saw fit. The Creeks furthermore must turn over to United States authorities those individuals who had instigated the war against the settlers.

If the chiefs did not accept his terms, he told them, they were free to move to Florida and ally themselves with the British or Spanish. He said he would give food and ammunition to any Indian deciding to make such a move. But, he warned, they needed to know that he would soon be marching his army into Florida, coming right behind them.

Having heard, through interpreters, Jackson's harsh words, the chiefs withdrew to consider them. The next day they made their protest to Jackson (whom they called Sharp Knife), telling him that most of them had been friendly and that most of the surviving Red Sticks had fled to Florida. Jackson was unmoved. The Creek Nation, he told them, must be isolated from the "mischief-makers from the [Great] lakes. . . . Until this is done, your nation cannot expect happiness, nor mine security. . . . This evening must determine whether or not you are disposed to become friendly. Your rejecting the treaty will show you to be the enemies of the United States—enemies even to yourself."[2]

Realizing the only alternative to accepting the treaty was a resumption of hostilities and the vengeance of Sharp Knife, the chiefs gave in. On August 9, 1814, thirty-five Creek chiefs—only one of whom was a Red Stick—made their marks on the document to indicate their acceptance of the Treaty of Fort Jackson.

True to his word, Jackson now marched south toward Florida. On August 27, 1814, he reached Mobile and there set up a new base of operations, where he could be closer to his sources of information and to whatever threat he might discover along the gulf coast. He then wrote to Governor Blount of Tennessee asking him to turn out the entire Tennessee militia and send them to Jackson in Mobile. His intelligence had reported from sources in Havana that thirteen British warships and transports, bearing 10,000 troops, were headed for the gulf coast, intending an assault on Mobile or Louisiana. He also learned that the British had landed an expeditionary force at the mouth of the Apalachicola River, in Spanish territory, and were building a fort and arming, supplying, and training fugitive Creeks to fight United States forces.

Jackson saw Spanish complicity in those British actions. He wrote to the secretary of war, James Monroe, requesting permission to carry the war into Florida, onto Spanish soil. He also wrote to Gonzalez Manrique, the Spanish governor, or commandant, of Pensacola, demanding that he hand over fugitive Indian chiefs and explain why they had been allowed refuge in Florida. Jackson also protested the permission of British activities on the Apalachicola.

The governor turned aside Jackson's demands and protests with countercharges of American connivance in the depredations of privateers upon Spanish shipping. Infuriated by that response, Jackson fired back with another letter, insulting and belligerent, accusing the governor of imbecility and falsehood and ending threateningly. "In the future," Jackson told Gonzalez Manrique, "I beg you to withhold your insulting charges against my government for one more inclined to listen to slander than I am; nor consider me any more as a diplomatic character, unless so proclaimed to you from the mouths of cannon."[3]

The governor, undaunted, wrote back calmly and bravely. "I have armed the Indians," he said,

> and have taken all the measures I have been obliged to take, not for the purpose of committing hostilities on the United States nor on their property, but to defend myself against the insults that may be offered. If the United States continue the aggressions they have begun, the officers and soldiers subject to my orders will do their duty, and support to the last extremity the great, heroic, and generous character of the Spanish Nation to which they belong.[4]

As that exchange of letters was going on, the British, on August 14, 1814, landed a force in Pensacola, whence the governor was writing, his courage perhaps stiffened by the British presence and by the expectation that the massive main body of the British invasion force would soon be arriving from Jamaica. The British attempt to capture Mobile failed, however, when the land assault, launched from Pensacola and led by Major Edward Nicholls, was repulsed at Fort Bowyer on September 15.

The four British warships meant to give support were driven off by Fort Bowyer's batteries, which crippled one of them, the *Hermes* (which lost thirty-one crewmen killed and forty wounded), and forced the squadron's commander, Sir William Percy, to set the ship ablaze to prevent its capture.

Jackson was now eager to get into Pensacola to eliminate any further threat and to make the British and the Spanish governor pay for the attack. Disregarding Spain's supposed neutrality in America's war with Britain and tired of waiting to receive approval for his request from Washington, he organized a campaign to capture Pensacola. His old friend Brigadier General John Coffee, responding to his call, began a southward march from west Tennessee, leading some 1,800 men, each riding his own horse and carrying his own rifle. "Every one of my boys wants to get within fair buckrange of a red coat!" Coffee wrote to his wife.[5] On the way south, Coffee's contingent was joined by companies of other troops, bringing the total reinforcements to upwards of 2,500 men.

To Jackson the British were an old foe, first encountered when he was a boy. "I owe to Britain a debt of retaliatory vengeance," he wrote to Rachel. "Should our forces meet I trust I shall pay the debt—she [Britain] is in conjunction with Spain arming the hostile Indians to butcher our women and children."[6]

On October 25, 1814, Jackson moved out of Mobile with some twenty-three hundred troops to rendezvous with Coffee at a place called Pierce's Stockade, on the Alabama River. There he halted and wrote to Secretary of War Monroe to explain his actions:

> As I act without orders of the government, I deem it important to state to you my reasons for the measure I am about to adopt. First I conceive the safety of this section of the union depends on it. The hostility of the Governor of Pensacola in permitting the place to assume the character of British territory by resigning the command of the fortress to them, permitting them to fit an expedition against the United States, and after its failure to return to the

> town, refit, and make arrangements for a second expedition. At the same time making me a declaration that he (the governor) had armed the Indians and sent them into our territory. Knowing at the same time that these very Indians had under the command of a British officer captured our citizens and destroyed their property within our own territory. . . .
>
> I feel a confidence that I shall stand Justified to my government. . . . Should I not . . . the consolation of having done the only thing in my own opinion which could give security to the country . . . will be ample reward for the loss of my commission.[7]

On November 2, 1814, General Jackson marched toward Pensacola with an army of some three thousand men (some sources say more than four thousand), seven hundred of them regular army troops. On the afternoon of November 6, he and his army reached Pensacola and halted so that he could send the governor a message. He selected a Major Peire of the Forty-fourth Infantry Regiment to deliver the message, under a flag of truce. The written message said that Jackson had come to Pensacola "to require that the different forts, Barrancas, St. Rose, and St. Michael, should be immediately surrendered, to be garrisoned . . . by the United States, until Spain . . . could preserve unimpaired her neutral character."[8]

Major Peire did not get a chance to deliver the message. British troops harbored by the governor opened fire on the flag of truce, and Peire withdrew to his lines.

Pensacola was a small town whose importance lay in its harbor, entered from Pensacola Bay, which opens into the Gulf of Mexico. Forts Saint Rose and Saint Michael protected the town from a mainland attack, and Fort Barrancas, which stood guard over the entrance to Pensacola Bay, protected it from a seaborne assault. The fortifications of the town were constructed on the assumption that a land attack would come from the west, along a broad, sandy beach. The opposite side of the town could be approached only by a narrow beach that made access from the east difficult. The British ships that stood ready to aid the defense of the town, seven men-of-war, were positioned so their guns could meet an attack from the west.

Jackson decided to attack from the east.

His army was encamped on the main road on the west side of Pensacola, just beyond the range of the guns of Fort Saint Michael and of the British warships. An hour before dawn on November 7 he marched the main body of his army around the town to the east side and ordered a contingent of some five hundred men to make a feint on the west side.

At daybreak the defenders discovered Jackson's maneuver, too late to reposition the seven British ships to meet the attack. Inside the town an artillery battery was rolled out to block entrance into the main street, and infantrymen were posted behind courtyard walls that faced eastward.

Jackson's troops advanced in three columns, one on the narrow beach and two above it. The defenders' artillery battery, firing grapeshot and solid shot, got off three rounds before it was overrun and captured by a company of Jackson's Third Infantry Regiment. Elsewhere in the streets the battle was brisk, but the Spanish troops were driven from their positions in the town's courtyards and houses. Within minutes, the town's defenses collapsed, and Jackson's troops were everywhere.

Governor Gonzalez Manrique, no longer defiant and now discovered to be old and infirm, grabbed up a white flag and began searching for General Jackson. The two men met at Pensacola's Government House, where the governor surrendered to Jackson the town, its arms, and its fortifications. Apparently stalling for time on behalf of his British allies, the governor took so long in surrendering Fort Michael that Jackson had to postpone an attack on Fort Barrancas, fourteen miles away, which he intended to capture along with its British garrison.

About three o'clock the next morning, November 8, as Jackson was preparing to march on the fort, the earth beneath his feet shuddered, and the air was filled with the noise of a massive explosion. The British had blown up Fort Barrancas to prevent Jackson's taking it. They then sailed safely off into Pensacola Bay while Jackson stood pondering his hollow victory. He blamed Gonzalez Manrique and wrote to him a mild protest that notified the governor he was returning Pensacola to the Spaniards:

> Finding that the Barrancas and fortifications adjacent to it, have been surrendered to and blown up by the British, contrary to the good faith I was induced to place in your promises, I find it out of my power to protect your neutrality as I was willing to have done. The Enemy having disappeared from your Town and the hostile Creeks fled to the forest, I retire from your Town, and you are again at liberty to occupy your Fort, as I received it for the protection of your citizens.[9]

Evidently humbled by the realization that he would get help from neither the British nor the fugitive Creeks, upon whom his previous boldness had rested, Governor Gonzalez Manrique answered: "Exmo Senor Don Andres Jackson. . . . Permit me . . . to sign myself, with additional consideration and respect, your most faithful and grateful servant, who kisses your hands."[10]

Jackson feared that the escaped British troops and vessels were now headed for Mobile. He remained convinced that the British plan was to land first at Mobile, push inland and recruit Indians on the way, then turn west and march on New Orleans and the Mississippi River. He intended to stop them at Mobile and thwart the entire plan.

Quickly departing Pensacola, he marched his army westward and reached the Tensaw River, just east of Mobile, on November 13. From there he moved into Mobile and prepared to meet a British assault. While waiting for it, he received new intelligence that the prime British objective was New Orleans, that Mobile would be bypassed. He also received letters from influential citizens of New Orleans, including Governor Claiborne, urging him to come help defend the city. In response, Jackson sent his inspector general, Colonel Arthur P. Hayne, to New Orleans to assay the city's defenses and needs. He ordered Lieutenant Colonel William McRae, a regular army officer, to go and take command of the city's defenses and put its forts in order. He sent General Coffee and his troopers to Baton Rouge, where they would be in a position to move swiftly to New Orleans or to Mobile, if the British were to come there after all.

Finally, though, after days without a sign of a British invasion at Mobile, Jackson decided New Orleans must indeed be the target, and he led his army overland toward New Orleans, some 150 miles to the west. He left Brigadier General James Winchester in command of a protective force that would remain at Mobile. Fort Bowyer, guarding Mobile Bay, was the key to communication between New Orleans and Mobile, Jackson told Winchester, and it must be held.

Jackson also wrote to his wife, asking her to come to New Orleans and bring with her beds, tables, a carriage, and servants. She was to bring Andrew Jr., too, and would make the trip by boat, accompanied by her niece, Rachel Hays Butler. Jackson planned to take twelve days to reach New Orleans, moving at a leisurely pace that would allow him to discover the most likely places where the British might land.

On November 22, 1814, he at last left Mobile and led his army toward New Orleans. Jackson would eventually learn that an invading army might approach New Orleans in a number of ways. Perhaps the most obvious was to come up the Mississippi from its mouth, an upriver voyage of more than one hundred miles. Invading vessels would not find the going easy. About sixty-five miles below New Orleans was Fort Saint Philip, manned by regular army troops who guarded the river with twenty-eight twenty-four-pounders. Closer to the city stood Fort Saint Leon, at a sharp twist in the river known as English Turn (or Detour des Anglais, the place where a shipload of English settlers supposedly was turned back by the French in the eighteenth century). The bend in the river there was so sharp that vessels had to stop and wait for a change in the wind to negotiate the change in the river's direction. While they waited, they were easy targets for the big guns of Fort Saint Leon.

A second possible route was Bayou Lafourche, which flows into the gulf about sixty miles west of the Mississippi's mouth and joins the river between New Orleans and Baton Rouge. The bayou was deep enough to allow oceangoing vessels passage, but it was narrow and could be easily obstructed.

A third possible route was through Barataria Bay, between the river's mouth and the mouth of Bayou Lafourche, and through a network of bayous and streams that joined the Mississippi across from New Orleans. Help from local guides would be necessary to follow that course, and those streams could also be easily blocked.

Two other channels together provided a fourth route from the gulf, paralleling the Mississippi on the east and joining it near English Turn. They had the disadvantage of being navigable only in small boats and also were easily obstructed.

Then there were the approaches by way of Lake Borgne, through the Rigolets and into Lake Pontchartrain, placing the invaders, should they get that far, at the rear of the city. One option allowed by that route would be to land a force on the relatively high, dry ground of the Gentilly plain, a ridge that ran northeast of the city and was traversed by a road called the Chef Menteur (Chief Liar), which would allow the invaders to march on the city from the north.

Another option of the Lake Borgne route was to continue into Lake Pontchartrain and down Bayou Saint John, which flowed from the lake to within two miles of the walls of the city. It, too, however, was navigable only by small boats and could be easily obstructed. Furthermore, Fort Saint John stood protecting it at its entrance from Lake Pontchartrain.

Jackson arrived in the outskirts of New Orleans on the morning of December 1, 1814, wan and haggard, having suffered from dysentery and the fatigue of travel and battle. One who saw him that morning described him as follows:

> A tall, gaunt man, very erect . . . with a countenance furrowed by care and anxiety. His dress was simple and nearly threadbare. A small leather cap protected his head, and a short blue Spanish cloak his body, whilst his . . . high dragoon boots [were] long innocent of polish or blacking. . . . His complexion was sallow and

> unhealthy; his hair iron grey, and his body thin and emaciated like that of one who had just recovered from a lingering sickness. . . . But . . . [a] fierce glare . . . [lighted] his bright and hawk-like eye[s].[11]

He was welcomed to the city by Governor Claiborne; Commodore Daniel Todd Patterson, commander of the naval station at New Orleans; Edward Livingston, a lawyer who was chairman of New Orleans's Committee of Public Defense; and the city's mayor, Nicholas Girod (who once had offered Napoleon refuge in New Orleans).

After welcoming speeches by Governor Claiborne and Mayor Girod, Jackson, from the gallery of the large house where he had been officially received, replied with a short speech of his own. It was translated into French by Livingston while a steady rain soaked his listeners, standing in the street to hear him. Jackson promised he would protect the city and would drive the enemy into the sea or perish in the effort.

Following his remarks, he mounted his horse and rode to the Place d'Armes. Riding beside him was Livingston, whom Jackson had known since 1796 when they both were members of the House of Representatives. Livingston had since become his guide, translator, adviser, secretary, and aide-de-camp and was given the rank of colonel in Jackson's army. At the Place d'Armes Jackson reviewed the smartly uniformed New Orleans militia, four companies made up mostly of the sons of the city's well-to-do but also including some veterans of Napoleon's armies, and the battalions of free men of color, whom Jackson complimented on their soldierly appearance. After that he went to dinner at Livingston's home, where he was introduced to many of the leaders of New Orleans society.

Jackson set up his headquarters in a building at 106 Royal Street and, in an effort to learn the geography of the city and its surroundings, summoned a number of citizens to inform him. He was disappointed by their apparently vague or false reports, commenting later that "the numerous bayous and canals appear almost as little understood by the inhabitants as by the Citizens of Tennessee. True every man will give you an exact description of the whole & every man will give you an erroneous one."[12] New Orleanians, Jackson discovered, were city folk, unlike the people of the frontier, who knew the lay of the land and its natural features. New Orleans, he decided, was "an opulent and commercial town" that had become soft through "the habits . . . of wealth."[13]

He conferred with his chief engineer and took a six-day tour to see for himself where the enemy might approach the city and what was the state of existing defenses, particularly along the river. Colonel Hayne, whom he had sent from Mobile to assay the defenses, had already reported that the fort at the mouth of the Mississippi was useless. Fort Saint Philip needed improvements, and with Major A. Lacarriere Latour, his chief engineer, Jackson drew up plans to strengthen it, adding two batteries of artillery. He also ordered additional batteries installed at Fort Saint Leon, at English Turn. Labor for the construction of the additional gun emplacements would be provided by slaves made available by planters in the area.

Jackson ordered details of the Louisiana militia, commanded by Major General Jacques Villere, to move out into the swamps and fell trees that would obstruct the multitudinous bayous and streams that might provide an approach to the city. The militia troops were to remain in the outlying area to serve as sentries.

To keep an eye on Lake Pontchartrain and Lake Borgne and the invasion routes that led to the north side of the city, he directed Commodore Patterson to post his six gunboats near the Rigolets. To patrol and guard the Chef Menteur road, he ordered into position an army unit of Choctaw Indians, commanded by Major Pierre Jugeat, and a battalion of free men of color, commanded by Major Pierre Lacoste. He ordered the splendidly uniformed New Orleans militia, commanded by Major Jean Plauche, to bolster the defenses at Fort Saint John, which guarded the entrance into Bayou Saint John, and Fort Petites Coquilles, which guarded the pass between the lakes at the Rigolets.

Popular support for and confidence in Jackson's efforts were growing in Louisiana, although the state's legislature seemed languid in realizing the seriousness of the British threat and appropriating money to defend against it. Bernard Marigny, perhaps the most influential Creole in New Orleans at the time, described the public's mood:

> When General Jackson arrived in New Orleans, all the inhabitants wished to fight. We know moreover that one cannot be French, or of French origin, without detesting the English domination. . . . In 1812 the territory of Orleans was erected into a State and henceforth its inhabitants were in the enjoyment of all their rights. But the desire to fight was not sufficient. There was among them a sense of uneasiness, arising from a defect of organization. Governor Claiborne was a very honest man of personal bravery, but he had not the energy necessary to give a great impulse to the population of Louisiana. Beside the Government of the United States had not sent us any means of providing for our defense. In the magazines of the United States there were not 500 guns to distribute.
>
> Such was the state of affairs when General Andrew Jackson launched the Proclamation in which he announced that he was hastening to the defense of our State. . . .
>
> Never was a general received with more enthusiasm. His military reputation, his well-known firmness of character contributed to call forth a spontaneous movement. From all quarters, the cry was "to arms!" The whole population arose in a body.[14]

The size of the army that Jackson was deploying to defend New Orleans is estimated at between 3,500 and 4,000.[15] It was steadily increasing with the arrival of new volunteers every day, yet the American force was far fewer in number than the imposing British invasion force bearing down on the Louisiana coast. The Americans' shortage in manpower was especially critical in Commodore Patterson's naval force. The schooner *Carolina,* which carried fourteen guns, and the ship *Louisiana,* carrying sixteen guns, the two naval vessels remaining in the river after Patterson's gunboats had been posted in the lakes, had not enough men to crew them. Both vessels could be vital to the city's defense yet were virtually unusable because of the lack of men.

There was a solution to that problem. It was to enlist the help of the privateers who inhabited the islands of Barataria. So far Jackson had been unwilling to do so.

The New Orleans Committee on Defense spent hours trying to talk Jackson into accepting help from the leader of the Baratarians, the notorious Jean Lafitte. Edward Livingston, who was now a key member of Jackson's staff and was also Lafitte's lawyer, did his best to persuade Jackson to use Lafitte and his men, most of whom were experienced sailors and skilled artillerymen who could provide invaluable help in the city's defense.

To Jackson, however, they were pirates. "Hellish banditti," he called them. He stubbornly refused to let them help, despite his needing all the help he could get.

# ∴ 14 ∴

# The Pirates of Barataria

ALONG the ragged coast of Louisiana, the waters of the Gulf of Mexico creep onto the land to form vast marshes where wild grasses grow taller than men and wetlands wildlife thrives. It is hard to see where the land ends and the sea begins. At some places the gulf invades the Louisiana coast with deep water, making inlets and bays. In these indentations along the edge of the land, seagoing sailing vessels of the nineteenth century could find shelter from the gulf's tempests and refuge from their adversaries.

Forty-five miles south of New Orleans and forty-five miles northwest of the mouth of the Mississippi River lies one such indentation—Barataria Bay, about fifteen miles long and twelve miles wide. Its entrance from the gulf is largely blocked by a short chain of islands, the major two of which are Grand Isle and Grande Terre. The land around the bay is called Barataria.

In 1810 privateers who had been driven by the British from their previous bases of operation in Martinique and Guadeloupe arrived in Barataria. Europe's wars had produced a class of men who with the color of legality preyed on the shipping of an enemy nation, depriving the enemy of the products and rewards of trade, as well as the ships themselves, and enriching the predators at the same time. In the early nineteenth century the Gulf of Mexico swarmed with privateers, acting—or so they claimed—under letters of marque issued by France. The letters of marque in effect licensed them to act on behalf of the French government and capture vessels of France's enemy countries. The Baratarians' activities, which amounted to nothing less than legitimized piracy, included the seizure of ships, cargoes, and passengers and sometimes the murder of crews.

About the time that the British ousted the privateers from their bases in Guadeloupe and Martinique, the Spanish province of Colombia declared its independence from Spain, and the government of the Colombian seaport town of Cartagena began granting letters of marque to privateers who would harass Spanish shipping. The land to which the privateers came for sanctuary, Barataria, had for half a century been the home of trappers and fishermen who discovered there was more money to be made in smuggling than in honest toil. In the myriad streams and lagoons that wind in and out of Barataria Bay and its surrounding marshes, the smugglers found tortuous channels that led them and their small boats, bearing contraband obtained from lawful sources or otherwise, through backwaters to markets in New Orleans.

Journeys in or out of Barataria were for the experienced only, however. The unknowing could become easily lost in Barataria's web of bayous and marshy streams. Having become trapped in a maze of reeds, marsh grass, and sluggish water, they could die of thirst or starvation before reaching safety.

The privateers made their base on the islands that stood at the gulf's entrance to the bay, protected by the nearly impassable marshes on the land side of the islands and by the privateers' gun emplacements on the seaward side. The two islands, Grand Isle and Grande Terre, rose from the gulf's waters like great heaps of earth grown over with moss-draped oaks, oleanders, palmettoes, and thick underbrush. Almost hidden amid the islands' lush flora were the simple houses of the inhabitants, the fishermen and trappers who dealt in contraband. Among them now settled the privateer newcomers, rough and violent seafarers, thieves, and plunderers whose very business was contraband.

The smugglers of Barataria needed an outlet where their goods, ill gotten or otherwise, could be turned into cash, and the Lafitte brothers, Pierre and Jean, provided one for them. Not much is known for certain about the brothers' background, except that they were born in France and had spent their youth there. They had come to New Orleans by way of the West Indies, arriving sometime before 1809 and opening a business not long afterward. They made connections with the smugglers of

Barataria and began using their place of business, a blacksmith shop on Saint Philip Street, as a warehouse for smuggled goods. In 1809 they opened a retail shop on Royal Street, where they displayed silk and linen fabrics and other items of merchandise, much of it, if not all, apparently contraband.

When the privateers began bringing Africans to Louisiana to be sold into slavery, the cargo of captured Spanish ships, the Lafitte brothers also sold them. Despite the laws prohibiting the importation of slaves, the Lafittes held weekly slave auctions at Barataria, selling hundreds of Africans who were smuggled into New Orleans or Baton Rouge after their sale.

Pierre Lafitte, the oldest of five brothers, was reportedly born in Bayonne, France, sometime before 1780, the approximate year that Jean was born. He is believed to have served in the French navy. Pierre was apparently a vigorous, strong, and forceful man, but he had suffered a stroke that left him weakened for many months and paralyzed one side of his face; as a result, he had no control over his left eye, which made him appear cross-eyed. Pierre kept a mistress, a Santo Domingan named Adelaide Maselari whom he had brought with him from the West Indies and by whom he had at least one son and a daughter. He later took another mistress, an eighteen-year-old quadroon named Marie Louise Villars, for whom he acquired a house. She bore him at least two children.

Jean Lafitte was a charismatic figure. A man of striking good looks, he was six feet tall, slender, dark-complexioned and dark-eyed, with sleek black hair and a classic profile. He had a reputation as an expert with the foil, and rumor had it that he had killed a man in a duel in Charleston. According to one source, he was born in Bordeaux, France, the second of the five Lafitte brothers, and had served briefly in both French and British navies.[1] He was a man of unusual charm, with an outwardly gracious manner and a ready wit, all of which captivated both men and women.

He was also an adroit businessman. His profits from the sale of seized, stolen, and smuggled goods, particularly from the sale of slaves, were enormous, but he was careful to split his take with the legitimate merchants in New Orleans and thereby forestall complaints from them and possible prosecution. His charm and his money had made him many influential friends.

His brains, ability, and contacts, plus his facility for disposing of contraband, made him the leader of the privateers of Barataria, whose numbers were estimated at about one thousand and who built for themselves a community, a village of thatched-roof dwellings and other structures, on Grande Terre, where Jean also built a house, overlooking the gulf. The men he led were a motley lot. They were French, Portuguese, Italian, even Spanish, many nationalities, including Americans, some of them deserters from the United States Navy. They were from the West Indies, Malta, and Catalonia, among other places. They were white, black, and in between. They were veteran seamen who had sailed in the vessels of a variety of nations. They spoke a variety of languages. Jean Lafitte insisted that they were not pirates; they were corsairs, his word for privateers.[2]

The man who became the best known of the Baratarians, other than the Lafittes themselves, was Dominique You, who joined Lafitte's band of "corsairs" in 1811. He was born in Port-au-Prince and had served in Napoleon's armies and had become an artillery expert, apparently renowned for his skill and bravery. He had tried his hand as a privateer, operating on his own with his own ship, but had been unsuccessful acting independently, and upon learning of Lafitte's enterprises at Barataria had sailed there to investigate.

According to one source, Jean Lafitte knew of You by his reputation and enthusiastically welcomed him into the fold.[3] The two men became close friends. Sailing under the flag of Bolivia with letters of marque from Cartagena, which granted him a license to "burn, destroy or sink any vessel belonging to Spain,"[4] You became one of the most feared of all the privateers operating in the Caribbean Sea. Accused of piracy upon vessels other than those of Spain, he was charged in a criminal proceeding but was never brought to trial. His seizure of slave ships, however, and the subsequent sale of Africans into slavery from the barracoon at Barataria was well known.

People in New Orleans generally accepted Jean Lafitte's sea rovers and smugglers, enthusiastically so by the many who enjoyed the cheap prices of the Baratarian merchandise or a cut of the profits. In November 1812, however, perhaps in response to the prodding of Governor Claiborne, federal authorities finally took action against the Baratarians. Evidently with a mandate from United States customs officials, a special forty-man armed force of uniformed dragoons was assembled under the command of army captain Andrew Hunter Holmes and directed to sail down the bayous to Barataria and raid the smugglers' sanctuary.

On the night of November 16, 1812, the Lafitte brothers themselves were leading a flotilla of five pirogues and skiffs loaded with contraband, headed for New Orleans. Captain Holmes surprised them en route. One of Lafitte's men was killed trying to escape. The others, including Jean and Pierre, were arrested on smuggling charges, their goods were confiscated, and all twenty-five of them were taken to New Orleans, where after bond was posted and a trial date scheduled, all were released.

Neither Jean nor Pierre showed up for the hearing. One of their influential friends, a Monsieur Sauvinet, who apparently was one of their bankers, represented them. Testimony against them was given by Captain Holmes. The court records contain mysterious gaps but show that months later the case against the Lafittes had not been resolved, nor had the brothers appeared before the court in three separate sessions. The court ordered their bonds, amounting to twelve thousand dollars, forfeited. During the period from November 1812 to October 1813, six writs were issued for the arrest of the Lafittes. Each of the writs came back to the court with a notation: "Not found in New Orleans."

Jean and Pierre Lafitte were now outlaws.

Governor Claiborne, apparently infuriated by their defiance and frustrated over attempts to apprehend them, issued a proclamation on March 15, 1813, aimed at stopping their illegal activities:

> Whereas I have received information that upon or near the shores of Lake Barataria, within the limits and Jurisdiction of this State, a considerable Banditti composed of Individuals of different nations, have armed and equipped several Vessels for the avowed purpose of cruising on the high Seas, and committing depredations and piracies on the Vessels of Nations at peace with the United States, and to the great injury of the fair trade of the Public Revenue. . .I have thought proper to issue this my Proclamation hereby Commanding the persons engaged as aforesaid, in such unlawful acts to cease therefrom and forthwith to disperse and separate. . .and I do caution the people of this State against holding any kind of intercourse, or being in any manner concerned with such high offenders.[5]

On October 14, 1813, a company of dragoons led by revenue officer Walker Gilbert came upon Jean Lafitte and a group of his men in a swamp near New Orleans, aboard a schooner loaded with contraband. Lafitte commanded his men to resist. Gilbert's detail quickly gained the upper hand and captured the schooner, but Lafitte's men opened fire on the dragoons, wounding one and driving the rest of them off. The Baratarians then continued on their way in their ship, leaving the wounded soldier in the swamp.

On November 24, 1813, Governor Claiborne issued a new proclamation, which was printed and posted around New Orleans. The proclamation cited the latest offense of Lafitte, prohibiting any contact with him or his men and offering a reward for his capture: "I do furthermore, in the name of the State, offer a reward of five hundred Dollars which will be paid out of the Treasury, to any person delivering the said Jean Lafitte to the Sheriff of the Parish of New Orleans, or to any other Sheriff in the State, so that the said Jean Lafitte may be brought to Justice."[6]

Two days later another printed proclamation was tacked up beside the governor's. It offered a reward of fifteen hundred dollars for the arrest of William C. C. Claiborne and for his delivery to Grand Terre. It was signed, "Jean Lafitte."

Lafitte committed more outrages in January 1814. On New Year's Day he had distributed in New Orleans handbills advertising an auction at which 415 slaves would be sold at the Temple, a well-known Indian mound in the swamp south of the city, on January 20. Claiborne conferred with the collector of customs, who subsequently sent an inadequate, twelve-man force of officers, led by a customs inspector named Stout, into the swamp to post themselves at the Temple and prevent the illegal sale.

Undeterred, Lafitte's Baratarians attacked the customs officers, killing Stout and two others and taking the rest of the officers prisoner. The auction was held as announced, and all the slaves were sold.

The collector of customs appealed to Governor Claiborne for help. Claiborne formed a grand jury, which promptly returned indictments against the two Lafittes and two of their top lieutenants, Dominique You and another ship captain, Renato Beluche. Acting swiftly before word got out about the indictments, a platoon of dragoons surprised Pierre Lafitte on the street, near the Place d'Armes, arrested him, and hauled him off to the parish prison. He was refused bail. After conferring with his friend and associate Sauvinet, and also with his legal representatives, former district attorney John Randolph Grymes and the estimable Edward Livingston, Jean Lafitte went into hiding and remained largely out sight throughout the summer of 1814, while Pierre languished in prison, awaiting trial.

On September 3, 1814, Jean Lafitte was on Grande Terre when, soon after sunrise, the *boom* of a signal cannon broke the silence. He quickly ordered a small boat out to investigate, and he climbed into it with four oarsmen. Moving out into the bay, they sighted a British navy sloop lying in the gulf, just outside the pass between Grande Terre and Grand Isle, and as Lafitte's boat drew nearer to it, the British vessel's gig appeared and started toward them. As the gig approached, Lafitte could make out two men in naval officer uniforms and one in a scarlet officer's coat. The gig bore a white flag in its bow and a Union Jack at its stern.

One of the officers called out and introduced himself as Captain Nicholas Lockyer of the Royal Navy. He was captain of the sloop

*Sophie.* The two others were introduced as a Royal Navy lieutenant and Captain McWilliams of the Royal Colonial Marines. Lockyer said they had come to speak with Jean Lafitte.

Without identifying himself, Lafitte told the officers, in French, that they could see Monsieur Lafitte on the island. The British followed him to shore, and after they arrived at Lafitte's house, he told them, "Messieurs, I myself am Lafitte."

Lockyer handed Lafitte four documents. One was the proclamation that had been issued by Lieutenant Colonel Edward Nicholls, calling on the people of Louisiana to join the British in opposing American forces. The second was a letter from Nicholls addressed to "Mr. Lafitte, or commandant at Barataria." Dated August 31, 1814, it was an offer to Lafitte to "enter into the service of Great Britain," along with Lafitte's men. "You shall have the rank of a Captain," the letter promised Lafitte. Nicholls also promised that "lands will be given to you in proportion to your respective ranks. . . . Your property shall be guaranteed to you and your persons protected."

In return, Nicholls asked Lafitte "to cease all hostilities against Spain or the allies of Great Britain. Your ships and vessels [are] to be placed under the orders of the commanding officer on this station."[7]

The third document was a letter from William Henry Percy, captain of HMS *Hermes* and senior British officer in the Gulf of Mexico. The letter, dated August 30, 1814, and addressed to Lockyer, contained his orders to meet with Lafitte and make him the offer under the terms stated in Nicholls's letter.

The fourth document, dated September 1, 1814, was also a letter from Captain Percy. It threatened the use of the stick if Lafitte did not accept the carrot:

> Having understood that some British merchantmen have been detained, taken into and sold by the inhabitants of Barataria, I have directed Captain Lockyer of his majesty's sloop Sophie to proceed to that place and inquire into the circumstances with positive

> orders to demand instant restitution, and in case of refusal to destroy to his utmost every vessel there as well as to carry destruction over the whole place. . . . I trust at the same time that the inhabitants of Barataria consulting their own interest, will not make it necessary to proceed to such extremities.[8]

Seeing Lafitte hesitate, as if almost sold, Captain McWilliams sweetened the written offer with an oral promise of thirty thousand dollars if Lafitte and the Baratarians would throw in with the British.

The officers finally returned to their ship while Lafitte seemed to be still mulling over the proposals. Not long after they reboarded the *Sophie,* a letter arrived from Lafitte. "If you could grant me fifteen days," it said, "to put my affairs in order . . . I will be entirely at your disposal."[9]

Now, perhaps for the first time, Lafitte realized the imminent peril from the British—New Orleans and a whole way of life were in danger of being lost, as were the vital Mississippi River and all of Louisiana, even, perhaps, the nation itself. Lafitte decided he must warn the Louisiana authorities. On the morning of September 4, the day after the visit from the British officers, Lafitte wrote two letters. One was to his friend Jean Blanque, a wealthy merchant who was a member of the Louisiana legislature. He described for Blanque the British officers' offer and enclosed the documents that Lockyer had brought to him. He also made a strong pitch for the release of Pierre.

The second letter he wrote that morning was addressed to Governor Claiborne:

> Sir:
>
> In the firm persuasion that the choice made of you to fill the office of first magistrate of this state was dictated by the esteem of your fellow-citizens and was conferred on merit, I confidently address you on an affair on which may depend the safety of this country. . . .

> This point of Louisiana, which I occupy, is of great importance in the present crisis. I tender my services to defend it; and the only reward I ask is that a stop be put to the proscription against me and my adherents by an act of oblivion for all that has been done hitherto. I am the stray sheep, wishing to return to the sheepfold.[10]

He enclosed the letter to Claiborne in the letter for Blanque, then handed the entire packet, including the British documents, to a courier, who made a fast voyage by pirogue from Barataria to New Orleans. Lafitte then penned a letter to Captain Lockyer, again asking for a fortnight to consider the British proposal.

Blanque received the packet within twelve hours. Alarmed, he immediately took it to Claiborne, who read the letters and quickly called together a committee to advise him. Included were Commodore Daniel Patterson of the United States Navy, Major General Jacques Villere of the Louisiana militia, and a Colonel Ross, of the United States Army. Villere said he believed the letters were genuine and urged Claiborne to accept Lafitte's offer to help defend Louisiana. Like other Creoles, Blanque was more sympathetic to Lafitte than were the English-speaking Americans of the community.

Patterson and Ross were strongly opposed to having dealings with Lafitte. They believed the letters were fake and the offer of help in defending the city was designed merely to gain Pierre's release from prison. Lafitte's offer was refused, though Claiborne made no reply to his letter.

That night, mysteriously and perhaps with the complicity of the warden, Pierre Lafitte managed to escape from the parish prison. A one-thousand-dollar reward was immediately offered for his capture and return.

On September 7 Jean Lafitte sent another note to Blanque, warning him of the three British warships now posted within sight of Grande Terre. On September 10 Pierre wrote to Blanque, pressing him for a reply to the earlier letters:

> Being fully determined to follow the plan that may reconcile us with the government, I herewith send you a letter directed to his excellency the governor, which I submit to your discretion, to deliver or not, as you may think proper. I have not yet been honored with an answer from you. The moments are precious; pray send me an answer that may serve to direct my measures in the circumstances in which I find myself.[11]

Days passed, and still no answer came from Blanque or the governor. In the meantime, the two weeks that Jean Lafitte had requested of the British were also passing. Lafitte feared that Lockyer would attack the Grande Terre base, as he had been ordered to do, if an acceptance of the British offer were not soon forthcoming. Anticipating a British attack, Lafitte loaded several of his ships with all the arms and ammunition he had stockpiled, plus some merchandise, and sailed off with them to Isle Derniere, about forty miles west of Grande Terre. Pierre, who was ill at the time, was taken by pirogue to a hideout on Bayou Lafourche. Left in charge of the base was Dominique You, with instructions to burn the warehouses and remaining ships if the British attacked.

Before dawn on September 11, 1814, Commodore Patterson and Colonel Ross, acting on orders from the United States secretary of the navy, embarked an armed force aboard three barges and floated down the Mississippi to rendezvous with Patterson's flotilla of six gunboats, sent from Lake Pontchartrain, and the schooner *Carolina,* waiting at Balize, near the mouth of the river. The entire force arrived off Grande Terre on the morning of September 16.

When the flotilla, flying the United States flag, was sighted by the Baratarians, Dominique You refused to fire on the American ships. Instead, as instructed by Lafitte, he had his men set fire to warehouses and ships before some five hundred of them fled into the trackless marshes just before the American forces landed. Not all of the Baratarians escaped; You and about eighty others were captured. The buildings that were not already burning were put to the torch by Patterson's troops, and twenty-six vessels were seized. Also seized was an estimated half-million dollars in contraband, which Patterson claimed as a prize of the raid. You and the other captive Baratarians were taken to New Orleans and imprisoned in chains.

When Captain Lockyer returned after the two weeks asked for by Lafitte, he found the Grande Terre village in ruins and deserted, and he sailed away, defeated in his mission.

To apprise General Jackson of the situation in Louisiana, Governor Claiborne sent him the documents from Lafitte, prior to Jackson's arrival in New Orleans. He also sent Jackson information concerning the attack on Barataria, which was then in the planning stage. Claiborne evidently was changing his mind about accepting Lafitte's help, either in desperation, as the British threat grew, or in response to public opinion in Louisiana and to the urgings of Edward Livingston, Lafitte's lawyer and chairman of the city's Committee on Defense. "In this city," Claiborne wrote to Jackson, "a much greater Spirit of Disaffection than I had anticipated, and among the faithful Louisianians there is a Despondency which palsies all my preparations. . . . Laffite and his associates might probably be made useful to us."[12]

Jackson was unmoved. Three months passed, and he remained adamant in his refusal to accept help from outlaws even as the British threat mounted and Edward Livingston vainly urged Jackson, now in New Orleans, to accept Lafitte's help.

Sometime in December 1814, after months of Jackson's refusals, Bernard Marigny, the influential Creole social leader, heard Jackson say something that sparked an idea in Marigny's mind. Jackson, he reported, "told us that these men [Lafitte and the Baratarians] are being prosecuted by the civil officers of the United States . . . and that he neither would nor could do anything in the matter."[13]

Marigny decided that if the big obstacle for Jackson was the federal court proceedings against Lafitte and his men, he—Marigny—and the Committee on Defense should see what they could do to quash those proceedings. Marigny and the committee went to see the judge of the United States District Court, Dominick Augustus Hall, who proved sympathetic. He told them they should get the state legislature to pass a resolution calling for the suspension of the prosecution of the Baratarians, and then he would do what he could.

The committee promptly appealed to the legislature, which unanimously passed a resolution demanding the proceedings against Lafitte and his men be suspended for four months. When that was done, Judge Hall directed the United States district attorney to cease prosecution, and he ordered that Dominique You and the other imprisoned Baratarians be released on one condition—that they join in the defense of New Orleans. Judge Hall also granted safe conduct to Jean Lafitte so he could return to the city without being subject to arrest.

In the minds of some, there was a question as to whether Lafitte, after having his base destroyed and his goods seized in Commodore Patterson's raid, would still be willing to fight on the side of the Americans. That question was resolved when Lafitte, his brother Pierre, and Dominique You strode up to Jackson's headquarters on Royal Street and made their offer in person to the general.

Jackson needed gunflints, gunpowder, cannon shot, artillery, small arms, and men. Lafitte had them all. He offered them and himself to Jackson. Major Lacarriere Latour, Jackson's chief engineer, summarized the meeting with Jackson:

> Mr. Lafitte solicited for himself and for all Baratarians, the honour of serving under our banners, that they might have an opportunity of proving that if they had infringed the revenue laws, yet none were more ready than they to defend the country. . . . Persuaded that the assistance of these men could not fail of being very useful, the general accepted their efforts.[14]

Jackson quickly incorporated Lafitte's resources into his defense plans. He ordered artillery units formed under the command of You and Renato Beluche. He ordered defensive positions strengthened between Barataria Bay and New Orleans, writing to a Major Reynolds that "Mr.

Jean Lafite [*sic*] has offered his services to go down [to Barataria] and give you every information." He instructed Reynolds that, once Lafitte had finished with his assistance at Barataria, Reynolds was to "dismiss him as soon as possible as I shall want him here."[15]

Jean Lafitte and the pirates of Barataria had entered the fight.

# ∴ 15 ∴

# The Invasion

ADMIRAL Alexander Cochrane, aboard HMS *Tonnant,* arrived in Negril Bay, Jamaica, on November 18, 1814, right on time for the scheduled November 20 rendezvous of the invasion force. He soon received two pieces of bad news. He discovered that his plan to attack New Orleans, far from being kept secret, as it was supposed to be, was well known in Jamaica, and thus had become known to the Americans. In a letter meant for members of the Admiralty, addressed to the secretary of the Admiralty, John Wilson Croker, he complained about that serious breach of security:

> I conceive it highly encumbent upon me to state to their Lordships that on my arrival at Jamaica, I found to my very great astonishment, the intention of sending an expedition against New Orleans and Louisiana which I had taken the utmost precautions to keep profoundly secret, publickly known throughout Port Royal and Kingston a very few hours after the arrival there of their Lordships instructions. . . .
>
> . . . a Mr. Hudson who is connected with a mercantile house in New Orleans sailed from Jamaica in a small schooner that cleared out for Pensacola, and I have to consider that through him . . . the information was brought . . . to General Jackson at Pensacola . . . ; this information . . . caused him [Jackson] to relinquish his intentions and proceed immediately for New Orleans.[1]

The loss of surprise in the attack against New Orleans was not the worst of the bad news, however. Somewhere along the chain of command a breakdown had occurred, and the shallow-draft flatboats that Cochrane had ordered had not arrived with the reinforcements that had been sent from Europe, as he had planned. These flatboats, needed to ferry troops from British transports across the shallow waters of Lakes Borgne and Pontchartrain to the northern edge of New Orleans, were essential to Cochrane's plan of attack. The deep-draft, oceangoing vessels of Cochrane's fleet could not navigate the lakes, the depth of which ranged from six to twelve feet. Without shallow-draft boats, an attack from Lake Pontchartain, which was Cochrane's plan, became highly impractical. Not only that, but efforts to hire enough light schooners that Cochrane could try to use in place of the absent flatboats were frustratingly futile.

He would have to draw a new attack plan. Knowing that Jackson had marched with his army from Mobile on November 22, Cochrane decided to race him to New Orleans. On November 25 and 26 he gathered his invasion force, the army and marine units that had sacked Washington and had turned back at Baltimore, plus the troops that had just recently arrived from Europe, and hastily sailed off for New Orleans. He did not wait for the arrival of the army's new commanding general, whom Cochrane would force to do his best to catch up with his command and who would be presented with Cochrane's plan as a fait accompli.

Cochrane's invasion fleet numbered some fifty to sixty vessels, both warships and transports, an impressive sight as they raised their canvas and their sails caught the wind. Once the ships were past the headlands of Negril Bay, a fair breeze sped them from the Jamaican coast. Aboard the vessels the men and officers, many of them accompanied by their wives, welcomed a speedy voyage, eager to depart the heat of Jamaica and enter cooler air. The farther they got from Jamaica, the cooler and, to them, more agreeable the temperature became. They knew their destination was New Orleans, and they were hoping that the weather there would not be as oppressively hot as they had been told to expect.

On November 29 they reached Grand Cayman Island and sailed past without stopping. On December 2 they sighted the western shore of

Cuba, admired the picturesque Cuban coast as they rushed past it, and continued on into the Gulf of Mexico. On December 10 they reached the Chandeleur Islands. Near there, close to the gulf entrance to Lake Borgne, the fleet dropped anchor. The weather there was much less than what the troops had hoped for; the temperature had dropped to a wintry level, and the sea had become rough.

Lieutenant Thomas ap Catesby Jones, commanding the flotilla of gunboats that General Jackson had posted in Lake Borgne to be his seaborne sentinels, had positioned his seven vessels near the entrance to Lake Borgne. They were sighted there by Cochrane's fleet. Jones's vessels, altogether, carried a total of twenty-three guns. Cochrane's flagship, the *Tonnant,* alone carried eighty guns. Faced with such a menace, Jones's vessels, upon sighting the British ships, hurriedly withdrew into Lake Borgne, where Cochrane's warships could not reach them. Jones then sent one of his boats, the *Alligator,* to Commodore Patterson to report that the invasion fleet had arrived at Lake Borgne.

Cochrane's plan now was to use his ships' launches and barges, many of which had to be rowed, to ferry the British troops from their transports off Cat Island to a landing spot on Pea Island (Isle aux Pois), about thirty miles across Lake Borgne, off its north shore, near the mouth of the Pearl River. That would be the first leg of an invasion route across the lake. But, first, the lake would have to be cleared of Jones's gunboats, highly maneuverable light vessels that would threaten a landing force borne in small boats.

Cochrane ordered Captain Lockyer to take all the forty-five launches and barges off the fleet's ships, load them with one thousand sailors and marines, and send them out to capture or destroy the American gunboats. Lockyer organized his force into three units, one commanded by Captain Henry Montressor, one by Captain John Roberts, and one that he would himself command. Each boat would be armed with one small gun. About three o'clock on the afternoon of December 12, the boats were put in the water, and the hardy oarsmen began rowing, continuing at their oars through the wintry night. By ten thirty the next morning the boats were closing on Jones's gunboats.

Unsure at first of the British intentions, Jones soon realized the fleet of small craft was headed not for land but for his gunboats. He detached the schooner *Seahorse* and sent it to remove stores from a base at Bay Saint Louis, then withdrew his remaining five gunboats toward the Rigolets and the protection of Fort Petites Coquilles, as Commodore Patterson had instructed him to do in the event his flotilla was threatened.

When *Seahorse* sailed away from the rest of Jones's vessels, the unit of seven barges commanded by Captain Roberts swung about to cut it off and capture it, while the two other units continued to row toward Jones's remaining five gunboats. The *Seahorse* drew in close to shore to seek protection of guns onshore and managed to hold off Roberts's assault for half an hour. Finally, *Seahorse*'s commander, Sailing Master Johnson, fighting a losing battle against superior numbers, ordered the vessel blown up, along with the stores onshore that he had come to retrieve.

Meanwhile, as the two other units of Lockyer's force pressed on toward the American gunboats, Lieutenant Jones discovered that three of his vessels had run aground in the lake's shallow water and were stuck fast. In desperation, Jones ordered everything not needed to stave off British boarding parties to be thrown overboard in an effort to lighten and refloat the vessels. About three thirty that afternoon, as the British boats came relentlessly toward the grounded gunboats, the tide turned, raising the American vessels from the lake bottom and allowing them to escape toward the Rigolets.

Lockyer's sailors kept pressing toward Jones's gunboats, not stopping until eight o'clock that evening, December 13. They then rested on their oars until four o'clock the next morning, when Lockyer awakened them and had them begin rowing again. At nine o'clock they were again in sight of the American vessels.

Jones attempted to withdraw closer to the Rigolets and the guns of Fort Petites Coquilles, but now, as the British boats came closer, the wind suddenly died, and Jones's vessels were unable to move against the ebbing tide. On Jones's command, his ships took a position just west of

Malheureux Island, anchoring in a formation intended to block the British boats from passing between the island and the mainland. There they waited for the invaders to come within range of their guns.

Then they sighted the *Alligator* to the southeast of their position, returning from having carried Jones's message to Commodore Patterson. The boats of Captain Roberts's unit also sighted the *Alligator* and quickly moved toward it to capture it. The *Alligator* got off a couple of ineffectual rounds with its lone four-pounder before the vessel was overwhelmed by the swarming British seamen and was soon forced to surrender.

The strong outgoing tide swung two of Jones's gunships out of their defensive formation, leaving them more vulnerable to the oncoming horde of enemy boats. At about ten fifty that morning, December 14, Lockyer's fleet of launches and barges, bearing their one thousand fighting men, closed in on the hapless American vessels. Jones's ships sank two of Lockyer's barges but could not prevent the overwhelming force of British marines and sailors from boarding the American vessels and overpowering their crews. By twelve forty that afternoon all the American gunboats had been captured. In the battle the British lost seventeen killed and seventy-seven wounded, Captain Lockyer among them. The Americans lost ten killed, thirty-five wounded, including Lieutenant Jones, and all surviving officers and crew were taken prisoner.

Lake Borgne having been cleared of the hostile presence of Jones's gunboats, Admiral Cochrane now attempted to move the invasion force into the lake with the few light sailing vessels that were available to him (including, presumably, the captured vessels of Lieutenant Jones's flotilla). In the end, however, as the sailing vessels grounded, one after another, British oarsmen had to assume the arduous task of rowing the invading army from the larger ships off Cat Island to the new jumping-off place on Pea Island.

The task of removing the troops from their ships to the assembly area on Pea Island, laboriously performed by sailors who spent four or five days continually at their oars, was not finished until December 21. The entire fleet of small boats manned by those sailors could carry no more than two thousand men at a time, thus necessitating repeated trips from the larger vessels across thirty miles of Lake Borgne to Pea Island.

While the troops were being ferried to Pea Island, a two-man reconnaissance party was sent out to scout a route to firm ground that would lead to New Orleans, Admiral Cochrane by now having abandoned altogether his hopes of approaching the city from Lake Pontchartrain. On December 16 the two men, army lieutenant John Peddie and navy captain Robert Spencer, guided by a resident of the area, began their reconnaissance. What they found was the entrance to Bayou Bienvenue, in the northwest corner of Lake Borgne. The bayou flowed mostly northwest to southeast, but a tributary of it, Bayou Mazant, angled off toward the Mississippi River. Bayou Bienvenue's width varied from 100 to 150 yards, and its depth ranged from six to nine feet, making it navigable for small vessels.

About a half mile inland from the mouth of Bayou Bienvenue was a fishing village composed of twelve large shacks where thirty to forty Spanish and Portuguese fishermen lived. Peddie and Spencer put on the fishermen's clothes that their guide procured for them; thus disguised, their uniforms hidden, they continued up Bayou Bienvenue in a pirogue paddled for them by two of the village's inhabitants.

They glided through a watery corridor that was hedged by reeds ten feet high, then veered off Bayou Bienvenue and into Bayou Mazant, which carried them into a cypress swamp and then past canals that drained the lands of the plantations that fronted on the Mississippi River, about ten miles below New Orleans. They paddled past a bayou that led into the Jumonville plantation, then past a canal that led into the plantation of Major General Jacques Villere, the commander of the Louisiana militia. They then entered a canal that ran through the plantation of Denis de Laronde and there drew up to the canal bank.

Peddie and Spencer got out of the pirogue and strode along the firm ground beside the canal, calmly making their way through the Laronde tract and taking a good look at the surrounding area. Before them, stretching into the distance, was a field covered with the stubble of newly harvested sugarcane, heaps of which dotted the field. Far in the distance they could see clusters of trees and several houses. They walked to the four-foot-high levee, crossed over it and stood on the bank of the river, broad and muddy, and peered across to the far side, also protected by a levee. Still undetected, they strode back across the field, stepped into the pirogue, and slipped back down the bayous to their vessel at the fishermen's village, then returned to Pea Island to report their findings.

Acting on their information, Admiral Cochrane and Major General John Keane, in command of troops pending the arrival of the new commanding general, on December 21 ordered an advance on New Orleans via the route taken by Peddie and Spencer. Keane divided his troops into three brigades. The first brigade, composed of the Eighty-fifth Light Infantry Regiment, the Ninety-fifth Rifle Regiment, a detachment of the Fourth Light Infantry Regiment, a rocket unit, and an artillery detachment armed with two three-pounders—about 1,600 men in all, commanded by Colonel William Thornton—would be first to embark and be rowed or sailed from Pea Island to the mouth of Bayou Bienvenue and then up the bayou as far as the boats could take them. The boats would then return to Pea Island to ferry the second, then the third brigade. General Keane and his staff would go with the first brigade. Admiral Cochrane would also go.

At nine o'clock in the morning on December 22, 1814, the officers and men of the first brigade began entering the launches, barges, and captured gunboats that stood waiting to receive them. When all were embarked, the stalwart sailors once more manned their boats and slowly pulled away from the island shore. As they gained room to maneuver, the boats moved into a formation that placed them in lines of ten abreast, with two light sailing ships (probably from Jones's captured flotilla) in the van, two more guarding the formation's flanks, and three others protecting the rear of the formation.

The drive to seize New Orleans was now beginning.

Eighteen-year-old British army lieutenant George Robert Gleig of the Eighty-fifth Regiment was aboard one of those boats that drew out into Lake Borgne bearing the first brigade. He described the lake crossing and the entry into Bayou Bienvenue:

> When we set sail, the sky was dark and lowering, and before long, a heavy rain began to fall. Continuing without intermission during the whole of the day, towards night it as usual ceased, and was succeeded by a sharp frost; which taking effect upon men thoroughly exposed, and already cramped by remaining so long in one posture, rendered our limbs completely powerless. Nor was there any means of dispelling the benumbing sensation, or effectually resisting the cold. Fires of charcoal, indeed, were lighted in the sterns of the boats, and were suffered to burn as long as day-light lasted; but as soon as it grew dark, they were of necessity extinguished, lest the flame should be seen by row-boats from the shore, and an alarm be thus communicated. Our situation was, therefore, the reverse of comfortable; since even sleep was denied us, from the apprehension of fatal consequences.
>
> Having remained in this uncomfortable state till midnight, the boats cast anchor, and hoisted awnings. There was a small piquet of the enemy stationed at the entrance of the creek, by which we meant to effect our landing. This it was absolutely necessary to surprise; and while the rest lay at anchor, two or three fast sailing barges were sent on to execute the service. Nor did they experience much difficulty in accomplishing their object. Nothing, as it appeared, was less dreamt of by the Americans than an attack from this quarter.[2]

Actually, General Jackson had considered the Chef Menteur road the likeliest invasion route, but he realized that Bayou Bienvenue was also a possible route of approach to the city. On December 17 he had issued specific orders for the bayou to be obstructed to bar passage by the British vessels. On December 18 the orders had been acknowledged by Major Gabriel Villere, son of the Louisiana militia commander, Major General Jacques Villere. Young Villere commanded a militia unit entrusted with guarding the approaches to the Villere plantation. Jackson's orders, inexplicably, had not been obeyed.

On December 21 young Major Villere had, however, ordered a twelve-man detachment of the militia's Third Regiment to take a boat down Bayou Bienvenue and set up a sentry post at the fishermen's village near the lake entrance to the bayou. The detachment was to keep an eye on the entrance and let the unit's commander know if the British attempted to come up the bayou.

On their arrival at the village late that day, Villere's men found it deserted except for one fisherman who was ill. He told the militiamen that the others of the village were away fishing. In fact, the others had apparently been recruited by Peddie and Spencer as guides for the British fleet of launches and barges. A three-man patrol from Villere's detachment scouted the area, found no sign of invaders, and returned to the village to spend the night.

The next day, December 22, a patrol again was sent out and again came back without having sighted the British. That night the members of the detachment went to sleep in the fishermen's shacks. Around midnight the British arrived.

The two main accounts of what happened next are in conflict. One account is by Lieutenant Gleig, the British eyewitness. The other is by General Jackson's chief engineer, Major Lacarriere Latour, who was not at the scene and evidently got his information later from one or more of the militiamen. Gleig's report states that:

> no persons could be less on their guard than the party here stationed. The officer who conducted the force sent against them, found not so much as a single sentinel posted; but having landed his men at two places, above and below the hut which they inhabited, extended his ranks so as to surround it, and closing gradually in, took them all fast asleep, without noise or resistance.[3]

Latour's version states that one militiaman was posted to watch the bayou while the eleven others slept. The man on guard duty waited until three of the invaders' barges had passed the village before running to alert his comrades, who grabbed their weapons and found a place to hide. After five more barges came by, the militiamen ran for their boat to try to escape. Eight of them were captured in the attempt. Four others plunged into the dark marsh, and three of them were later captured. One managed to survive in the swamps and emerged on the Chef Menteur road three days later. In either case, in the early hours of December 23, 1814, the first brigade of the British invasion force stole into Bayou Bienvenue without allowing a warning to be given to the commanders of the American forces guarding the city.

The captured militiamen were confined in the fishermen's shacks, and some of them, including one named Joseph Rodolphe Ducros, were taken to General Keane and Admiral Cochrane and interrogated about the strength of Jackson's army. Ducros told them General Jackson had twelve to fifteen thousand men in the city and four thousand posted at English Turn. The other militiamen who were interrogated gave similarly exaggerated reports (as did seamen captured from Lieutenant Jones's gunboats). Cochrane responded by ordering his troop-bearing boats to proceed up the bayou as swiftly as possible.

Lieutenant Peddie was guiding the barges as they crept up Bayou Bienvenue in the darkness. When they veered off into Bayou Mazant, the channel was too narrow for the sweep of the oars, and the barges had to be punted through the dark water, the crewmen picking their way along as those on the lead barge sought the canal leading to the Laronde plantation.

Now came a bit of a problem. Since Peddie and Spencer had been there the day before, the water in Bayou Mazant had fallen and was not deep enough to float the barges, the first of which soon grounded. Behind it, in single file, the others were stopped also, blocked by the lead barge. This was the end of the line for the barges. The troops would have to disembark and try to find ground solid enough to walk on beside the bayou.

The men were formed up in a column, and they then walked from barge to barge, stern to bow, until they reached the lead barge, where they jumped onto the soft ground. They waited while a detail of engineers, commanded by Captain Robert Blanchard, assembled to precede them and hack out, fill, and bridge a path for the infantrymen.

General Keane by now had decided that the Laronde plantation was too far to reach by a march on the marshy ground. Instead of marshaling his troops on the Laronde tract, as planned, he would have them proceed along the nearer canal that led into the Villere plantation and would form up his army there.

By nine o'clock on the morning of December 23, the troops were ready to move out from the spot where the barges had halted. Lieutenant Gleig described what the troops faced:

> The place where we landed was as wild as it is possible to imagine. Wherever we looked, nothing was to be seen except one huge marsh, covered with tall reeds; not a house, nor a vestige of human industry could be discovered; and even of trees, there were but a few growing upon the banks of the creek. Yet it was such a spot as, above all others, favoured our operations. No eye could watch us, or report our arrival to the American General. By remaining quietly among the reeds, we might effectually conceal ourselves from notice; because, from the appearance of all around, it was easy to perceive that the place which we occupied was seldom, if ever before marked with a human footstep.[4]

By noon the Eighty-fifth and Ninety-fifth regiments had slogged off single file into the swamp, following an indistinct path beside the canal, and the elements of the Fourth Regiment were ready to follow them. With all men of the first brigade out of the boats and on land, the barge crews began poling their vessels, stern first, back down Mazant Bayou to return to Pea Island to embark the second brigade.

The entire operation was way behind schedule. General Keane had expected that by dawn all three brigades would have been landed at the mouth of the Laronde canal. He had figured that by noon his whole army, all three brigades, would have assembled in the stubbled field of the Laronde plantation, ready to march on New Orleans. The plan, he knew, would have to be adjusted.

As the troops advanced, the marsh ended, the ground became firmer, and cypress trees stood around them instead of the marsh's tall reeds. Finally they reached the open field. Soon the advancing troops sighted a grove of orange trees and, beyond them, a couple of houses. One was the Villere home, where, on the gallery, Major Gabriel Villere sat smoking a cigar and talking to his brother Celestin. Upon sighting the houses, Colonel Thornton, the brigade's commander, immediately ordered his troops to rush the buildings, surround them, and take as prisoners anyone found inside.

Gabriel caught sight of flashes of scarlet as the British infantrymen ran through the orange grove, headed toward the river. Instantly he realized he was seeing British soldiers. He leaped from his chair on the front gallery and ran through the house. As he reached the back door, he was met by Colonel Thornton and several of Thornton's soldiers, who quickly seized him. Also captured were several other men who were in the house at the time. Gabriel, with the others, was held under guard to await the arrival of General Keane, who doubtless intended to interrogate the prisoners.

During the awful minutes while he waited, Gabriel undoubtedly felt painful regret for not having followed General Jackson's orders to obstruct Bayou Bienvenue. The invasion army had reached the Villere plantation because of his failure. (Some sources argue that he deliberately disobeyed because he was involved in smuggling operations that depended on access to the city through Bayou Bienvenue.) General Jackson, he knew, must be warned. The fate of New Orleans depended on it.

The doors of the room where he and the others were being held were blocked by guards, but the windows offered a way of escape. Gabriel suddenly sprang for a window and dived through it, knocking over several soldiers in the process. He picked himself up off the ground and sprinted for the cypresses at the edge of the swamp, British bullets whizzing past him and British soldiers in hot pursuit. Gabriel dashed into the cypress woods and disappeared into the swamp, where he hid himself in the dense underbrush.

Once he was satisfied he had eluded his pursuers, he resumed his flight, hurrying to the nearby Laronde plantation, where he found the militia colonel Denis Laronde and told him what was happening. The two of them ran for the river, jumped into a small boat, and rowed to the safety of the opposite bank, where they borrowed horses from Dussau de la Croix, a member of the Committee for Public Safety, who owned a plantation on the west bank. Gabriel, Laronde, and de la Croix then sped up the west bank, racing for the city and for the ears of General Jackson.

They recrossed the river at New Orleans and hurried to General Jackson's headquarters at No. 6 Royal Street. Minutes later a soldier on guard duty at the headquarters rapped on the door of the room where General Jackson sat in a meeting with some of his staff. The soldier announced to the general that three gentlemen were there with important intelligence to deliver. Jackson ordered them admitted.

As Gabriel Villere, Laronde, and de la Croix, all of them spattered with mud, entered the room, Jackson asked, "What news do you bring, gentlemen?"

"The British have arrived at Villere's plantation, nine miles below the city, and are there encamped," de la Croix told him. "Here is Major Villere, who was captured by them, has escaped and will now relate his story."

In French, translated by de la Croix, Gabriel Villere gave General Jackson the bad news in full.[5]

## ∴ 16 ∴

# The Night Assault

VILLERE's report of the invaders' arrival was confirmed by other intelligence coming to Jackson's headquarters. Even before Villere had reached Jackson, Colonel Laronde had sent word that militia pickets on the river had sighted several British vessels near Bayou Terre aux Boeufs, in position to threaten the American forces at English Turn. Jackson had ordered Major Latour, his chief engineer, and Major Howell Tatum, a topographical engineer, to ride down the river road and check on the situation at English Turn and at all the bayous between Bayou Terre aux Boeufs and Lake Borgne.

At the Bienvenue plantation, just above Laronde's, the two officers stopped to hear an urgent report by slaves from the Lacoste plantation, situated between Laronde's and Villere's, who told them that the British were at the Villere plantation. Tatum rushed back to Jackson with the news, and Latour continued toward the Villere plantation to investigate further.

Augustin Rousseau had also given the alarm. He had defiantly ridden through British troops at Laronde's plantation to get the news of the invaders to General Jackson. Reports were coming into the city from many individuals.

Upon hearing Gabriel Villere's report, Jackson immediately took action. He believed an attack from the Villere plantation might be only a feint, with the main thrust to come along the Chef Menteur road, but he quickly issued orders for all available troops to assemble in the city to meet the immediate threat. General Coffee was directed to bring to the city his brigade of Tennesseans from its encampment four miles above New Orleans. Summoned from that same position were Brigadier General William Carroll and his three thousand Tennessee militiamen. Together, those commands would form the backbone of Jackson's army of defense. Summoned to the city from their post at Fort Saint John were the five companies of uniformed Louisiana volunteers commanded by Major Jean Baptiste Plauche.

Just in case the main British thrust would come from Gentilly, Jackson ordered General Carroll's militiamen and units of Louisiana militia to guard the Chef Menteur road. Earlier he had posted there a battalion of free blacks, which had drawn a protest from an assistant paymaster, who objected to Jackson's using black troops. Jackson had squelched him with a stinging order: "Be pleased to keep to yourself your Opinions upon the policy of making payments to particular Corps. It is enough for you to receive my order for the payment of the troops with the necessary muster rolls without inquiring whether the troops are white, Black or Tea."[1]

Commodore Patterson was directed to order all available navy vessels to support Jackson's attack. The schooner *Carolina,* carrying fourteen guns, was moored on the river's west bank, across from New Orleans, and would move downriver to a position opposite the Villere plantation and anchor there. *Carolina* was now manned mostly by Jean Lafitte's Baratarians and was commanded by Captain John D. Henley of the United States Navy. It would drift with the current, the wind being too slight to fill its sails. The Navy sloop *Louisiana,* its steering mechanism apparently insufficient to guide the ship in the river's current without wind in its sails, would remain at its mooring opposite the city until the wind rose. Patterson ordered its skipper, Lieutenant C. C. B. Thompson, to take it to join the *Carolina* downriver as soon as the wind allowed.

Within the city an alarm cannon was fired, and New Orleans's defenders, men of many descriptions, turned out in prompt response. Besides the 563 troopers of Coffee's Tennessee mounted rifles, there were Major Thomas Hinds's 107 Mississippi dragoons; 62 men of Captain Thomas Beale's New Orleans rifle company (composed largely of businessmen and lawyers); 465 regular troops of the Seventh U.S.

Infantry Regiment, 331 regulars of the Forty-fourth U.S. Infantry Regiment; 18 Choctaw Indian soldiers commanded by Captain Pierre Jugeant (who was himself half Indian, half French); 210 men of Major Jean Daquin's battalion of free blacks; 287 members of Major Plauche's five Louisiana militia companies (many of them Creoles and all of them having double-timed most of the ten miles from their post at Fort Saint John); 66 United States Marines; and 22 artillerymen commanded by Lieutenant Samuel Spotts and armed with two six-pounder field pieces. That total force that Jackson would lead against the British consisted of 2,131 men, by the count of Major Latour.

By four o'clock that afternoon—Friday, December 23—Jackson was astride his mount, reviewing his troops as they marched past Fort Saint Charles, on the lower edge of the city (a site later designated as 600 Esplanade Avenue, where a United States mint was later built), from which they headed to meet the invaders. With him were his aides: Edward Livingston, Major John Reid, Auguste Davezac (Livingston's brother-in-law), Pierre Duplessis, Colonel Robert Butler (Jackson's adjutant general), and Captain Harry Chotard of the Louisiana militia.

First in the line of march was the Seventh Infantry Regiment, acting as a vanguard. It would be first to engage the enemy should the British advance toward the city while Jackson's army was en route. With the Seventh marched the United States Marines and the artillerymen. Behind it came the Forty-fourth Regiment, then Beale's rifle company, then the mounted troops of Hinds and Coffee. Next came Major Plauche's handsomely uniformed militiamen. Behind them came Major Daquin's battalion of free blacks and Captain Jugeant's Choctaws, bringing up the rear.

Shortly after the column of soldiers had passed Fort Saint Charles, the crewmen aboard the *Carolina* weighed anchor and began drifting with the current, moving at four miles an hour, easing toward the British position. Commodore Patterson, aboard the *Carolina,* would soon get a request from Jackson to commence firing on the British position at seven thirty in the evening. The shots from the *Carolina*'s guns, booming into the far distance, would be the signal for Jackson's troops to launch their assault.[2]

The army commanders had received their orders. They were to advance down the river road to the Rodriguez canal, about two miles above the Villere plantation. There they were to halt, move into their assigned positions, and await the signal from *Carolina*'s guns. Jackson waited until the last of his troops had marched by him, then galloped off behind them.

General Keane, the interim British army commander, and Colonel Thornton, commanding the first British brigade, had moved into the Villere house and established their headquarters there. Thornton, eager to attack, wanted to rest his men for a short time and then march on the city, before Jackson had time to position his army. Keane, perhaps thinking of the inflated reports of Jackson's strength, was opposed to an immediate attack. He wanted to wait until the rest of the invasion force could be assembled and join the first brigade, then advance on New Orleans and its defenders with the army's full force.

While Keane made himself comfortable at the Villere house, the men of the Fourth, Eighty-fifth, and Ninety-fifth regiments spread out to the Lacoste plantation, adjacent to and just above Villere's, and there made camp.

The British posted sentinels, established defensive outposts across their front, and sent out reconnaissance patrols, which returned with reports that they had been unable to find any Americans. At that report, the commanders allowed the troops to make themselves comfortable and to light cooking fires, which they soon did, gathering fence boards to build their fires and water from the river for cooking. They not only ate their rations but also raided the dwellings around them and feasted on stolen hams, chickens, and wine. About three o'clock that afternoon, having fed themselves, many of the British troops took advantage of the mild temperature and bathed in the nearby streams. Others stretched out on the ground and napped.

Later in the afternoon a bugled alarm from a forward outpost signaled the approach of an American patrol, and the brigade swiftly stood to arms and prepared for battle. Sounds of gunfire were heard, but then the bugle sounded an all clear. The American patrol had been chased off with a few rounds from the British sentinels.

The short winter day passed into deepening darkness, and the British troops put more wood on their fires to give light and to cook their evening meal. Comfortable and relaxed, their second hot meal of the day having been eaten, the officers and men of the first brigade prepared for a good night's sleep.

Not long before seven thirty, some of them noticed the shadowy hulk of a ship on the river, slowly moving to a position opposite their bivouac. They watched as it furled its sails and dropped its anchor not far from the east bank of the river, about midway down the Villere tract. They thought it must be one of their vessels that had crept up the river and managed to slip unobserved past the American guns at English Turn, coming to support the army's advance on New Orleans. Some of the soldiers hailed the ship, shouting across the river to its crew. There was no response, arousing suspicions about the vessel.

Quickly an alarm spread through the camp, and the troops began to rise from where their lay. Several muskets were fired in hopes of drawing a response from the vessel. None came.

Now the ship menacingly swung its broadside toward the British encampment, illumined by the soldiers' glowing campfires. From the vessel, across the dark water and into the ears of the invaders, came words cried out in a commanding voice, distinctly heard: "Give them this for the honor of America!"[3]

In an instant the guns of the *Carolina,* three hundred yards away from the mass of British troops, flashed bright and ghastly in the night, their *boom* resounding through the night air. In a continuous barrage, the *Carolina*'s five broadside guns and its two swivel-mounted, long twelve-pounders began raining murderous grapeshot and round shot down on the British troops, caught exposed in the open field, lighted by their own campfires.

Unable to defend themselves, their two field pieces too light to inflict damage on the *Carolina,* their muskets useless at three hundred yards, and their Congreve rockets beautiful to see but ineffectual, the British troops were ordered to run for cover behind the levee. There hundreds of them lay crowded together, wherever they could find room, listening to the shrieks and groans of their wounded comrades and the repeated *boom* of the *Carolina*'s guns. So much shot was falling on the bivouac area that the campfires were extinguished by it, and with the moon covered by clouds, the night had become blindingly black. Minutes later, musket fire broke out from the British pickets' advance positions. Soon after, someone yelled from the darkness, and suddenly a volley of rifle and musket fire ripped into the main body of the British brigade, the muzzle flashes forming a semicircle of fire around the bivouac area. In the confusion caused by the darkness and the constant cannonade, General Keane and Colonel Thornton had lost communication with their subordinate officers and were unable to direct a defense or counterattack. It was up to individual officers to lead their troops against the encircling host of enemy riflemen.

The American assault was led by Coffee, commanding a 732-man force composed of his own Tennessee rifles, now dismounted, Hinds's Mississippi dragoons, also dismounted, and Beale's New Orleans rifle company. Following Jackson's orders, they had turned their column to the left, leaving the river road, and had moved toward the swamp, guided through the darkness by Colonel de Laronde, taking a position midway between the British advance guard, which was posted just behind the forward sentinels, and the main body of the invaders' troops. Coffee's objective was to turn the British right flank and force the invaders to the bank of the river. At the sound of the *Carolina*'s guns, Coffee wheeled his force to the right to strike the British flank and rear.

On the American right, commanded by Jackson himself, were the two regiments of regulars, Plauche's militia companies, the battalion of free blacks, the marines, Jugeant's Choctaws, and the artillery unit, some fourteen hundred men. About two miles above the British bivouac, Jackson waited for the *Carolina*'s signal; when it came, he ordered his troops to advance on the British outposts about a mile to their front. They struck the outposts a few minutes before eight o'clock and formed a line extending from the levee to the right end of Coffee's line.

As Jackson's troops advanced, the clouds scattered to reveal a bright moon, and a company of the Seventh Regiment quickly pushed forward, across the lower end of the Laronde plantation and onto the Lacoste plantation, adjacent to Villere's. The company ran into heavy fire from an eighty-man British outpost, but returning the enemy's volleys, it managed to drive back the invaders. Reinforced by two hundred men, the British unit turned and stood to deliver a devastating fire on the Americans, forcing them back and allowing the British to recapture their outpost.

Jackson's artillery, supported by the marines, had moved down the forty-foot-wide river road and opened fire on the outposts, but stiff resistance forced the marines back, leaving the artillery pieces exposed. Seeing the inadequately protected guns, a contingent of British reinforcements swiftly moved to capture them. The marines, now joined by a company of the Seventh Infantry Regiment, rallied and turned to rescue the guns and haul them off beyond the enemy's reach.

The Americans were meeting increased resistance all across their lines. By now the second brigade of the British invasion force had reached the battlefield, having run to the sound of the guns from where they had disembarked on Bayou Mazant. They had rushed in to reinforce their embattled comrades. Gleig, the eyewitness, gave his account of the fighting:

> Rushing from under the bank [the levee], the 85th and 95th flew to support the piquets, while the 4th, stealing to the rear of the encampment, formed close column, and remained as a reserve. But to describe this action is altogether out of the question, for it was such a battle as the annals of modern warfare can hardly match. All order, all discipline, were lost. Each officer, as he was able to collect twenty or thirty men round him, advanced into the middle of the enemy, when it was fought hand to hand, bayonet to bayonet, and sword to sword, with the tumult and ferocity of one of Homer's combats.[4]

There was confusion in the American lines as well as in the British. An American eyewitness, Major Tatum, the topographical engineer, reported, "The moon shone on the back of the enemy and gave them a decided advantage in discovering our situation, when it was difficult to see them from our lines."[5] That disadvantage to the Americans, Tatum claimed, added to the "confusion and derangement of our lines."

In Coffee's sector, on the extreme left of the American line, the fight was going somewhat better than in the center and on the right. Coffee's troops had driven down across the Lacoste plantation as far as the boundary separating it from the Villere tract. Some of his units penetrated as far as the center of the enemy bivouac and were forced to fight hand-to-hand combat when troops of the British Eighty-fifth Regiment rushed to oppose them. Coffee's men drove them back, but the British were reinforced by four companies of the Twenty-first Regiment, and the attack by Coffee's units was blunted.

The British resorted to trickery, identifying themselves as Americans when they encountered American troops in the darkness. The American army captain John Donelson Jr. related his experience:

> I charged on near [Keane's] quarters, made several prisoners and killed several. . . . The enemy having discovered my position immediately fell on my rear . . . [shouting] that they were General Coffee's men, having by some means learned the General's name. They advanced within about ten steps, ordered us for d——d rebels to lay down our arms. . . . I answered them, they be d——d, and ordered my men to open a fire.[6]

Although the moon was shedding some light on the battlefield, the gunfire of both sides had become so heavy that the resulting thick gunsmoke, together with fog that began floating across the fields, presented a new problem of visibility. By nine o'clock the fighting had begun to wane. The guns of the *Carolina,* which since the outbreak of combat had been trained upon the British left flank, fell silent. Finally, after hours of only sporadic exchanges of gunfire, General Jackson at four o'clock in the morning on Christmas Eve ordered his troops to pull back behind the Rodriguez canal, about two miles toward the city, between the Macarty and Chalmette plantations.

The British were quick to claim victory. "The victory was decidedly ours," Lieutenant Gleig reported, "for the Americans retreated in the greatest disorder, leaving us in possession of the field."[7] Gleig conceded that the victory had come at a high cost, calling the British loss "enormous." His estimate of casualties, however, proved exaggerated, the actual number being comparable to that of American casualties, except in the number killed. British losses were 46 killed, 167 wounded, and 64 captured, making a total of 277 casualties. American losses were 24 killed, 115 wounded, and 74 captured, or a total of 213 casualties.

Jackson had failed to make good on his vow to smash the British force. Even so, there was success to be found in the American assault, as Major Latour pointed out:

> The result of the affair of the 23d was the saving of Louisiana, for it cannot be doubted but that the enemy, had he not been attacked with such impetuosity, when he had hardly effected his disembarkation, would, that very night, or early next morning, have marched against the city, which was not then covered by any fortification, and was defended by hardly five thousand men, mostly militia, who could not, in the open field, have withstood disciplined troops.[8]

Jackson knew that he and his army would get another chance. In a letter to the United States secretary of war, James Monroe, written on December 26, Jackson briefly reported the action he had taken. Then, in conclusion, he told Monroe, "I expect something far more important will take place. I hope to be able to sustain the honour of our arms and to secure the safety of this country."[9]

Then began the tense wait for events to prove him correct or not.

# .·. 17 .·.

# The New British Commander

On April 18, 1814, the day that England's war with France ended and one week after Napoleon's abdication had allowed the Bourbons to regain the throne of France, Major General Sir Edward Pakenham wrote to his mother to tell her that his job as Wellington's adjutant general would prevent his quick return to Ireland, since he had to handle the chore of getting Wellington's army back to Britain. Even so, he told her, he expected to be home within three months.

By the time he wrote to her two months later, he apparently had heard there was a chance he would be going to America, perhaps instead of back to Ireland. That letter to his mother, written in June 1814, indicated, however, that he believed he had managed to avoid the American assignment. "I think I have escaped America," he wrote, "and shall consider myself vastly fortunate to have been spared such a service."[1]

It was not until early fall that he finally returned to Ireland, no doubt happy to be home. The happiness was short-lived. In October, from London, he wrote again to his mother, this time with unpleasant news:

> It was my expectation when I left you to have returned to your little party at the Lodge. Public Events have otherwise determined my private movements. The Affairs in America have gone ill—staff officers have become necessary, and I have been called on by the Ministers to proceed to the other side of the Atlantic. I confess to you that there is nothing that makes this employment desirable—but under the circumstances of my improved health, I cannot resist a National call or the feelings of my Personal Duty.[2]

The particular public event that had caused his assignment to the war in America was the death of Major General Robert Ross, killed by a sniper's bullet on the morning of September 12, 1814, outside Baltimore.

Service in America was not all of the unpleasantness facing Pakenham. Making matters worse was the fact that he would be serving with a man who was himself unpleasant, the arrogant Vice Admiral Alexander Cochrane. In his attitude toward Cochrane, Pakenham probably had been influenced by the opinions of his brother-in-law, the Duke of Wellington, who believed that Cochrane had originated the plan to capture New Orleans and that the plunder of the city's warehouses filled with cotton, sugar, tobacco, and other commodities (worth, according to one estimate, three to four million British pounds; by another estimate, twenty million United States dollars) was Cochrane's primary objective and motivation. Distrustful of the self-seeking Cochrane, Pakenham had doubts about the wisdom as well as the legitimacy of the Louisiana campaign. He confided to an old friend, George Napier, that he "much doubted the policy of the expedition or the correctedness of the information upon which the Government had decided to make an attempt on that place [New Orleans]."[3]

Nevertheless, Pakenham accepted the distasteful assignment that Wellington had turned down. Among the British troops in America there was a rumor that Pakenham had been enticed by the government's promise of a handsome reward for victory at New Orleans. The rumor had it that he had been promised the governorship of Louisiana and a British earldom.

Pakenham sailed from Portsmouth, England, on All Saints' Day—November 1—of 1814 aboard the frigate *Statira.* By then he was already three weeks late for the rendezvous of the invasion force at Negril Bay, Jamaica. The ship was crowded not only with its crew and Pakenham and his staff and their staffs but also with 30 other passengers. Most were provided with cots and slept in the ship's steerage compartments. Pakenham was given a cabin but had to share it with four staff officers—Major General Sir Samuel Gibbs, a veteran soldier who had served on four continents; Lieutenant Colonel John Fox Burgoyne, who was Pakenham's chief engineer and the bastard son of the Revolutionary War British general Gentleman Johnny Burgoyne; Lieutenant Colonel Alexander Dickson, Pakenham's chief of artillery; and the surgeon who was Pakenham's medical inspector general, John Robb—plus the *Statira*'s commander, navy captain Spelman Swaine. Also sailing on *Statira*, but accommodated elsewhere on the ship, was Pakenham's assistant adjutant general, Major Harry Smith, who had served on General Ross's staff and was one of the British officers who had objected to Ross's burning of Washington, D.C.

Not everyone sailing with Pakenham knew the ship's destination, but on the third day out, Captain Swaine broke the seal on his orders and announced they were headed for Jamaica, despite being considerably late for the rendezvous (a fact that leads observers of the war to believe Cochrane, who had sailed from Jamaica on November 25, had been expected by his superiors to wait at Negril Bay for Pakenham's tardy arrival). It was a long, boring voyage, made even longer by the captain's navigating error that threw the ship temporarily off course.

Pakenham's impatience with the speed of the voyage was obvious. Burgoyne later reported that Pakenham "showed great anxiety on the voyage to arrive at the scene of operations before the troops had been put to shore." He passed some of the time by poring over maps, at least one of which he had borrowed from the Spanish archives. It was a map showing New Orleans as it was in 1769, under the rule of the Spanish governor, Alessandro O'Reilly.

On December 6, 1814, the *Statira* passed the West Indies island of Saint Lucia and met the British brig *Swaggerer*, which had sailed out of Guadeloupe. In the exchange of news between the vessels, Pakenham learned from *Swaggerer*'s captain, Lieutenant Alexander Sandilands, that the Louisiana expedition force, or at least a part of it, commanded by General Keane, had stopped at Guadeloupe a month earlier, had taken aboard some black troops, and had proceeded to Jamaica. Pakenham's anxiety grew.

On December 13, twenty-three days late for the November 20 rendezvous, *Statira* arrived at Negril Bay. Waiting there were Major General

John Lambert and the two thousand British troops under his command. They had sailed from England a week earlier than Pakenham. In a conference of the three generals—Pakenham, Gibbs, and Lambert—held aboard the *Statira,* Pakenham decided to push on to the Louisiana coast without going ashore at Jamaica. Lambert, needing to resupply his troops with water and provisions, would sail later.

On December 22 the *Statira* reached the mouth of the Mississippi River, where it came upon the British sloop *Herald,* anchored there. Its officers told Pakenham that Cochrane's fleet was anchored at the north end of the Chandeleur Islands and that the army which Pakenham was appointed to command had already been put ashore.

After two days spent sailing against head winds, *Statira* reached the northernmost Chandeleur Islands only to find that Cochrane's fleet had moved. It was now December 24, and the army that was Pakenham's to command had already fought the opening battle of New Orleans without him.

The *Statira* at last reached Cochrane's fleet, spread out from Cat Island (off the coast from present-day Gulfport, Mississippi) westward to Pea Island in the northeast corner of Lake Borgne. Pakenham, with Gibbs, Burgoyne and Dickson, set out in *Statira*'s gig and by ten o'clock that night, Christmas Eve, reached HMS *Anaconda,* near the entrance to Lake Borgne, and was told of the battle of the night before. Pakenham, ever more eager, instructed the gig crew chief to continue on, braving a biting wind that brought freezing temperatures to a clear, moonlit night.

According to one account, the gig followed the shore of Lake Borgne until it reached a spot marked by a red flag on a tall pole, indicating the entrance to Bayou Bienvenue, the route to the battlefield. Pakenham and his party then proceeded up the bayou to the fishermen's village, which they reached about eight o'clock on Christmas morning and where Admiral Cochrane had established a headquarters. His flag was attached to a tall tree there. Cochrane offered them breakfast and filled them in on the battle of December 23, particularly mentioning the devastation caused by the guns of the American ship *Carolina.* Pakenham's chief of artillery, Colonel Dickson, asked if Cochrane could have guns removed from one of the ships of his fleet and brought up to the battlefield. Cochrane said he could quickly provide four eighteen-pounders, and Dickson recommended that it be done. Breakfast finished, Pakenham, with his party, continued up Bayou Bienvenue and on to the Villere plantation to take command of his army and of the campaign to capture New Orleans.

Pakenham's army consisted of the troops that had served in the Chesapeake Bay campaigns—the Eighty-fifth (Shropshire Light Infantry) Regiment, the Fourth (the King's Own) Regiment, the Forty-fourth (Essex) Regiment and the Twenty-first (Royal Scots Fusiliers) Regiment—and the reinforcements General Keane had brought with him to Jamaica. Those troops included the Ninety-third (Argyll and Sutherland Highlanders), six companies of the Ninety-fifth Regiment, the Fifth West India Regiment, a company of the First West India Regiment, a squadron of the Fourteenth Light Dragoons, dismounted, a company of artillery, a company of engineers, and a rocket detachment. That force would soon be augmented by the troops of General Lambert—the Seventh and Forty-third regiments—and by the rest of the First West India Regiment.

As Pakenham and his party continued up Bayou Bienvenue on Christmas morning, he saw for himself how unusual the invasion route was, having already traversed some eighty miles of Lake Borgne's shallow waters in a small boat and now having to row upstream through an otherwise virtually impenetrable marsh and, finally, when Bayou Mazant could no longer float their vessel, having to slog across about four miles of swampy terrain subject to flooding. Besides that, an insufficient number of small craft prevented the army and its equipment, ammunition, and provisions, upon which the army depended, from moving together. Instead, everything, including the troops, had to be transported piecemeal, the small craft required to make repeated, time-consuming trips to accomplish the army's movement.

Having reached the site of the British position, Pakenham, Gleig reported, had "arrived in time to see his troops brought into a situation from which all his abilities could scarcely expect to extricate them." The troops, Gleig continued, realized they were caught in "unfavourable circumstances," but they took heart from Pakenham's assumption of command. "Hoping everything, therefore, from a change, they greeted their new leader with an hearty cheer; while the confidence which past events had tended in some degree to dispel, returned once more to the bosoms of all."[4]

While other officers pooled their meager stock of provisions to attempt some semblance of a Christmas feast, using a barn as a dining hall, Pakenham immediately set about examining, with the eye of a professional soldier, everything to be seen about and from the British position. Gleig noticed General Pakenham's attentiveness to his army's situation:

> Of the American army nothing whatever could be perceived, except a corps of observation, composed of five or six hundred mounted riflemen, which hovered along our front, and watched our motions. The town itself was completely hid, nor was it possible to see beyond the distance of very few miles, either in front or rear, so flat and unbroken was the face of the country. Under these circumstances, little insight into the state of affairs could be obtained by reconnoitering. The only thing, indeed, which he could learn from it was that while the vessels kept their present station upon the river, no advance could be made; as he felt that every moment's delay was injurious to us, and favourable to the enemy, he resolved to remove these incumbrances, and to push forward as soon as possible.[5]

Pakenham's initial reaction to the situation, according to his twentieth-century biographer, was anger.[6] The seemingly impossible situation in which the army was now caught served to confirm his worst fears about the New Orleans expedition.

On Christmas night, according to another source, Pakenham met with General Keane and Admiral Cochrane at Keane's headquarters in the Villere plantation house and asked for a briefing by Keane, questioning him about details of the situation. Implicit in his questions, apparently, was criticism of Cochrane's plan for capturing New Orleans. During the discussion it became obvious that Pakenham not only preferred the Chef Menteur invasion route, the one that General Jackson had thought would be taken, but was considering moving the army from its present position to the Gentilly plain. With Cochrane present, however, Keane was in no position to provide negative comments about the present position or question decisions that Cochrane had made.

Cochrane himself spoke up, explaining that the Chef Menteur route offered the city's defenders more mobility and more speed of movement than it did the British. He claimed that the system of moving the expedition's troops, equipment, and supplies by small boats was working well and that soon it would bring up the needed artillery pieces. He told Pakenham that if he, Pakenham, needed more room to maneuver, Cochrane, would have his sailors dig a canal from Bayou Mazant to the river so that the troops could be ferried to the west bank of the Mississippi.

It was apparent, however, that Cochrane believed such was not necessary, that the present position was satisfactory, and that if the army would only get on with the business of overrunning the American position, a disciplined British attack would demolish the amateur army that was attempting to defend New Orleans. "If you wish," Cochrane is reported to have derisively told Pakenham, "I will take the city with my sailors and marines, and the army can bring up the baggage."[7]

Cochrane was a crusty, white-haired veteran of thirty-six years of military service. He had commanded ships for thirty-two years and had been an admiral for ten. Haughty (he had already boasted he would eat Christmas dinner in New Orleans) and domineering, he nevertheless had won the confidence of his government with his methods and results. He was a man of immense authority and influence, and he was not to be criticized or second-guessed.

Stung and challenged to defend the army's abilities, Pakenham decided not to contest the admiral or his ill-drawn plan. Instead, he acquiesced. (Some students of the battle doubt the meeting at Keane's headquarters took place or that Cochrane made such a remark to Pakenham. Whether he did or did not, however, the fact remains that Pakenham acquiesced to Cochrane's plan of attack.)

Pakenham's first objective on the morning after taking command was to silence the guns of the *Carolina* and *Louisiana,* against the enfilading fire of which it would be impossible to advance his troops. But before he got to that matter, he had to deal with the cut in the levee made during the night on Jackson's orders to Major Latour. Jackson's purpose was to allow the river to flow through the levee opening and flood the fields of the Chalmette plantation in front of the American lines, thereby preventing a British advance. But through some foul-up, the American work party had cut the levee not forward of the British lines but to their rear. The cut allowed a considerable stream of river water to rush onto the fields some two hundred yards behind the British position, but it was soon noticed by General Keane, and a work party was quickly ordered to fill the gap and halt the flow.

The potential danger to Pakenham's army was so great that Pakenham ordered the arrest of the officer in charge of the sentries who had failed to see and report the activity of the American work party. Perhaps the sentries were confused by the work taking place on the levee that night, for Colonel Dickson had ordered embrasures cut in the levee to accommodate the artillery he intended to bring to bear against the American ships in the river. That work also took place on the night of December 25.

The following night, Dickson moved his guns into position beside the levee, two nine-pounders, four six-pounders, and two five-and-a-half-inch howitzers. The promised eighteen-pounders had not yet arrived.

Before dawn on December 27, Dickson's artillerymen lighted fires and began to heat shot for the nine-pounders' salvos against the *Carolina,* which would be the artillery's first target, eight hundred yards away. Hot shot was a favorite weapon of Dickson, who had used it with great effect in the Battle of Salamanca.

About eight o'clock in the morning on December 27, the British guns opened fire, the nine-pounders with hot shot, the six-pounders and howitzers with cold round shot and shells. Under that bombardment, the *Carolina*'s crew, unable to move the ship out of range, after about fifteen minutes of bombardment took to the vessel's small boats and rowed to safety on the west bank of the river. The hot shot had repeatedly pierced the wooden hull and superstructure of the vessel and had set it afire. About ten thirty, as smoke and flame billowed from its decks and hull, the *Carolina* exploded in a fiery spectacle and sank in the muddy river. Troops of the British Eighty-fifth Regiment ran up atop the levee and cheered wildly as the blazing, broken hulk slipped beneath the water.

Meanwhile, the Baratarian crew of the *Louisiana,* which had been anchored about a mile upstream of the *Carolina,* managed to tow the ship farther upstream and out of range of Dickson's artillery. The smaller American gunboats that had been supporting *Carolina* and *Louisiana* also escaped.

His primary mission accomplished, though he had expended nearly a third of his guns' ammunition, Dickson now moved his artillery pieces from their batteries beside the levee to positions at the front of the British lines, where they could support an advance on Jackson's line. The job of actually manhandling the ponderous guns into new emplacements was given to the black troops of the First West India Regiment, who were suffering severely from the cold, being ill clad and unused to the frigid temperatures of the Louisiana winter.

Pakenham organized his army into two brigades, placing one on the British right, next to the swamp, and the other on the left, closest to the river. He put Major General Gibbs in command of the brigade on the right, which included the Fourth, Twenty-first, and the Forty-fourth regiments and the First West India Regiment. He put Major General Keane in command of the brigade on the left, which was composed of the Eighty-fifth, Ninety-third, and Ninety-fifth regiments, plus the Fifth West India Regiment. With the *Carolina* disposed of and his artillery in place, Pakenham would wait no longer to attack, believing delay favored the city's defenders, allowing them time to strengthen their fortifications and receive reinforcements.

On the night of December 27 the two brigades formed into columns in preparation for an advance toward General Jackson's line, which ran along the Rodriguez canal—which was little more than a dry ditch, usually, behind which a breastworks had been raised. The breastworks extended from the river to the swamp, about three-quarters of a mile. Near the levee and situated so as to block the river road, a redoubt had been built in front of Jackson's line, protecting his right flank and enabling the defenders posted there to deliver a crossfire with the redan constructed near the swamp on Jackson's left flank.

Pakenham had little or no knowledge of the position or strength of the American line, his patrols being so harassed that they were prevented from observing it, which they attempted to do once more during the night of December 27–28. Pakenham's reconnaissance in force would let him discover what he was facing. He hoped the advance would prove more than a reconnaissance, though. He had ordered his men to cook two days' rations of meat, in case the reconnaissance would turn into a pursuit of the Americans all the way into New Orleans. With his staff at his side, Pakenham would position himself at the center of the two advancing brigades, where he could observe and direct the advance.

At daylight on December 28 Pakenham's troops moved out. The two columns crossed the frosty fields of the Villere and Lacoste plantations and, employing their three-pounder field pieces and Congreve rockets, drove back the Americans' forward outposts on the Laronde and Bienvenue plantations. The British line pushed steadily forward, past the blazing Bienvenue buildings, which the American sentries had set afire as they fell back, and advanced a distance of some four miles without resistance. As the forward elements on the British left rounded a bend of the river road, passing several houses, General Keane could see, for the first time, the American line, about seven hundred yards in front of him. Lieutenant Gleig described the sight:

> At length we found ourselves in view of the enemy's army, posted in a very advantageous manner. About forty yards in their front was a canal, which extended from the morass to within a short distance of the high road. Along their line were thrown up breastworks, not indeed completed, but even now formidable. Upon the road, and at several other points were erected powerful batteries; while the ship [*Louisiana*], with a large flotilla of gun-boats, flanked the whole position from the river.
>
> . . . on the left, a few houses built at a turning in the road, entirely concealed him [the enemy]; nor was it till they had gained that turning, and beheld the muzzles of his guns pointed towards them, that those who moved in the direction were aware of their proximity to danger.[8]

On the right of Jackson's line four artillery batteries were emplaced. Their guns included two twenty-four pounders. Dominique You and Renato Beluche and a twenty-man crew of Baratarians manned one of them, Battery No. 3. Another crew of Baratarians and navy sailors, who had been aboard the *Carolina* and were commanded by Lieutenant Otho Norris, manned the other twenty-four-pounder battery. Further firepower would come from the guns of the *Louisiana,* which had eased downriver to a position where its broadsides could enfilade the British ranks as they advanced.

As the troops of Pakenham's left continued past the turn of the river road, about six hundred yards from the Rodriguez canal, the American artillery, from Jackson's line and from the *Louisiana,* opened fire. Gleig, advancing in that left column, was an eyewitness to the devastating effects:

> Scarcely had the head of the column passed the houses, when a deadly fire was opened from both the battery and the shipping. That the Americans are excellent shots, as well with artillery as with rifles, we have had frequent cause to acknowledge; but,

> perhaps, on no occasion did they assert their claim to the title of good artillerymen more effectually than on the present. Scarce a bullet passed over, or fell short of its mark, but all striking full into the midst of our ranks, occasioned terrible havoc. The shrieks of the wounded, therefore, the crash of firelocks, and the fall of such as were killed, caused at first some little confusion; and what added to the panic, was, that from the houses beside which we stood, bright flames suddenly burst out. The Americans expecting this attack, had filled them with combustibles for the purpose; and directing one or two guns against them, loaded with red-hot shot, in an instant set them on fire. . . . A tremendous cannonade mowed down our ranks and deafened us with its roar; while two large chateaux and their out-buildings almost scorched us with the flames, and blinded us with the smoke which they emitted.[9]

Pakenham ordered his infantrymen off the road and into the cane field to continue their advance, and he brought up his artillery to answer the American fire. "But the contest," Gleig reported, "was in every respect unequal, since their artillery far exceeded ours, both in numerical strength and in weight of metal."[10] Within a half hour three British artillery pieces had been crippled by the American fire, several artillerymen had been killed, and the remainder of the outmatched artillery had been forced to retire to the rear.

According to Gleig, the advance on the British left was stopped by a water-filled canal, the unknown depth of which deterred the troops from moving farther, since they were uncertain they could ford it. A halt was called, and the troops were ordered to find whatever cover they could. Many of them simply lay on the ground to duck beneath the withering fire. Others, including Gleig, hurried into a ditch knee-deep in water, where they hid in the high weeds growing on its bank.

On Pakenham's right, General Gibbs's column, out of range of *Louisiana*'s guns, pushed almost all the way to the American line, despite taking heavy rifle fire. Pakenham, after conferring with General Keane on the left side, galloped to the right side to observe the Americans' line opposite it. With him were Colonel Dickson and Lieutenant Peter Wright of Pakenham's engineers. Pakenham directed Wright to climb a tree to be able to see the American position. When Wright came down, he told Pakenham that the canal in front of Jackson's line was filled with water (probably from recent heavy rains) and that the swamp on the Americans' left would prevent Pakenham from turning Jackson's left flank.

Pakenham then thought he would concentrate his artillery and pound the left side of Jackson's line, it being less protected than the right, and he ordered Dickson, his artillery chief, to move his guns from where they were on the left to new positions on the right. Dickson rode off and soon returned with the bad news that the two six-pounders had been disabled and the nine-pounders had been pulled back to the rear.

Now Pakenham decided to call off the advance, for the present. He ordered both brigades to withdraw and seek cover. His reconnaissance in force having proved less than what he had hoped for, he would wait for the arrival of the eighteen-pounders promised by Admiral Cochrane. Then he would try again.

## ∴ 18 ∴

# Preparing for Battle

GENERAL Jackson never stopped working on his defenses. He ordered a massive thirty-two-pounder emplaced in the center of his line, and during the night of December 28, after Pakenham's reconnaissance in force, Lieutenant Charles Crawley of the United States Navy, who had been commanding the howitzer crew at Battery No. 1, directed the construction of a platform for the thirty-two-pounder, mounted it, and took command of the battery.

Construction was started on a second line of defense, on the Dupre plantation, about two miles behind the Rodriguez canal line. As the second line was nearing completion, a third defensive line was begun, about a mile below New Orleans at the Montreuil plantation. Nine hundred slaves were put to work building those two lines.

To form platforms for his field pieces, which he realized would be crucial in repelling an attack, Jackson removed about 150 bales of cotton from a merchant ship in the river. They would serve as a stable base in the rain-sodden mud, and planks would be laid atop them, on which the guns would be mounted.

More artillery pieces were brought up to Jackson's line at the Rodriguez canal. By the end of the day on December 31, seven batteries were ready for service on the line. They bristled with the thirty-two-pounder, three twenty-four-pounders, one long brass eighteen-pounder, three twelve-pounders, and a six-inch howitzer. Two twelve-pounders were removed from the *Louisiana* and emplaced behind the levee on the west bank of the river, opposite Jackson's line, and on the night of December 30 another twenty-four-pounder was mounted in the battery that commanded Pakenham's left flank.

Jackson also ordered additional fortifications to be established on the west bank of the Mississippi, to prevent the British from turning his right flank by crossing the river. Major General David B. Morgan commanded a reinforced regiment of Louisiana militia posted across the river from the Chalmette plantation, and now Major Latour, Jackson's chief engineer, set about establishing a new defensive line at the Boisgervais canal, about three miles below New Orleans and nearly the same distance behind Morgan's line. By Latour's own account, "One hundred and fifty negroes, under the direction of Mr. Lefevre, in six days completed the parapet, the whole length of the canal, and levelled the earth to form a glacis on the opposite side [of the parapet]."[1]

Also on the west bank, opposite the city, at the edge of the river, a square redoubt was constructed from a brick kiln. A moatlike fosse, twenty feet wide, was dug around it, and the earth removed by the digging was used to form a steep glacis extending from the parapet to the edge of the fosse. The redoubt was mounted with two twenty-four-pounder artillery pieces, which commanded the west bank river road and the river itself. The former skipper of the *Carolina*, Captain John Henley, was placed in command of the redoubt.

Meanwhile, the harassing fire of Jackson's artillery and sniper fire from his patrols continued relentlessly. The *Louisiana* slipped downriver every day to join the artillery in bombarding the British positions. "Whenever a group of four or five men showed themselves," Major Latour reported, "they were instantly dispersed by our balls or shells. . . . Our gunners annoyed the enemy to such a degree that he could not work at any fortification . . . by day, and was deprived of all repose during the night."[2] In the hours of darkness, Tennessee sharpshooters, the "dirty shirts," as the elegantly uniformed British soldiers scornfully called them, stalked Pakenham's sentries and picked them off like game. British officers were especially targeted.

Besides being deprived of sleep and suffering from the cold, the damp, and disease, Pakenham's army also had to deal with inadequate provisions. While Jackson's men ate from a bounteous supply of meat, meal, flour, vegetables, and fruit, received from stocks in New Orleans, the British, after consuming all the cattle and other food from the plantations they occupied, were eating horse meat, from the stolen horses they had butchered, to keep from starving.

Following the repulse of his reconnaissance in force on December 28, General Pakenham had determined he must silence Jackson's artillery if an attack on the American line was to be successful. At a council of war called by Pakenham and attended by, among others, Admiral Cochrane, General Gibbs, Rear Admiral Pultney Malcolm, and General Keane, the senior officers reached a decision to assault Jackson's fortified parapet in the same way they would a walled and fortified city. The first thing that must be done was to bring up more heavy guns to hammer the Americans' defensive wall until it was breached.

According to one account,[3] General Pakenham exhibited some depression at the war council, apparently defeated not only on the field during his reconnaissance in force but also in his confidence of a British victory. Cochrane, however, was undaunted. He was sure that the reconnaissance in force had failed mainly because the Americans possessed superior artillery firepower. The addition of his big naval guns, he was certain, would reverse that situation. He issued orders for some thirty of his fleet's heaviest guns to be removed from his vessels and laboriously carried across Lake Borgne and up bayous Bienvenue and Mazant and manhandled into positions from which they could assault Jackson's defenses.

While Cochrane's guns were being fetched from his ships, from December 28 to December 30, Pakenham's army remained inactive in its position. Jackson's army, however, kept busy. Lieutenant Gleig recorded its activities:

> Day and night we could observe numerous parties employed in strengthening his [the enemy's] lines; while from the increased number of tents, which almost every hour might be discerned, it was evident that strong reinforcements were continually pouring into his camp. Nor did he leave us totally unmolested. By giving to his guns a great degree of elevation, he contrived at last to reach

> our bivouac; and thus were we constantly under a cannonade which, though it did little execution, proved nevertheless extremely annoying.[4]

On December 31, the naval guns having been delivered to the field, General Pakenham ordered preparations made for the artillery assault on Jackson's line, and the British camp now came alive with activity. Gleig recalled that night:

> One half of the army was . . . ordered out . . . and marched to the front, passing the piquets, and halting about three hundred yards from the enemy's line. Here it was resolved to throw up a chain of works; and here the greater part of the detachment, laying down their firelocks, applied themselves vigorously to their tasks, while the rest stood armed and prepared for their defence.
>
> . . . six batteries were completed long before dawn, in which were mounted thirty pieces of heavy cannon; . . . falling back a little way, this force united itself to the remainder of the infantry, and lay down behind some rushes, in readiness to act, as soon as it should be wanted.[5]

Along Jackson's line the increased enemy activity had not gone unnoticed. British deserters had already reported that Pakenham was expecting reinforcements and was bringing up heavy guns for an artillery assault. During the night of December 31–January 1, the noises of construction and men working could be heard. Two of the British batteries were set up about 600 yards from Jackson's line, beside a ditch that ran along the side of the Chalmette plantation, one positioned about 350 yards from the river, the other about 300 yards farther toward the center of Jackson's line. Other batteries were erected as close as 300 yards away.

The light of dawn on New Year's Day, 1815, filtered dimly through an unusually thick, lingering fog that did not start to lift until around eight o'clock and did not clear completely until about two hours later. The most forward British units could then plainly see the American position. Jackson's regiments were in a parade formation, their bands playing, their colors displayed, and mounted officers riding back and forth before the ranks.

Once their targets were in sight, Pakenham's artillery suddenly opened fire, scattering the American troops from their formation. Major Latour described the action:

> The enemy opened a very brisk fire from his three batteries, of which the left, established on the road, mounted two twelve-pounders; the centre, eight eighteen-pounders, and twenty-four-pound carronades, and that on the right towards the wood opposite our lines, mounted eight pieces of cannon and carronades. A cloud of Congreve rockets accompanied the balls, and for fifteen minutes the fire was kept up with unexampled celerity. The first discharges of the two batteries nearest the river, were principally directed against Macarty's house, where the headquarters were established. In less than ten minutes, upwards of one hundred [cannon] balls, rockets and shells struck the house, and rendered it impossible to remain there. The general-in-chief [General Jackson] and all his staff were in the apartments when the firing began; but though bricks, splinters of wood and furniture, rockets and balls, were flying in all directions, not a single person was wounded.[6]

The surprised American troops quickly regrouped and hastened to their posts along the line. About ten minutes after the British bombardment had begun, most of Jackson's artillery was ready to answer. An account based on interviews with eyewitnesses details the American response:

> Presently the American lines broke their ominous silence. Humphrey led off on the right with his twelves, firing several volleys before the other guns began. . . . But soon Dominique [You],

> and [Navy Lieutenant Otho] Norris, and [Army Lieutenant Samuel] Spotts . . . with their larger guns joined the chorus. Next, the veteran Garrigue [militia general Garrigues Fleaujac, a member of the Louisiana legislature and a former artillery officer in Napoleon's army] with his twelve-pounder, directed his particular attention to the redoubt on the British right and in his front, whilst [navy lieutenant Charles] Crawley [commanding the thirty-two-pounder battery] made the earth tremble under the reverberations of his huge piece. And now once fairly opened, the batteries of the Americans poured forth, without pause or cessation, a constant stream of fiery missiles. . . . There is nothing in this brilliant campaign more remarkable than the vigor, destructiveness, and complete success of this cannonade on the part of the Americans.[7]

Jackson's artillery had also suffered. "We had the carriage of a twenty-four-pounder broken by one of their balls, at captain Dominique's battery," Latour reported, "and that of the thirty-two-pounder . . . was also damaged by a ball; the fore-train of the twelve-pounder of general Garrigues was likewise broken by the balls of the enemy."[8]

Colonel Dickson, Pakenham's artillery chief, reported that his guns "only ceased for want of Ammunition" and claimed that he had "not one piece of heavy Ordnance disabled, or even struck." However, the American fire had killed thirteen of Dickson's artillerymen, including one officer, and had wounded another thirteen. "Even if there had been Sufficient Ammunition," Dickson said, "the nature of our Batteries was such the men could not have gone on for many hours longer." Cochrane's naval guns had proved less effectual than the admiral and General Pakenham had apparently believed, for the hastily constructed platforms on which they rested proved "uneven and loose," and the eighteen-pounders' carriages, meant for shipboard use, "were found very Awkward and unmanageable," Dickson reported. The result, he said, was that "during the Cannonade, or at least until the latter part of it, our fire did not attain the precision it ought, neither could it be kept up with the rapidity necessary to Silence the Enemies Guns."[9]

General Pakenham had assembled his infantry on the field in position to advance on Jackson's line once the Americans' murderous artillery had been silenced. Following the failure of Admiral Cochrane's big guns and the rest of the British artillery to accomplish their mission, new orders called the infantrymen back from the front, their only action having been a probe in the woods on the American left flank, where they had waited until the general advance was aborted.

The furious artillery exchange left Pakenham's forces with forty-four killed and fifty-five wounded. American casualties were eleven dead and twenty-three wounded, some of them civilians who had come to witness the spectacle. The British artillerymen, eager to catch the American forces by surprise with their opening fire, had not taken time to bracket their rounds and fire for effect only after having zeroed in on their targets. As a result, many of the British rounds had overshot their targets by a considerable distance and had landed among the civilian spectators.

Pakenham's decision to withdraw his infantry without a fight disappointed his troops, who were eager to take the fight to the American lines. Lieutenant Gleig reported his feelings and the effects on morale:

> We retired, therefore, not only baffled and disappointed, but in some degree disheartened and discontented. All our plans had as yet proved abortive; even this, upon which so much reliance had been placed, was found to be of no avail; and it must be confessed, that something like murmuring began to be heard through the camp.... Be it observed, however, that these were not the murmurs of men anxious to escape from a disagreeable situation by any means. On the contrary, they resembled rather the growling of a chained dog, when he sees his adversary, and cannot reach him; for in all their complaints, no man ever hinted at a retreat, while all were eager to bring matters to the issue of a battle, at any sacrifice of lives.[10]

According to the report of Major Harry Smith, whom Pakenham had ordered to command a detail to retrieve the cannon left on the field, the troops were so demoralized that they refused to obey Smith and move the guns. Humiliated, Smith had to go get Pakenham to come use his imposing influence on the men, which he did, before the guns were successfully retrieved.

Pakenham knew that Major General John Lambert, whom he had left behind when he sailed from Jamaica, should be arriving any time now, bringing two regiments with him, the Seventh and the Forty-third. The big push against Jackson's lines would need those reinforcements. So with his army pulled back from the American lines, Pakenham decided to wait for Lambert. He also decided that a new plan of attack, to be carried out as soon as feasible, would have to be devised.

Jackson's army was being reinforced by some twenty-three hundred Kentucky militiamen, who arrived on January 4, 1815. Commanded by Major General John Thomas, the militiamen trooped into New Orleans cold and ragged, lacking rifles, warm clothing, blankets, tents, and equipment. To their enormous disappointment, they learned that Jackson had none of those things to provide them. Jackson angrily ordered a detachment to go to Natchez, where a ship loaded with supplies was docked, its captain afraid to enter the war zone to deliver the badly needed goods. In a rage, Jackson ordered the ship captain arrested and brought to him in irons.

Jackson was astonished that so many of the Kentuckians had come without weapons. "I never in my life seen a Kentuckian without a gun, a pack of cards and a jug of whiskey," he claimed.[11] The estimated 550 Kentucky militiamen who did have rifles or muskets were sent to reinforce the line at the Rodriguez canal. The others were posted as backups to the defenders manning the lines closer to the city.

The people of New Orleans were so moved by the plight of the Kentuckians that one of their state legislators, Louis Louaillier, persuaded the Louisiana legislature to immediately appropriate six thousand dollars, to be dispensed by a special committee for the relief of the Kentuckians. The public also contributed. With cloth and other material purchased with the contributions, the women of New Orleans sewed hundreds of trousers, shirts, and shoes for the men who had come to defend them.

To arm as many of the weaponless Kentuckians as he could, Jackson asked the women of New Orleans to scour their attics, closets, and basements for every pistol, hunting rifle, antique musket, and sword they could find and bring them, along with whatever flints and ramrods they could turn up, to him.

On January 3, 1815, Jackson wrote a report to Secretary of War James Monroe to inform him of the situation. "The enemy occupy their former position and are engaged in strengthening it; our time is spent in the same employment and in exchanging long shot with them. . . . I do not know what may be their further design—Whether to redouble their effort, or apply them elsewhere. . . . I am preparing for either event."[12]

General Lambert and the two additional British regiments arrived on January 4. By then a new plan of attack had been devised, and Pakenham had begun implementing it. The plan had been drawn up by Admiral Cochrane, and Pakenham had approved it. In his own words, Cochrane described the British position and gave his superiors a barebones explanation of the new plan:

> The Mississippi is here about eight hundred yards wide, and they [the Americans] had on the right [west] bank a heavy battery of twelve guns, which enfiladed the whole front of the [American] position on the left bank.
>
> Preparations were made on our side with very considerable labour, to clear out and widen a canal that communicated with a stream [Bayou Mazant] by which the boats had passed up to the place of disembarkation, to open it into the Mississippi, by which means troops could be got over to the right bank, and the co-operation of armed boats would be secured.
>
> The disposition for the attack [on the American fortifications on the west bank] was as follows: a corps consisting of the 85th light infantry, two hundred seamen, and our hundred marines, the 5th West-India regiment, and four pieces of artillery, under the

> command of colonel Thornton of the 85th, was to pass over during the night, and move along the right bank towards New Orleans, clearing its front, until it reached the flanking battery of the enemy on that side [the west bank], which it had orders to carry.
>
> The assailing of the enemy's works in front of us was to be made by the brigade composed of the 4th, 21st and 44th, under major-general Gibbs, and the 3d brigade, consisting of the 93d, two companies of the 95th, and two companies of the fusiliers, and the 43d, under major-general Keane. Some black troops were . . . to skirmish in the wood on the right;—the principal attack to be made by major-general Gibbs;—the first brigade and the 43d formed the reserve;—the attacking columns were to be provided with scaling-ladders and rafts;—the whole to be at their stations by daylight. An advanced battery in our front of six eighteen-pounders was [to be] thrown up during the night, about eight hundred yards from the enemy's line. The attack was to be made at the earliest hour.[13]

The plan called for Jackson's artillery on the west bank to be captured by Colonel Thornton's force and then to be turned on Jackson's main line on the east bank. Jackson's flank would be turned by advancing on the opposite side of the river, and his guns that had enfiladed the British ranks would be used to enfilade Jackson's line of troops. The seizure of those guns, plus the two new regiments, could provide that additional element that Pakenham knew he needed for success.

The enormously arduous task of extending the Villere canal, which led from Bayou Mazant, so that it reached the river and was deep enough to float the boats that would carry Thornton's men and artillery, had begun on January 2, the large work parties apparently equipped with little more than their entrenching tools to dig out the canal for a distance of about two miles. The men were divided into four shifts that worked around the clock, until the canal was lengthened and deepened. Once the deepened canal reached the levee, the levee would be cut, and the river diverted into the canal to fill it. The work proved torturously backbreaking and was made even more burdensome by a continuing heavy rain and by the harassing fire of Jackson's artillery.

While the digging proceeded nonstop, Colonel Dickson's supply of artillery ammunition was being replenished, a considerable amount of it being brought up by hand by Lambert's newly arriving infantrymen. Dickson set up six eighteen-pounders and two twenty-four-pounders with which he intended to command the river from the east side and to support Thornton's attack on the American position on the west side of the river.

Work on the canal was evidently going well enough, despite continual cave-ins of its rain-sodden banks, that Pakenham and his staff planned to have Colonel Thornton embark his troops and take them across the Mississippi on the night of January 6. The general assault on Jackson's line could then be launched at daybreak on January 7. The plan called for a signal rocket to be fired by Thornton's force once it had seized the American guns on the west bank. On that signal, Pakenham's main force would commence its all-out attack on Jackson's line.

Before the end of the day on January 6, however, Pakenham's staff determined that the work on the canal would not be finished in time for an attack on the west bank that night. Thornton's mission therefore was postponed for twenty-four hours. The all-out assault on Jackson's line at the Rodriguez canal was rescheduled for January 8.

Jackson was anxious to avoid overlooking some possible move of the British. He thought they might send a force back to Bayou Bienvenue and attempt to get behind his line by following the bayou upstream from Bayou Mazant. The canal of the Piernas plantation, about a mile to the rear of Jackson's line, extended from the river to Bayou Bienvenue, a distance of some four miles, and could possibly provide access from the bayou to a position behind Jackson's line. Jackson ordered Colonel Reuben Kemper to take a detachment to the Dupre plantation, about a mile upriver from the Piernas tract, and after following the Dupre canal by canoe as far as it went, cross the swamp to determine whether there was a route the British could take either to turn Jackson's left flank or that would provide an approach to New Orleans via the

Chef Menteur road. Kemper's difficulty in penetrating the swamp persuaded him, and apparently Jackson, that no such route across the swamp existed.

On the night of January 3, however, Jackson received intelligence that the British had ascended Bayou Bienvenue as far as its junction with the Piernas canal and had landed a considerable force there. Jackson immediately ordered his assistant inspector general, Major Davis, to take two hundred men from General Coffee's brigade and quickly march overland to the reported British position to determine if the report was accurate. Struggling through a heavy rain and mud in which the men sank up to their knees, Davis's detachment reached the junction of the Piernas canal and Bayou Bienvenue and found no sign of British soldiers.

Still not convinced that the British planned no flanking movement by way of the bayous, Jackson ordered Colonel Kemper to come down the Piernas canal to its junction with Bayou Bienvenue, then proceed to the spot where Bayou Mazant split off from Bayou Bienvenue. That reconnaissance revealed a fortification erected by the British near the junction of bayous Bienvenue and Mazant. A magazine for stores had been built into the fortification, and a strong detachment of troops left to guard it. The British had also posted a sentinel high up in a tall tree, to keep watch over the bayous and the marsh. In a brief engagement with the British guards, Kemper's detachment was forced to make a hurried retreat, and one of his men was taken prisoner. No troop movement was observed, though, and Kemper and the remainder of his detachment returned to the encampment behind the Rodriguez canal.

While Pakenham was discovering from Kemper's man who had been captured that Jackson's force had been swelled by the arrival of 2,250 Kentucky militiamen, Jackson was learning of the arrival of General Lambert and his two regiments of British reinforcements. The resulting totals gave Pakenham the advantage in numbers. The British force totaled approximately 5,400 soldiers (some sources put the number at 8,000 to 15,000 soldiers, plus 2,000 seamen and marines). The men in Pakenham's army also had the advantage in experience, most of them veterans of Britain's battles with the armies of Napoleon. Jackson's forces, on the other hand, numbered about 4,000, most of them militiamen and volunteers.

The superior numbers of the British force, however, were facing a determined foe, frontier hunters and fighters renowned for their deadly marksmanship with rifles and muskets. They were also facing Jean Lafitte's skilled Baratarian gunners, as well as the artillerymen of the United States Navy and Army.

What was more—significantly more—Jackson held the advantage of position. To beat the Americans, Pakenham's troops would have to advance across about two thousand yards of open fields in the face of withering artillery and musket and rifle fire. If they got as far as Jackson's line, they would have to negotiate the Rodriguez canal and scale a crude but formidable rampart fashioned of mud and logs.

When Pakenham went out from his headquarters to inspect the work on the Villere canal late in the day on January 7, he asked the engineer (apparently Colonel Burgoyne) about something that was troubling him. Harry Smith, an eyewitness, recorded the conversation.[14] "Are you satisfied," Pakenham wanted to know, "the dam will bear the weight of the water which will be upon it when the banks of the river are cut?" The dam would have to hold back the diverted river water so that the flooded canal would be deep enough to float the forty-two boats that had been brought from Admiral Cochrane's fleet to transport Colonel Thornton's attack force across the Mississippi.

"Perfectly," Pakenham's engineer replied.

Pakenham was doubtful. "I should be more so if a second dam was constructed."

The engineer assured Pakenham a second dam, a backup in case the first dam failed, was unnecessary.[15] After that, Pakenham completed his check of the preparations for the next day's battle and retired to his headquarters to sleep.

Jackson observed the flurry of British activity through his telescope while peering from the upper floor of the Macarty plantation house. He could see the British troops constructing fascines and "working on pieces of wood, which we concluded must be scaling ladders."[16] As daylight faded into concealing darkness, Jackson and his staff could hear British details working at the sites of the artillery batteries that had been evacuated on New Year's Day. A large number of men were seen laboring to move something unwieldy, apparently artillery. Also, the number of British pickets near the wood to Jackson's left had been increased and posted closer to each other, and officers were seen riding about the fields giving orders.

Clearly, Pakenham's army was about to make a move. Jackson's officers issued orders for their troops to be ready. "Half the troops," Major Latour reported, "passed the night behind the breastwork, relieving each other occasionally. Every one waited for day with anxiety and impatience, but with calm intrepidity, expecting to be vigorously attacked."[17]

Jackson, having alerted his officers and men to what he believed to be an imminent British assault, retired to a couch in the Macarty house and fell asleep in his worn and rumpled uniform.[18]

## .·. 19 .·.

# The Battle

On the morning of Sunday, January 8, 1815, Major General Sir Edward Pakenham awoke at five o'clock and learned the evil news. Colonel Thornton's brigade, which was to cross the river during the night, attack the American positions on the west bank, capture their artillery, and signal for the general assault on General Jackson's line before dawn, was still on the east side of the river.

Something had gone wrong while Pakenham slept. The accounts do not agree on the cause, but the Villere canal either had not filled or had not retained the river's diverted water when the cut was made in the levee. According to Major Harry Smith, the dam that Pakenham had feared might collapse, despite his engineer's confidence that it would not, had indeed burst and allowed the river water to flow past the waiting boats without filling the canal. Burgoyne, the engineer, reported that "the banks of the new cutting" had fallen in, blocking the flow of river water.[1] Other reports, including Colonel Dickson's, also concluded that the collapse of mud into the channel at the levee had prevented the canal from filling with water.

In any event, because there was insufficient water to float them, the boats had to be laboriously, exhaustingly dragged through the thick mud by Admiral Cochrane's sailors. It was a hugely difficult, enormously time-consuming task, and as dawn drew near, Thornton was still waiting for the entire fleet of forty-two boats to be put into the river before embarking his force, about twelve hours behind schedule.

During the nearly twelve hours of delay, no one evidently had seriously thought about awakening Pakenham to apprise him of the problem, which he might have solved by sending Thornton's force piecemeal across the river. But apparently Pakenham's staff felt that to wake their exhausted commander would be, as Harry Smith put it, "as bad as the loss of a leg."[2]

Pakenham believed that the dam had failed, and he was, in Smith's words, "greatly distracted" over the turn of events. At first he doubted that any good purpose could be served by having Thornton cross the river at this late hour—some thirty minutes before daybreak. "The dam, as you heard me say it would, gave way," he told Smith that morning, "and Thornton's people will be of no use whatever to the general attack."[3]

He considered canceling the entire Thornton mission but then decided it could be useful as a diversion from the main attack. After sending for information on the current status of the mission and learning that the troops of the Eighty-fifth Regiment were aboard their boats, as were the marines, a total of 460 men, and that the thirty-three boats already in the river could carry another one hundred men, he ordered those boats to cross the river and proceed with the mission.

Four artillery pieces that Thornton's force was to take across the river were still waiting to be placed aboard the boats, and Colonel Dickson successfully urged Pakenham to keep them on the east side of the river to support the main attack. Pakenham was also receiving advice from Major Smith, who urged him to withdraw the troops from the front, where they were poised, and to postpone the general assault. "So obvious is it in every military point of view," Smith told him, "[that] we should possess the right [west] bank of the river, and thus enfilade and divert the attention of the enemy; there is still time before daylight to retire the columns now. We are under the enemy's fire as soon as discovered."[4]

Pakenham conceded the validity of Smith's argument but rejected his advice. "This may be," he said in concession, "but I have twice deferred the attack. We are strong in numbers now comparatively. It will cost more men, and the assault must be made."[5]

Smith continued to urge a postponement, as streaks of sunlight pierced the cloudy sky. Pakenham would not consider it. "Smith," he said, "order the rocket to be fired." It was the rocket that was to be the signal to launch the general assault. Again Smith pleaded for a postponement.

"It is now too late," Pakenham told him. "The columns would be visible to the enemy before they could move out of fire, and would lose more men than it is to be hoped they will in an attack. Fire the rocket, I say, and go to Lambert."[6]

Smith ordered the signal rocket fired, as commanded, and then reported to General Lambert, reaching him, Smith recalled, "just when the stillness of death and anticipation was broken."[7]

Pakenham's disciplined army began its advance in tight columns, the bagpipes of the Ninety-third, the tartan-trousered Highlander Regiment, flooding the morning's damp air with the shrieking notes of "Monymusk," the regiment's sound to charge. On their backs Pakenham's soldiers bore forty-pound packs; in their hands they carried their nine-and-a-half-pound, four-foot-seven-inch-long, seventy-five-caliber muskets, the East India Pattern musket, modeled after the Brown Bess that had been the primary weapon of British infantrymen during the American Revolutionary War. More feared than its shot was its eighteen-inch bayonet, with which British soldiers were lethally proficient and the mere sight of which in the hands of an advancing army often sent enemy troops fleeing.

Beyond the muddy rampart that rose along the Rodriguez canal, the movement of Pakenham's army was now seen through the wisps of morning fog by members of Jackson's army of defenders, including Major Lacarriere Latour, who gave this eyewitness account of the commencement of the battle:

> At last the dawn of day discovered to us the enemy occupying two-thirds of the space between the wood and the Mississippi. Immediately a Congreve rocket went off from the skirt of the wood, in the direction of the river. This was the signal for the attack. At the same instant, the twelve-pounder of battery No. 6, whose gunners had perceived the enemy's movement, discharged a shot. On this all his [the enemy's] troops gave three cheers, formed in close col-

> umn of about sixty men in front, in very good order, and advanced nearly in the direction of battery No. 7, the men shouldering their muskets, and all carrying fascines, and some with ladders. A cloud of rockets preceded them, and continued to fall in showers during the whole attack. Batteries Nos. 6, 7 and 8, now opened an incessant fire on the column, which continued to advance in pretty good order, until, in a few minutes, the musketry of the troops of Tennessee and Kentucky, joining their fire with that of the artillery, began to make an impression on it, which soon threw it into confusion. It was at that moment that was heard that constant rolling fire, whose tremendous noise resembled rattling peals of thunder.[8]

Harry Smith, at General Lambert's command post in the rear of the center of Pakenham's massed troops, gave his own report of the commencement of the battle: "The rocket was hardly in the air before a rush of our troops was met by the most murderous and destructive fire of all arms ever poured upon column."[9]

The main thrust of the assault, according to Pakenham's battle plan, was to be made by General Gibbs's brigade on the left side of Jackson's line, which was believed to be the most vulnerable part of the line. Included in Gibbs's brigade were the Fourth, the Twenty-first, and the Forty-fourth regiments and three companies of the Ninety-fifth Rifles, a total of about twenty-two hundred men. The Forty-fourth, an Irish regiment commanded by Lieutenant Colonel Thomas Mullens, was to form the advance unit of the brigade, protected on its right flank by the rifle companies, which would also make a diversionary attack at the extreme left of Jackson's line.

The task of the Forty-fourth was spelled out in Pakenham's orders to Mullens issued the day before the assault: "The Advance Guard is to carry forward with it, six long Ladders with planks on them & ten small Ladders, as well as the Fascines. The officer commanding the 44th Regt. must ascertain where these requisites are, this evening, so that there may be no delay in taking them forward tomorrow to the old Batteries."[10]

Mullens had no enthusiasm for his regiment's assignment and upon reading Pakenham's orders commented, "It is a forlorn hope, and the regiment must be sacrificed."[11] Another account reports his saying, "My regiment has been ordered to execution. Their dead bodies are to be used as a bridge for the rest of the army to march over."[12] As he led his men onto the battlefield on the morning of the assault, Mullens took them past the redoubt where the ladders and fascines were stored and formed them into their attack position while the ladders and fascines still rested in the redoubt. Lieutenant Gleig recounted Pakenham's discovery of Mullens's failure and the events that followed:

> Instead of perceiving every thing in readiness for the assault, he [Pakenham] saw his troops in battle array, indeed, but not a ladder or fascine upon the field. The 44th, which was appointed to carry them, had either misunderstood or neglected their orders; and now headed the column of attack, without any means being provided for crossing the enemy's ditch, or scaling his rampart.
>
> The indignation of poor Pakenham on this occasion may be imagined, but cannot be described. Galloping towards Colonel Mullens, who led the 44th, he commanded him instantly to return with his regiment for the ladders, but the opportunity of planting them was lost, and though they were brought up, it was only to be scattered over the field by the frightened bearers. For our troops were by this time visible to the enemy. A dreadful fire was accordingly opened upon them, and they were mowed down by hundreds, while they stood waiting for orders.
>
> Seeing that all his well-laid plans were frustrated, Pakenham gave the word to advance, and the other regiments, leaving the 44th with the ladders and fascines behind them, rushed on to the assault.[13]

General Gibbs, enraged by Mullens's disobedience and seeing his men fall under the deadly American fire, shouted an angry vow: "Let me live till tomorrow and I'll hang him to the highest tree in that swamp!"[14] He urged his troops forward, despite the terrible losses being inflicted on them.

On the left side of Pakenham's front, near the levee, General Keane commanded the brigade composed of the Ninety-third Regiment—the vaunted Highlanders—the remaining companies of the Ninety-fifth Regiment, the light infantry companies of the Seventh and Forty-third regiments, and units of the West Indian regiment, about twelve hundred men altogether. The brigade's advance guard, commanded by Lieutenant Colonel Robert Rennie, was to storm the redoubt that Jackson had had constructed on his extreme right and spike the guns that enfiladed the British ranks as they advanced.

Seeing Gibbs's brigade under heavy fire and taking severe casualties, Pakenham now ordered the bulk of Keane's brigade—all but the advance unit that was attempting to take Jackson's redoubt—to execute a massive right oblique across the open field and attack Jackson's line just to the left of Gibbs's position, hoping apparently to spare Keane's brigade from the murderous American fire coming from the west bank (as one account saw the move)[15] or else to give needed assistance to Gibbs's riddled brigade, or both. The move away from the left and toward the right, however, left Colonel Rennie's advance unit without support in its storming of the redoubt. The action and the result were recorded by Gleig:

> On the left, a detachment of the 95th, 21st, and 4th, stormed a three gun battery and took it. Here they remained for some time in the expectation of support; but none arriving, and a strong column of the enemy forming for its recovery, they determined to anticipate the attack, and pushed on. The battery which they had taken was in advance of the body of the works, being cut off from it by a ditch, across which only a single plank was thrown. Along this plank did these brave men attempt to pass; but being opposed by overpowering numbers, they were repulsed; and the Americans, in turn, forcing their way into the battery, at length succeeded in recapturing it with immense slaughter.[16]

Gleig's account then turned its attention to the right side of Pakenham's line, where the main body of Keane's brigade had entered the fight beside Gibbs's brigade:

> On the right, again, the 21st and 4th being almost cut to pieces and thrown into some confusion by the enemy's fire, the 93d pushed on and took the lead. Hastening forward, our troops soon reached the ditch; but to scale the parapet without ladders was impossible. Some few, indeed, succeeded in entering the works, but these were instantly overpowered, most of them killed, and the rest taken; while as many as stood without were exposed to a sweeping fire, which cut them down by whole companies. It was in vain that the most obstinate courage was displayed. They fell by the hands of men whom they absolutely did not see; for the Americans, without so much as lifting their faces above the rampart, swung their firelocks by one arm over the wall, and discharged them directly upon their heads. The whole of the guns, likewise, from the opposite bank, kept up a well directed and deadly cannonade upon their flank; and thus were they destroyed without an opportunity being given of displaying their valour, or obtaining so much as revenge.[17]

Major Latour recounted the action on Jackson's left as seen from the defenders' side of the muddy rampart:

> Some of the enemy's troops had advanced into the wood towards the extremity of our line, to make a false attack, or to ascertain whether a real one were practicable. These the troops under general Coffee no sooner perceived, than they opened on them a brisk fire with their rifles, which quickly made them retire. The greater part of those who, on the column's being repulsed, had taken shelter in the thickets, only escaped our batteries to be killed by our musketry. During the whole hour that the attack lasted, our fire did not slacken for a single moment; and it seemed as though the artillery and musketry vied with each other in vivacity.[18]

An account by Alexander Walker, based on interviews with eyewitnesses, describes the vigorous American defense on the left of Jackson's line:

> The American batteries . . . were now playing upon them with awful effect, cutting huge gaps in their flanks. These intervals were, however, quickly filled up by the gallant Redcoats. The column advanced without pause or recoil steadily towards Spotts' long eighteen, and Chauveau's six. . . . Carroll's men were all in their places, with guns sighted on the summit of the parapet, whilst the Kentuckians, in two lines, stood behind, ready to take the places of the Tennesseans as soon as their pieces were discharged, thus making four lines in this part of the entrenchment. There they stood all as firm as veterans, as cool and calculating as American frontiersmen. All the batteries in the American line, including Patterson's marine battery on the right bank, began now to join those on the left in hurling a tornado of iron missiles into that serried, scarlet column, which shook and oscillated like a huge painted ship tossed on an angry sea.[19]

Jackson, on the line with his men, shouted instructions and exhortations to them: "Stand to your guns! Don't waste your ammunition! See that every shot tells!" Then, shouting again, he urged his troops, "Give it to them, boys! Let us finish this business today!"[20]

"Their bullets," Walker reported, "swept through the British column, cutting down the men by scores, and causing its head and flanks to melt away, like snow before a torrent."[21]

Latour described the action on Jackson's right, where the redoubt, with its enfilading guns, had been the first objective of Keane's brigade:

> After the attack on our left had commenced, the enemy made a column advance on the right by the road, and between the river and the levee. This column precipitately pushing forward, drove in our out-posts, following them so closely that it came up to the

> unfinished redoubt before we could fire on it more than two discharges of our cannon. A part of the column leaped into the ditch, and got into the redoubt through the embrasures, and over the parapet, overpowering with their numbers the few men they found there: others advancing along the brink of the river, killed the soldiers of the 7th, who bravely defended their post at the point of the bayonet, against a number much superior, and continually increasing.
>
> To get into the redoubt was not a very arduous achievement: the difficulty was to maintain possession of it, and clear the breastwork of the entrenchment in the rear of the redoubt, which still remained to be attacked. Already several British officers, though wounded, were bravely advancing to encourage their men by their example.
>
> Colonel Renee [Rennie], followed by two other officers of high rank, had begun to mount the breastwork, when the gallant volunteer riflemen under captain Beale, who defended the head of the line, made them all find their graves in that redoubt which they had mastered with so much gallantry. Meanwhile, captain Humphreys' battery No. 1, lieutenant Norris's No. 2, and the 7th regiment, which was the only one within musket-shot, kept up a tremendous fire on that column, which, like that on the left, was obliged to fall back in disorder, leaving the road, the levee, and the brink of the river, strewed with its dead and wounded.[22]

Pakenham's artillerymen were servicing their guns in emplacements that were as much as eighteen inches deep in muddy water, and their support of the infantry's advance proved no more effective than it had been on January 1. When Keane had been ordered to have his column execute a right oblique, marching diagonally across the field of fire, most of Pakenham's artillery was forced to cease firing, lest Keane's troops be hit by shot from their own guns. The battery that the British had erected on the river road on December 28 and the one they had established behind the demolished buildings of the Chalmette plantation on January 1 opened a brisk fire directed mainly against the Macarty house, Jackson's headquarters, evidently hoping to catch and strike Jackson and his staff there. They had long since left the building to take posts along the muddy rampart, however, and the British fire did no more than injure Jackson's assistant adjutant general, Major Chotard, and knock down four or five pillars of the house.

The American batteries on the right side of Jackson's line, Batteries 2, 3, and 4, directed their fire principally on Pakenham's artillery emplacements and dismounted several of the guns positioned near the Chalmette buildings. Jackson's Battery 1, on the far right of his line, poured grapeshot on the troops of Keane's advance unit as it retreated after being forced to relinquish the redoubt it had captured and briefly held. That done, the battery redirected its fire to strike the British battery directly opposite it and, after a two-hour bombardment, forced the British crew to abandon their gun.

Pakenham's troops were taking a bloody beating all along their front, Keane's brigade toward the center and Gibbs's brigade on the right. Colonel Robert Dale, commanding the Ninety-third Regiment, led his troops in their oblique advance across the bloodied field, expecting to assault the muddy rampart, but had to halt them when he discovered there were no fascines to cross the ditch or ladders to scale the mud wall. No sooner had he called the halt than he was shot dead. Earlier that morning he had handed his watch and a letter to the regimental physician, telling him, "Give these to my wife. I shall die at the head of my regiment."[23]

With their commander dead, the Highlanders simply stood on the battlefield, awaiting orders, while the fire from Jackson's line continued to riddle their ranks. One account said that "most of the men [were] crying from rage and vexation at seeing their comrades fall so fast, with no chance of a fight."[24]

Major Latour's account describes the battlefield at eight thirty that morning:

> The whole plain on the [American] left, as also the side of the river, from the road to the edge of the water, was covered with the British soldiers who had fallen. About four hundred wounded prisoners were taken, and at least double that number of wounded men escaped into the British camp; and, what might perhaps appear incredible, were there not many thousands ready to attest the fact, is that a space of ground, extending from the ditch of our lines to that on which the enemy drew up his troops, two hundred and fifty yards in length, by about two hundred in breadth, was literally covered with men, either dead or severely wounded.[25]

In the center of the battlefield and to the rear stood Pakenham's reserve, General Lambert's brigade, poised and ready, but Pakenham was not yet ready to press them into the failed assault. These were the troops about whom Pakenham had said to Major Harry Smith, "Those fellows would storm anything. But, indeed, so will the others, and when we are in New Orleans, I can depend on Lambert's reserve."[26] In anticipation of victory, Pakenham apparently planned to use Lambert's men to police the troops of the other brigades, to prevent the looting, rape, and breakdown of discipline that Pakenham had witnessed following victories in the Peninsular War. Pakenham would not tolerate such behavior by an army he commanded.

The men of Gibbs's brigade, recoiling from the massive fire from the American line, at last refused to pursue the charge against the rampart. Pakenham, riding toward the head of the stalled column and seeing the disorder of the troops of the Forty-fourth, cried out to them, "For shame! Recollect that you are British soldiers!" Pointing to the front, he shouted, "*This* is the road you ought to take!"[27]

Farther toward the front, Pakenham was met by Gibbs, angry and frustrated. "I am sorry to have to report to you that the troops will not obey me," Gibbs told his commander. "They will not follow me."[28]

Pakenham then, on horseback, grasping his hat in his hand, rushed forward to the front of Gibbs's column to take command, accompanied by several of his staff. Angered by what he was seeing, he exclaimed to anyone within hearing, "Lost from want of courage."[29]

As they rode, one of his staff officers shouted to the Highlanders, "Ninety-third! Have a little patience and you shall soon have your revenge!"[30]

At the head of the wavering column, in the face of the heavy American fire, Pakenham shouted for the troops to rally behind him. He rode to their front to lead them in a new attempt on the muddy rampart, some two hundred yards away. Suddenly a shot struck Pakenham (some sources say he was hit in his right arm, others say in the knee, and one account says he was hit twice, in both arm and knee). Another shot felled his horse. His senior aide-de-camp, Major Duncan Macdougall, quickly dismounted and helped Pakenham mount Macdougall's horse, which Pakenham did with difficulty. With a shattered right arm, he could not hold the reins, and Macdougall, on foot, led the horse forward, with Pakenham astride it, shouting, "Come on, brave Ninety-third!"

Seconds later he was struck again, this time in the spine. He toppled from the saddle and fell into Macdougall's arms. Unconscious, he was carried away from the line of fire and placed on the ground, under a large oak tree, where he was examined by a surgeon, who pronounced the wound mortal.

Moments later General Pakenham was dead.

General Gibbs still had not given up. In another attempt to rally his troops, he charged to within twenty yards of Jackson's line, where he was shot. Carried in agony from the field, he lingered through the rest of the day and a painful night and died the next day.

When Major John Tylden, who had succeeded Harry Smith as Pakenham's assistant adjutant general, went searching for General Keane to tell him of Pakenham's death, Tylden discovered that Keane, too, had been severely wounded and removed from the battle. The American fire was taking a terrible toll on British officers. The list of killed or wounded included not only three major generals but eight colonels and lieutenant colonels, six majors, 18 captains, and 54 lieutenants and other subalterns.[31]

According to some accounts, Pakenham's last words before being mortally wounded were orders for Major Macdougall to pass to General Lambert, instructing him to throw his brigade, the reserve, against Jackson's line. Other sources say Pakenham instructed Major Tylden to have Lambert order the advance. The sources further disagree on whether the reserve actually made the advance. Some accounts say that Tylden, upon receiving Pakenham's order, directed the bugler to sound the call for Lambert's brigade to advance, but as the bugler lifted his instrument to his lips, he was shot in the arm, the bugle fell to the ground, and the signal for the advance was never given. In any case, either following a march forward in which Lambert's brigade began taking casualties and which Lambert soon halted, or because Lambert never received an order to advance, his brigade did not attempt to assault the American line. Lambert had apparently decided that the destruction of two more regiments, those of the reserve, would be pointless. Thus he held his ground but stood ready to cover the withdrawal of the two other brigades, both now broken, their troops disorganized and having effectively quit the fight.

Lambert was now the senior army officer in the field, and command of His Majesty's army devolved upon him. Unsure of what to do, Lambert left his brigade on the field and withdrew to confer with Admiral Cochrane. Following the meeting with Cochrane, Lambert ordered Colonel Dickson, of Pakenham's staff, to cross the river and find out if whatever position Colonel Thornton had gained could be held. Dickson did so, learning in the process that Colonel Thornton, as well as Captain James Money, commanding a naval detachment in Thornton's brigade, had both been seriously wounded and taken back to the east side of the river.

When Dickson returned and reported to Lambert that the British position on the west bank required 2,000 men to hold it, Lambert conferred again with Cochrane and then issued orders for all troops to return to the east side of the river. He also ordered Dickson to destroy the four eighteen-pounders and four twenty-four-pounder carronades that Pakenham's forces had so laboriously moved into forward positions to support the failed assault on Jackson's line. General Lambert, it now was clear, believed His Majesty's forces had had enough in their disastrously vain attempt to take New Orleans.

Not long after noon, the guns and musketry of both sides having fallen silent, a three-man British detail—an officer, a bugler, and a soldier carrying a white flag—approached Jackson's muddy rampart and halted some three hundred yards from it. There the bugler sounded a loud blast that brought a host of defenders to the rampart to peer over it. General Jackson ordered an aide, Colonel Butler, and two other officers to go see what the British detail had in mind. After a courteous exchange of greetings, the British officer handed Butler a letter addressed to the American commander in chief.

Jackson was at the Macarty house when he received the letter. It contained a proposal for a twenty-four-hour cease-fire, so that the dead and wounded could be removed from the field. It was signed, "Lambert, Major-General."

Jackson had no idea who Lambert was or what authority he had for offering a cease-fire. It took him three days to find out. In the meantime, many of the British wounded were being attended to by the Americans. Major Latour reported that nearly four hundred wounded British prisoners were nursed in New Orleans by civilian volunteers, who provided mattresses, "all kinds of refreshments and every attendance that their situation required."[32]

On January 11, after days of stalling by Jackson to give American reinforcements time to reach the embattled defensive posts on the west bank of the river and by Lambert to hide the fact that the British had lost their commander in chief, Jackson dispatched a note to Lambert saying that in order for their exchange of communications to continue, the commanders in chief of both armies would have to identify themselves. "I have the honor to Command the American forces in this quarter," he told Lambert.[33]

Lambert quickly responded. "I have the Honor to . . . inform you that I am Commr. of the Forces on the left Bank of Mississippi."[34]

Jackson more or less dictated the terms of an agreement, which stipulated, among other things, that hostilities on the east side of the river—but not on the west side, where things had not gone so well for the defenders—would cease until noon the next day. During that time, the wounded would be collected and the dead would be buried.

Now came the hours of horror that revealed how grotesquely one-sided the battle had been. Driven from the field by the intense American fire, the columns of His Majesty's army had left behind on the stubbled cane fields of Chalmette, by the British count, 291 killed and 1,262 wounded. The British also reported 484 taken prisoner, making a casualty total of 2,037. The illustrious Ninety-third, the Highlander Regiment, had suffered worst, losing half its men. The American estimate of the British casualties, reported by Jackson to Secretary of War James Monroe, was more than 2,600, counting 400 killed, 1,400 wounded, and 500 taken prisoner.

Reports of American losses vary. Jackson reported to Monroe that he had lost 7 killed and 6 wounded in the main battle, fought on the morning of January 8, but had lost a few more men in the skirmishing that continued for the next few days. The official report of American casualties, filed by Jackson's adjutant general, Colonel Robert Butler, put total American losses on both sides of the river on January 8 at 71, including 13 killed, 39 wounded, and 19 missing. Losses for four days of fighting on both sides of the river were listed as 333, including 55 killed, 185 wounded, and 93 missing.[35]

Lieutenant Gleig witnessed the dramatic one-sidedness of the battle as he sat in the saddle of his mount and watched the recovery of the dead:

> Parties were immediately sent out to collect and bury their fallen comrades. Prompted by curiosity, I mounted my horse, and rode to the front; but of all the sights I ever witnessed, that which met me there was beyond comparison the most shocking, and the most

> humiliating. Within the small compass of a few hundred yards, were gathered together nearly a thousand bodies, all of them arrayed in British uniforms. Not a single American was among them; all were English; and they were thrown by dozens into shallow holes, scarcely deep enough to furnish them with a slight covering of earth. . . . I confess that when I beheld the scene, I hung down my head half in sorrow, half in anger. . . . I turned my horse's head and galloped back to the camp.[36]

Jackson's victory—America's victory—had been simply overwhelming.

## ∴ 20 ∴

# The Retreat

Colonel Thornton's mission, which had begun so unpromisingly, had gone remarkably well. He had finally crossed the river as the sun rose on January 8, and after being carried off course by the river's powerful current, he had landed his 560 men, apparently all that the available boats could hold, at Andry's plantation, some one thousand yards below the spot he had intended. He immediately set out to capture the American batteries, which already were firing across the expanse of the river into the ranks of Pakenham's advancing troops.

Thornton's men, outnumbering the defenders, had quickly routed the first thin lines of American troops they encountered on the Morin plantation and by ten o'clock that morning had approached the main line of defense established by Major General David Morgan, commanding Jackson's troops on the west side of the Mississippi. The line, which included Commodore Patterson's artillery batteries, was directly opposite the Chalmette battlefield. Feinting an attack on Morgan's left, the strong side of the line, and simultaneously attacking the center, Thornton had at the same time sent Lieutenant Colonel Richard Gubbins with two infantry companies to turn the Americans' right flank, which they did, routing the Kentucky militiamen posted there.

Morgan's line had then disintegrated, his troops hurriedly falling back to the next line of defense, at the Boisgervais plantation, and the batteries of Commodore Patterson on the left side of the line being so quickly overrun there was not enough time to spike the guns, which had been bombarding Pakenham's troops on the east side of the river. Thornton had captured sixteen pieces of artillery, including a ten-inch howitzer that was inscribed, "Taken at the Surrender of York Town 1781."

Some twelve hundred yards beyond the overrun line, the British pursuit of the defenders had been halted on General Lambert's orders, delivered by Major Harry Smith. The orders called for a withdrawal from the west bank, back across the Mississippi. By then Thornton had been wounded and had already been taken back to the east side of the river. Lieutenant Colonel Gubbins had taken over for him. Not long after the halt, Colonel Dickson, on his mission for General Lambert, had arrived on the west bank, surveyed the situation, and returned to Lambert to report that the British position could not be held with fewer than two thousand troops.

American reinforcements, meanwhile, were on the way. Jackson had ordered General Jean Marie Humbert, a veteran of the army of the French Republic, to lead a force of four hundred men across the river to support General Morgan. He also dispatched Jean Lafitte to the west bank to help plan a defense against a British advance up the west side of the river. Jackson apparently was hopeful that Humbert would get the job done, and he stalled the cease-fire negotiations until Humbert and Morgan had recaptured the former position opposite the Chalmette plantation.

The withdrawal ordered by Lambert, however, made Humbert's a moot mission, though Jackson remained alert to British moves on both sides of the river. On January 10 he sent word to General Morgan instructing him "to set fire to and destroy every house, and remove the fences, in front of your position which may in the Smallest degree interfere with its defence. . . . Your post must be defended—the safety of the Country and my army in a great measure depends on it."[1]

While Jackson worried about a possible flanking action on his line by the British on the west side of the Mississippi, Admiral Cochrane, who thought Lambert's order to withdraw from the west bank was a big mistake, was planning to do exactly what Jackson worried about. The headstrong Cochrane believed he could send a fleet up the Mississippi from the gulf, bombard New Orleans into submission, and attack

Jackson from the rear—*if* the British ships could get past Fort Saint Philip and the American fortification at English Turn, Fort Saint Leon. It was a big "if."

On January 9 a flotilla composed of two bomb ships, a brig, a sloop of war, and a tender moved into position to bombard Fort Saint Philip from a bend in the river about four thousand yards away and just out of the effective range of the fort's guns. From that position Cochrane's ships opened fire, launching shells at a rate of one every two minutes for hours. The bombardment stopped at nightfall but resumed the next day and continued throughout the day, all without substantial effect on the fort or its garrison. The bombardment was renewed every day until the morning of January 18, when the effort was finally given up as futile. Its losses were two killed and seven wounded and not as much as ten feet of it had been left unmarked by the more than one thousand shells rained upon it, but defiant Fort Saint Philip and its forbidding guns were intact. The river route to New Orleans was still barred to the enemy. Cochrane and his navy had been thwarted.

Ever since the ending of the cease-fire, Jackson's army had continued its harassing fire on Lambert's troops on the east side of the river. Gleig recorded the misery of the British troops still encamped at the Villere plantation. "We never closed our eyes in peace," he wrote, "for we were sure to be awakened before many minutes elapsed, by the splash of a round shot or shell in the mud beside us. . . . Besides all this, heavy rains now set in, accompanied with violent storms of thunder and lightening, which . . . gave place to keen frosts. Thus we were alternately wet and frozen; wet all day, and frozen all night."[2]

What was more, the Mississippi, swollen with rainwater, spilled over the levee early one morning and flooded the crude shelters that the tentless British troops had erected in the field. There was water everywhere, covering everything, and it did not begin to recede until sunset.

In such miserable conditions, desertions were occurring in alarming numbers. General Lambert, slowly deliberating what his next move should be, at last decided that it was time to pull out. He began making preparations for a withdrawal, which he would make stealthily, not allowing Jackson a chance to attack while His Majesty's troops were in flight.

On January 17 Lambert sent a message to Jackson proposing an exchange of prisoners; Jackson, agreeing, appointed Edward Livingston to work out the details with Lambert's representative, Harry Smith. The next day, while Jackson's mind was presumably on the prisoner exchange, Lambert began the withdrawal of his army.

Unseen by the Americans, British troops had been extending the road they had built along Bayou Mazant when they had first arrived. With insufficient boats to evacuate his troops quickly, Lambert had decided to have his men march out, and to do so required construction of a road across the marshes, all the way to the shore of Lake Borgne. The road's construction was a feat of make-do engineering and human perseverance as work parties collected reeds and tied them together to form fill on the watery morass and built crude bridges from tree limbs.

After nine days of practically continuous labor, during which Lambert's troops made no response to the American harassment of their encampment and sentry outposts, Lambert began evacuating all his wounded who could be moved, carrying them to the ships of Cochrane's fleet anchored on the margin of Lake Borgne. Behind the wounded came the baggage and stores and then the light artillery. The heavy guns, about ten pieces that were mounted in front of the British encampment and along the levee, were left in place, too cumbersome to move.

By January 17 all except Lambert's infantry units had been evacuated. At the last minute the big guns that were being left behind were spiked. On January 18, in the gloom of early evening, the infantry regiments began moving out across the jerry-built road, the Twenty-first going first, followed at one-hour intervals by the Fourth, then the Ninety-third, then the Eighty-fifth, which was Lieutenant Gleig's regiment. He recounted the desperate march:

> While our route lay along the high road and beside the brink of the river [bayou], the march was agreeable enough; but as soon as

> we began to enter upon the path through the marsh, all comfort was at an end. Being constructed of materials so slight, and resting upon a foundation so infirm, the treading of the first corps unavoidably beat it to pieces; those which followed were therefore compelled to flounder on in the best way they could; and by the time the rear of the column gained the morass, all trace of a way had entirely disappeared. But not only were the reeds torn asunder and sunk by the pressure of those who had gone before, but the bog itself, which at first might have furnished a few spots of firm footing, was trodden into the consistency of mud. The consequence was that every step sunk us to the knees, and frequently higher. . . . I myself beheld an unfortunate wretch gradually sink till he totally disappeared. I saw him flounder in, heard his cry for help, and ran forward with the intention of saving him; but before I had taken a second step I myself sunk at once as high as the breast. How I contrived to keep myself from smothering is more than I can tell, for I felt no solid bottom under me, and continued slowly to go deeper and deeper, till the mud reached my arms. Instead of endeavoring to help the poor soldier, of whom nothing could now be seen except the head and hands, I was forced to beg assistance for myself; when a leathern canteen strap being thrown to me, I laid hold of it, and was dragged out, just as my fellow sufferer became invisible.
>
> Over roads such as these did we continue our journey during the whole of the night; and in the morning reached a place called Fisherman's Huts, upon the margin of the lake. . . . Here at length we were ordered to halt; and perhaps I never rejoiced more sincerely at any order than at this.[3]

After Gleig's regiment had passed through the ordeal, the last of the regiments, the Ninety-fifth, the Forty-third, and the Seventh, followed by the army's rearguard pickets, forced their way through the dangerous morass. It took those troops more than ten hours to trudge and slog across the nine miles of marsh and mud.

So stealthily and deceptively had Lambert's army slipped away from the field of battle that its absence was not discovered by General Jackson until dawn on January 19. The British forward outposts appeared suspiciously still, and a reconnaissance patrol confirmed that Lambert's forces had quit their positions and moved out. Soon after that, a British physician came to Jackson from the Villere plantation and delivered a letter from Lambert. In it Lambert told Jackson that he had yielded the field and, for the time being, abandoned the assault on New Orleans. He also asked Jackson to assume care for about eighty British soldiers whose wounds were too severe to allow them to be evacuated. Jackson passed to his surgeon general, Doctor David Kerr, the burden of the British wounded, many of whom were loaded aboard a river steamboat and transported to New Orleans to be treated for their wounds.

To verify Lambert's statements, Jackson ordered Colonel Hinds and his Mississippi cavalrymen to ride up along the Villere canal and on as far as possible along the route Lambert's army had taken in its retreat. Major Pierre Lacoste and a detachment of experienced hunters were sent to search the woods for stragglers. Jackson himself, with his staff, rode over to examine the empty British encampment.

Jackson had no intention of pursuit. The British strength, he realized, was combat in an open field, which he had not permitted Pakenham or Lambert to exercise. His strength, he also realized, was his army's ability to defend a narrow front behind a fortified wall. Jackson refused to be drawn from that advantageous defensive position. He distrusted Cochrane and Lambert both and believed that they still might, he said, "attempt some act of madness."[4] He would stay put a while and see what transpired.

But His Majesty's beaten army was not coming back. Those members of it fortunate enough to have survived all the hazards of battle and of nature retraced the wearisome route they had traveled with great expectations seven weeks earlier. Regiment after dejected regiment embarked in small boats and were ferried across Lake Borgne to where the ships of Admiral Cochrane's fleet lay at anchor near the gulf's entrance to the lake. Lieutenant Gleig again captured the mood of his comrades as they boarded their navy's vessels and prepared to leave:

> By the end of the month [January], we were all once more on board our former ships. But our return was far from triumphant. We, who only seven weeks ago had set out in the surest confidence of glory, and, I may add, of emolument, were brought back dispirited and dejected. Our ranks were woefully thinned, our chiefs slain, our clothing tattered and filthy, and even our discipline in some degree injured. A gloomy silence reigned throughout the armament, except when it was broken by the voice of lamentation over fallen friends; and the interior of each ship presented a scene well calculated to prove the shortsightedness of human hope, and human prudence. . . .
>
> . . . so great was the despondency which had taken possession of men's minds, that not even a rumour respecting the next point of attack, obtained circulation; while a sullen carelessness, a sort of indifference as to what might happen, seemed to have succeeded all our wonted curiosity, and confidence of success, in every undertaking.
>
> In this state we remained wind-bound till the 4th of February, when, at length, getting under weigh, the fleet ran down as far as Cat Island.[5]

Although the departing soldiers did not yet know it, the war was over. The diplomats had ended it even before the Battle of New Orleans was fought. All the carnage, all the misery had been for nought. But at least the men would soon be going home.

With them, returning to Ireland, his disemboweled corpse borne in a barrel of rum, their gallant fallen commander, Major General Sir Edward Pakenham, was also going home.

# ∴ 21 ∴

# The Celebration

In New Orleans, jubilation burst into the streets. When the big guns, whose thunderous fire could be heard miles away, had fallen silent, people in the city received their first notice that the battle was over. Many New Orleanians had earlier left the city and gathered at a distance behind Jackson's line to watch the battle.

News of the battle's end had spread quickly into the city. People poured from their houses and into the streets to join their neighbors in cheering the city's defenders and the happy conclusion of their efforts. Alexander Walker, who was in New Orleans at the time, described the city's outburst of exultation:

> The anxious spectators and listeners in the rear [of Jackson's line] quickly comprehending the glorious result, caught up the sounds of exultation and echoed them along the banks of the river, until the glad tidings reached the city, sent a thrill of joy throughout its limits, and brought the whole population into the streets to give full vent to their extravagant joy. The streets resounded with hurras. The only military force in the city, the veterans, under their indefatigable commander, the noble old patriot soldier, Captain De Buys, hastily assembled, and with a drum and fife paraded the streets amid the salutes and hurras of the people, the waving of the snowy handkerchiefs of the ladies, and the boundless exultation and noisy joy of the juveniles. . . .
>
> From the city the news of Jackson's triumph flew rapidly through the neighboring country.[1]

Amid the cheering and merrymaking in the city came more sobering news from the battlefield. Walker described it, too:

> There came a messenger, whose horse had been severely taxed, who inquired for the residences of the physicians in the city, and dashed madly through the streets in pursuit of surgeons and apothecaries. All of the profession, whether in practice or not, were required to proceed to the lines, as their services were needed immediately. "For whom?" was the question which agitated the bosom of many an anxious parent and devoted wife, and for a moment clouded and checked the general hilarity. Soon it was known, however, that this demand for surgeons was on account of the enemy. All who possessed any knowledge of the curative art, who could amputate or set a limb, or take up an artery, hurried to the camp. Next there came up a message from the camp to dispatch all the carts and other vehicles to the lines. . . .
>
> It was late in the day before the purpose of this order was clearly perceived, as a long and melancholy procession of these carts, followed by a crowd of men, was seen slowly and silently wending their way along the levee from the field of battle. They contained the British wounded; and those who followed in the rear were the prisoners.[2]

General Jackson, remaining vigilant and cautious, unaware of Lambert's intentions to withdraw, shifted his troops so as to command every approach to the city, in case Lambert should try a new route of attack. But at last satisfied there would be no new assault, on January 19, from his headquarters beside the battlefield, he wrote to Secretary of War Monroe to advise him of the British withdrawal, telling him that "there is very little doubt but his last exertions have been made in this quarter, at any rate, for the present season."[3]

On that same day, Jackson also wrote to Abbé Guillaume Dubourg, the chief administrator of the Catholic diocese of Louisiana, asking that he arrange a service in Saint Louis Cathedral to give public thanks for "the signal interposition of Heaven, in giving success to our arms against the enemy." The service, Jackson said, would be "in token of the great assistance we have received from the Ruler of all events, and of our humble sense of it."[4]

To his victorious army Jackson was also publicly grateful. Each corps had read to it Jackson's general orders, which praised their accomplishments and thanked them for their efforts. His thanks and praise also went to the Baratarians, to Dominique You, Renato Beluche, and the Lafitte brothers in particular.

On Saturday, January 21, 1815, leaving the Seventh Infantry Regiment at the rampart on the Rodriguez canal and a Louisiana militia unit guarding the Villere plantation, Jackson formed up the remainder of his troops and marched them in a long column to New Orleans. The streets were lined with the city's grateful residents, welcoming and cheering the troops. "Every countenance," Major Latour reported effusively, "was expressive of gratitude—joy sparkled in every feature, on beholding fathers, brothers, husbands, sons, who had so recently saved the lives, fortunes, and honour of their families, by repelling an enemy come to conquer and subjugate the country."[5] The curfew that Jackson had earlier ordered was lifted, and the celebrations around the city went on through the night.

Monday, January 23, was the day set aside for the thanksgiving service at the cathedral, but the service became just one event in the day's long program of celebration. An artillery salute in the morning sounded the commencement of the festivities. Alexander Walker described the scene and the ceremonies:

> The old cathedral was burnished up for the occasion. Evergreens decorated the entrance and the interior. The Public Square, or Plaza, blazed with beauty, splendor and elegance. In its centre stood a graceful triumphal arch, supported by six Corinthian columns and festooned with evergreens and flowers. Beneath the arch stood two young children on pedestals, holding a laurel wreath, whilst near them, as if their guardian angels, was a bright

> damsel, representing Liberty, and a more sedate one personifying Justice. From the arch to the entrance of the cathedral the loveliest girls of the city had been ranged in two rows, to represent the various States and Territories. They were dressed in pure white, with blue veils and silver stars on their brows. Each bore a small flag, inscribed with the name of the State she represented, and a small basket trimmed with blue ribands and full of flowers. . . .
>
> Precisely at the appointed time, Gen. Jackson appeared with his staff at the gate of the plaza fronting the river. He was received with salvos of artillery. Entering the square, he was conducted to the arch, where the two little girls, reaching forward with blushing, smiling faces, placed the laurel wreath on his brow. . . .
>
> . . . the Hero, supported by his staff, is led to the entrance of the Cathedral. Here he is met by the patriotic and revered Abbé Dubourg, clad in pontifical robes and supported by a college of priests. . . . He is then conducted into the Cathedral and escorted to a conspicuous seat near the altar. *Te Deum* is then chanted in the grand and impressive manner in which that melodious outburst of gratitude is usually rendered by the choirs of the Roman Catholic church. The people join in a noble hymn.[6]

At last the ceremony was concluded, and Jackson, no doubt fatigued, retired to his quarters in the Faubourg Marigny, a suburb of the city. The revels, however, continued throughout the day. When night came, the city was illuminated, and the celebration continued until, Walker wrote, "At last the people, wearied by the wild enthusiasm and inexhaustible joyfulness of the great event, sunk into slumbers that were no longer disturbed by dreams of sack, ruin, bloodshed and devastation."[7]

The battle was won, the thanks said, and the celebration made. The next day, January 24, 1815, General Jackson returned to his duties as commander of his victorious army.

# Conclusion

THE beaten British army that General Pakenham had so briefly and disastrously led withdrew from Louisiana and sailed to Dauphin Island, near the entrance to Mobile Bay. There the troops encamped and recovered. Still harboring hopes for the capture of New Orleans, Admiral Cochrane persuaded General Lambert they should attack Mobile; once it was captured, they would proceed inland on a new march against New Orleans.

On February 8, 1815, they opened an assault on Fort Bowyer in Mobile Bay, the first step of an attack on Mobile. Three days later, the American commander surrendered the fort and its garrison of 370 men.

On March 14, before Cochrane's planned attack on Mobile could be executed, a British frigate brought news that the war was over. The next day the British invaders reembarked aboard their ships and sailed for home.

In Ghent, Belgium, on December 24, 1814, the negotiations between the United States and Britain that had begun on August 8, 1814, had been concluded with a treaty that ended the War of 1812. The United States had withdrawn its insistence on an end to the impressment of seamen; Britain had dropped its insistence on *uti possidetis,* the provision that meant each country would retain whatever territory it held at the end of the war. The treaty failed to even mention any of the maritime issues that had provoked the United States to go to war. It merely restored the *status quo ante bellum;* the situation between the two nations would be again as it was before the war.

Unfortunately for those who died or were maimed at the Battle of New Orleans, news of the agreement did not reach America until weeks after the battle had been fought. Unofficial reports of the treaty reached New Orleans on February 10. On February 16 the United States Senate ratified the treaty, and General Jackson received confirmation of the ratification on March 13. He then revoked martial law in New Orleans and dismissed the militias. On April 6, 1815, Jackson, with his wife, Rachel, and adopted son, Andrew Junior, left New Orleans and returned to the Hermitage, their home in Nashville.

From his victory at New Orleans, which vaulted him into national prominence, Jackson went on to other successes, seizing Florida from the Spanish in 1818 and thereby forcing Spain to yield Florida, for a price, to the United States. He then became Florida's governor. In October 1823 he was elected to the United States Senate from Tennessee; he was elected president of the United States in 1828 and reelected in 1832.

Those who had fought in Jackson's army at New Orleans moved on with their lives as well. The pirates of Barataria, on Jackson's recommendation, were pardoned for their previous offenses. Most of them, however, resumed their piracy. Renato Beluche joined the forces of South American liberator Simón Bolívar and became a distinguished admiral. Dominique You returned to the sea for a time, but in poor health retired to New Orleans and operated a bar.

The Lafitte brothers became paid Spanish agents, as did Lacarriere Latour. The Lafittes later returned to piracy, with their base at Galveston, but were forced out by the United States Navy. From there they slipped out of public notice.

Jackson's friend and aide Edward Livingston served in the House of Representatives, in the Senate, and as secretary of state in Jackson's administration. William Claiborne continued as governor of Louisiana until he died of a liver ailment at age forty in 1817. Daniel Patterson rose to the rank of captain in the United States Navy, commanded a squadron in the Mediterranean Sea, and was commander of the Washington Navy Yard when he died in 1839.

Those who served with Pakenham also went on with their lives. Though his career languished, Vice Admiral Sir Alexander Cochrane was promoted to admiral in 1819. Major General John Lambert served under Wellington at the Battle of Waterloo, was promoted to general in 1841, took over a command in Jamaica, and died in 1847. Major General John Keane recovered from his wounds and later distinguished himself in the British campaign in Afghanistan and was created a baron. Colonel William Thornton became a lieutenant general and was knighted in 1836. Lieutenant Colonel Thomas Mullens was court-martialed and dismissed from the army for disobedience and neglect.

Among all those who fought at New Orleans, none was a more tragic figure than the British army commander himself, Sir Edward Pakenham. Cut down at age thirty-six, he had no chance to redeem his reputation after the enormous failure at New Orleans, no opportunity to write a memoir to explain it. He had, however, died a hero, gallant to the end. He and his fallen comrade-in-arms, Major General Sir Samuel Gibbs, were posthumously honored by their country with a statue of them both, which stands in Saint Paul's Cathedral in London.

Some who have written about the battle have tried to explain the spectacular British failure. Pakenham, as commander, gets the blame. What is clear is that Pakenham was presented with a plan of attack that was not his, that he acquiesced to it despite misgivings, and that his death foreclosed any possibility of his redesigning the British attack after its initial failure. The flaw in Pakenham's personality that allowed him to be intimidated by Cochrane into accepting Cochrane's attack plan is also clear. Pakenham's apparent meekness, or fearfulness, toward Cochrane stands in bold contrast to the aggressiveness and take-charge personality of Jackson.

At the heart of the British failure, however, was British arrogance and disdain for Americans and their fighting ability, feelings that apparently pervaded the British officer corps at New Orleans, from Cochrane down to Lieutenant Gleig. That arrogance let them believe the ragtag American forces were no match for the veteran warriors of Wellington's armies. It let them believe they would take New Orleans no matter the disadvantages of their position or attack plan.

Andrew Jackson and his makeshift army of American patriots, of many backgrounds, like the people of the nation they served, changed that way of thinking about Americans. They convincingly showed the world and their fellow citizens the strength and character of America, a people, a nation, made proud and confident by Jackson's triumph.

Because of the monumental victory at New Orleans, the young nation that Jackson felt it was his mission to defend became, for the first time, a respected member of the world community of nations.

# NOTES

### NOTES TO CHAPTER 1

1. James Parton, in *General Jackson,* says that Andrew and Elizabeth landed in Charleston, South Carolina.
2. James, *Andrew Jackson the Border Captain,* p. 7.
3. Some sources say the Crawfords' house was in North Carolina; others say it was in South Carolina. Jackson himself claimed to have been born in South Carolina.
4. James, *Andrew Jackson the Border Captain,* p. 11.
5. Parton, *General Jackson,* p. 5.
6. James, *Andrew Jackson the Border Captain,* pp. 18–19.
7. Buell, *History of Andrew Jackson,* vol. I, p. 64.
8. Parton, *General Jackson,* p. 11.
9. James, *Andrew Jackson the Border Captain,* p. 30.
10. Buell, *History of Andrew Jackson,* vol. I, p. 56.

### NOTES TO CHAPTER 2

1. Buell, *History of Andrew Jackson,* vol. I, p. 63.
2. Parton, *General Jackson,* p. 18.
3. James, *Andrew Jackson the Border Captain,* p. 36.
4. Ibid.
5. Ibid.
6. Ibid.
7. Parton, *Life of Andrew Jackson,* vol. I, p. 104.
8. Buell, *History of Andrew Jackson,* vol. I, p. 68.
9. Parton, *General Jackson,* p. 21.
10. James, *Andrew Jackson the Border Captain,* p. 40.
11. Buell, *History of Andrew Jackson,* vol. I, p. 68.
12. Parton, *Life of Andrew Jackson,* vol. I, pp. 122–23.
13. James, *Andrew Jackson the Border Captain,* pp. 54–55.
14. Parton, *Life of Andrew Jackson,* vol. I, p. 133.
15. Ibid., pp. 168–69.
16. Remini, *Life of Andrew Jackson,* p. 18.
17. Ibid., p. 23.

### NOTES TO CHAPTER 3

1. Scott, *Pakenham,* p. 6.
2. Ibid., p. 7.
3. Ibid.
4. Ibid., p. 6.
5. Ibid., p. 7.
6. Ibid., p. 8.
7. MacManus, *Story of the Irish Race,* p. 500.
8. Ibid., p. 499.
9. Scott, *Pakenham,* p. 11.
10. Ibid.
11. Ibid., pp. 12–13.

12. Ibid., p. 13.
13. Ibid.
14. Ibid.
15. Ibid., p. 15.
16. Hibbert, *Wellington,* p. 56.
17. Ibid.
18. Scott, *Pakenham,* p. 16.
19. Hibbert, *Wellington,* p. 57.
20. Ibid., pp. 62–63.
21. Ibid., p. 228.
22. Scott, *Pakenham,* p. 17.

### NOTES TO CHAPTER 4

1. James, *Life of Andrew Jackson,* p. 70.
2. Ibid.
3. Remini, in *The Life of Andrew Jackson,* pp. 25–26, makes a strong case for the wedding, if there actually was one, having taken place in 1790, a year earlier than John Overton put it and a year before Robards received approval to sue for divorce. Remini insists there is no documentary evidence of the wedding having occurred in either year and leaves much doubt that one did occur. Andy and Rachel, he suggests, may have simply cohabited, although doing so would have been entirely inconsistent with Jackson's character, with his ambitions, and with the high regard in which he and Rachel were both later held in Nashville. The whole truth remains beyond the grasp of research.
4. James, *Andrew Jackson the Border Captain,* pp. 70–71.
5. Ibid., pp. 74–75.
6. Ibid.
7. Ibid., p. 77.
8. Remini, *Life of Andrew Jackson,* p. 22.
9. Ibid., p. 19.
10. James, *Andrew Jackson the Border Captain,* p. 74.
11. Blount to Robertson, November 22, 1794, quoted by Alice B. Keith, "The North Carolina Blount Brothers in Business and Politics, 1783–1812" (Ph.D. diss., University of North Carolina at Chapel Hill, 1940), p. 412.
12. Remini, *Life of Andrew Jackson,* p. 32.
13. Remini, *Andrew Jackson and His Indian Wars,* p. 38.
14. *Annals of Congress,* 4th Cong., 2nd sess., pp. 1738–39.
15. Ibid., p. 1742.
16. Ibid.
17. Letter to Robert Hays, November 2, 1797, Jackson Papers, Library of Congress.
18. Bassett, *Life of Andrew Jackson,* p. 32.

### NOTES TO CHAPTER 5

1. Cronin, *Napoleon,* p. 47.
2. Ibid.
3. Ibid., p. 77.
4. Markham, *Napoleon,* p. 28.
5. Schom, *Napoleon Bonaparte,* p. 49.
6. Cronin, *Napoleon,* p. 120.
7. Ibid., p. 126.
8. Ibid.
9. Schom, *Napoleon Bonaparte,* p. 65.
10. Ibid., p. 63.
11. Ibid.
12. Ibid.
13. Ibid., p. 69.
14. Cronin, *Napoleon,* p. 144.
15. Schom, *Napoleon Bonaparte,* p. 73.
16. Ibid., pp. 81–82.
17. Ibid., pp. 289–90.
18. Louis Antoine Fauvelet De Bourrienne, *Memoirs of Napoleon Bonaparte, to Which Are Added an Account of the Important Events of the Hundred Days of*

*Napoleon's Surrender to the English and of His Residence and Death at St. Helena* (London, 1885), vol. V, pp. 62–63.
19. Schom, *Napoleon Bonaparte,* p. 293.
20. Ibid., p. 333.
21. D. A. Bingham, *A Selection from the Letters and Despatches of Napoleon* (London, 1884), vol. II, p. 324.

NOTES TO CHAPTER 6

1. Hibbert, *Wellington,* p. 68.
2. Ibid.
3. Ibid., p. 73.
4. Ibid.
5. Ibid., p. 74.
6. Ibid.
7. Scott, *Pakenham,* p. 16.
8. Ibid., p. 17.

NOTES TO CHAPTER 7

1. Hibbert, *Wellington,* p. 102.
2. Scott, *Pakenham,* p. 21.
3. Ibid.
4. Ibid., p. 22.
5. Ibid., p. 23.
6. Ibid.
7. Hibbert, *Wellington,* p. 104.
8. Scott, *Pakenham,* p. 26.
9. Ibid.
10. Ibid.
11. Ibid., p. 27.
12. Ibid.
13. Ibid.
14. Ibid.
15. Ibid., p. 30.
16. Ibid.
17. Ibid., p. 31.
18. Muir, *Salamanca 1812,* p. 41.
19. Ibid.
20. Hibbert, *Wellington,* p. 123.
21. Muir, *Salamanca 1812,* p. 85.
22. James Campbell, *The British Army As It Was—Is—and Ought to Be* (London: T & W Boone, 1840), pp. 224–25.
23. Ibid.
24. Weller, *Wellington in the Peninsula,* p. 227.
25. Muir, *Salamanca 1812,* p. 101.
26. Duke of Wellington, *The Dispatches of Field Marshal the Duke of Wellington* (London: Parker, Furnivall and Parker, 1844–47), vol. VI, p. 55.

NOTES TO CHAPTER 8

1. Rakove, *James Madison,* p. 139.
2. Hickey, *War of 1812,* p. 11.
3. Ibid.
4. Ibid., p. 21.
5. Ibid., p. 24.
6. Rakove, *James Madison,* p. 155.
7. Hickey, *War of 1812,* pp. 25–26.
8. Ibid.
9. Ibid.
10. Ibid., p. 25.
11. Ibid., p. 26.
12. Ibid.
13. Ibid.
14. Letter from a Federalist dated January 6, 1812, printed in the *Richmond Enquirer,* January 23, 1812.
15. Rakove, *James Madison,* p. 157.

NOTES TO CHAPTER 9

1. Remini, *Andrew Jackson and His Indian Wars,* p. 55.
2. Ibid., p. 56.
3. Ibid., p. 58.
4. Ibid.
5. Remini, *Life of Andrew Jackson,* pp. 65–66.
6. Remini, *Andrew Jackson and His Indian Wars,* p. 59.
7. Ibid., p. 60.
8. Bassett, *Life of Andrew Jackson,* p. 84.

9. Ibid., p. 86.
10. Remini, *Andrew Jackson and His Indian Wars,* p. 60.
11. Parton, *General Jackson,* p. 60.
12. Ibid., pp. 59–63. See also James, *Andrew Jackson,* pp. 161–63.
13. Bassett, *Life of Andrew Jackson,* p. 69.
14. Parton suggests it was hours later; James suggests it was days later.
15. Remini, *Life of Andrew Jackson,* p. 72.
16. Sources differ on the number killed.
17. James, *Andrew Jackson the Border Captain,* p. 168.
18. Ibid.
19. Remini, *Andrew Jackson and His Indian Wars,* p. 64.
20. Sources differ on who the officers were who were summoned, whether brigade commanders only, all field-grade officers, or all officers.
21. James, *Andrew Jackson the Border Captain,* p. 172.
22. Owsley, *Struggle for the Gulf Borderlands,* p. 68.
23. Ibid., p. 69.
24. James, *Andrew Jackson the Border Captain,* p. 176.
25. Ibid., p. 183.
26. Ibid.
27. Parton, *General Jackson,* p. 119.

### NOTES TO CHAPTER 10

1. George M. Troup, speech, April 30, 1812, *Annals of Congress: Debates and Proceedings in the Congress of the United States, 1789–1824,* 12th Cong., 1st sess., pp. 1359–62.
2. Hickey, *War of 1812,* p. 76.
3. Ibid.
4. Ibid.
5. Ibid., p. 8.
6. Ibid., p. 81.
7. Ibid., p. 84.
8. Ibid., p. 88.
9. Reilly, *British at the Gates,* p. 73.
10. Hickey, *War of 1812,* p. 131.
11. Sources give different numbers on the two ships' guns. The numbers here are from Hickey, p. 131.
12. Adams, *War of 1812,* p. 218.

### NOTES TO CHAPTER 11

1. Adams, *War of 1812,* p. 217.
2. Ibid., p. 223.
3. Ibid.
4. Sources differ on the total, from thirty-two hundred to more than five thousand.
5. Adams, *War of 1812,* p. 237.
6. Hickey, *War of 1812,* p. 193.
7. Lord, *Dawn's Early Light,* p. 299.
8. Ibid.
9. Ibid.
10. Ibid.
11. Adams, *War of 1812,* p. 285; Hickey, *War of 1812,* p. 205.
12. Adams, *War of 1812,* p. 285.
13. Ibid.
14. Hickey, *War of 1812,* p. 205.
15. Lord, *Dawn's Early Light,* pp. 313–14.

### NOTES TO CHAPTER 12

1. This origin of the word is according to *Encyclopaedia Britannica.*
2. This is the date agreed on by city officials in 1968, when New Orleans celebrated its 250th anniversary.
3. Garvey and Widmer, *Beautiful Crescent,* pp. 23–24.
4. Ibid.
5. Cowan, Chase, Dufour, LeBlanc, and Wilds, *New Orleans,* p. 98.
6. Garvey and Widmer, *Beautiful Crescent,* p. 60.

7. Cowan et al., *New Orleans,* p. 95.
8. Gleig, *Narrative of the Campaigns of the British Army,* pp. 255–56.

NOTES TO CHAPTER 13

1. Owsley, *Struggle for the Gulf Borderlands,* p. 89.
2. Remini, *Life of Andrew Jackson,* p. 85.
3. Bassett, *Life of Andrew Jackson,* p. 130.
4. Ibid., p. 131.
5. James, *Andrew Jackson the Border Captain,* p. 210.
6. Remini, *Life of Andrew Jackson,* p. 86.
7. Ibid., pp. 137–38; James, *Andrew Jackson,* p. 210.
8. James, *Andrew Jackson the Border Captain,* p. 210.
9. Bassett, *Life of Andrew Jackson,* pp. 140–41.
10. James, *Andrew Jackson the Border Captain,* p. 212.
11. Ibid., p. 216.
12. Ibid., p. 223.
13. Ibid.
14. Owsley, *Struggle for the Gulf Borderlands,* p. 129.
15. Remini, *Life of Andrew Jackson,* p. 92.

NOTES TO CHAPTER 14

1. James, *Andrew Jackson the Border Captain,* p. 198.
2. Saxon, *Lafitte,* p. 43.
3. Ibid., p. 45.
4. Ibid.
5. Ibid., p. 94.
6. Ibid., p. 102.
7. Ibid., p. 134.
8. Ibid., p. 136.
9. James, *Andrew Jackson the Border Captain,* p. 200.
10. Saxon, *Lafitte,* pp. 145–46.
11. Ibid., p. 151.
12. Reilly, *British at the Gates,* p. 196.
13. Remini, *Battle of New Orleans,* p. 47.
14. James, *Andrew Jackson the Border Captain,* p. 229.
15. Ibid.

NOTES TO CHAPTER 15

1. Owsley, *Struggle for the Gulf Borderlands,* p. 137.
2. Gleig, *Narrative,* pp. 276–79.
3. Ibid., pp. 277–78.
4. Ibid., pp. 278–79.
5. Parton, *General Jackson,* pp. 159–60.

NOTES TO CHAPTER 16

1. Chidsey, *Battle of New Orleans,* p. 118.
2. Bassett, *Life of Andrew Jackson,* p. 178.
3. Gleig, *Narrative,* p. 288.
4. Ibid., pp. 290–91.
5. Remini, *Battle of New Orleans,* p. 77.
6. James, *Andrew Jackson the Border Captain,* p. 243.
7. Gleig, *Narrative,* p. 296.
8. Latour, *War in West Florida,* p. 112.
9. Ibid.

NOTES TO CHAPTER 17

1. Reilly, *British at the Gates,* p. 210.
2. Ibid.
3. Ibid.
4. Gleig, *Narrative,* p. 305.
5. Ibid., pp. 306–7.
6. Scott, *Pakenham,* p. 39.
7. Walker, *Jackson and New Orleans,* p. 212.
8. Gleig, *Narrative,* pp. 312–13.
9. Ibid., pp. 313–14.
10. Ibid.

NOTES TO CHAPTER 18

1. Latour, *War in West Florida,* p. 124.
2. Ibid., p. 143.

3. Walker, *Jackson and New Orleans,* p. 239.
4. Gleig, *Narrative,* pp. 316–17.
5. Ibid., p. 318.
6. Latour, *War in West Florida,* p. 132.
7. Walker, *Jackson and New Orleans,* pp. 256–58.
8. Latour, *War in West Florida,* pp. 133–34.
9. Reilly, *British at the Gates,* pp. 272–73.
10. Gleig, *Narrative,* pp. 321–23.
11. Buell, *History of Andrew Jackson,* vol. I, p. 423.
12. Reilly, *British at the Gates,* p. 276.
13. Latour, *War in West Florida,* appendix LXVI, letter 4.
14. Reilly, *British at the Gates,* p. 282.
15. Ibid.
16. Latour, *War in West Florida,* p. 153.
17. Ibid., p. 154.
18. Parton, *General Jackson,* p. 208.

### NOTES TO CHAPTER 19

1. Reilly, *British at the Gates,* p. 283.
2. Scott, *Pakenham,* p. 42.
3. Ibid.
4. Ibid.
5. Ibid., p. 43.
6. Ibid.
7. Latour, *War in West Florida,* pp. 154–55.
8. Scott, *Pakenham,* p. 43.
9. Reilly, *British at the Gates,* p. 286.
10. Ibid.
11. Parton, *General Jackson,* p. 211.
12. Gleig, *Narrative,* pp. 328–29.
13. Walker, *Jackson and New Orleans,* p. 326.
14. Reilly, *British at the Gates,* p. 287.
15. Gleig, *Narrative,* p. 329.
16. Ibid.
17. Latour, *War in West Florida,* pp. 156–57.
18. Walker, *Jackson and New Orleans,* pp. 326–27.
19. Ibid.
20. Ibid.
21. Latour, *War in West Florida,* pp. 157–58.
22. Parton, *General Jackson,* p. 212.
23. Reilly, *British at the Gates,* p. 291.
24. Latour, *War in West Florida,* p. 159.
25. Reilly, *British at the Gates,* p. 287.
26. Parton, *General Jackson,* p. 215.
27. Ibid.
28. Reilly, *British at the Gates,* p. 291.
29. Ibid.
30. Parton, *General Jackson,* p. 226.
31. Latour, *War in West Florida,* p. 177.
32. Remini, *Battle of New Orleans,* p. 166.
33. Ibid.
34. Latour, *War in West Florida,* appendix XXIX.
35. Gleig, *Narrative,* pp. 336–37.

### NOTES TO CHAPTER 20

1. Remini, *Battle of New Orleans,* p. 164.
2. Gleig, *Narrative,* pp. 341–42.
3. Ibid., pp. 345–47.
4. Reilly, *British at the Gates,* p. 308.
5. Gleig, *Narrative,* pp. 351–53.

### NOTES TO CHAPTER 21

1. Walker, *Jackson and New Orleans,* pp. 345–47.
2. Ibid.
3. Latour, *War in West Florida,* appendix XXXII.
4. Ibid., appendix XXXIII.
5. Ibid., appendix LXIX.
6. Walker, *Jackson and New Orleans,* pp. 386–88.
7. Ibid., p. 388.

# BIBLIOGRAPHY

Adams, Henry. *The War of 1812.* New York: Cooper Square Press, 1999.

Bassett, John Spencer. *The Life of Andrew Jackson.* New York: Macmillan, 1925.

Brooks, Charles B. *The Siege of New Orleans.* Seattle: University of Washington Press, 1961.

Buell, Augustus C. *History of Andrew Jackson: Pioneer, Patriot, Soldier, Politician, President.* 2 vols. New York, 1904.

Chase, John. *Frenchmen, Desire, Good Children . . . and Other Streets of New Orleans.* New Orleans: Robert L. Crager, 1949.

Chidsey, Donald Barr. *The Battle of New Orleans.* New York: Crown, 1961.

Cowan, Walter G., John C. Chase, Charles L. Dufour, O. K. LeBlanc, and John Wilds. *New Orleans Yesterday and Today.* Baton Rouge: Louisiana State University Press, 1983.

Cronin, Vincent. *Napoleon.* New York: HarperCollins, 1994.

Durant, Will, and Ariel Durant. *The Age of Napoleon.* New York: MJF Books, 1975.

Garvey, Joan B., and Mary Lou Widmer. *Beautiful Crescent: A History of New Orleans.* New Orleans: Garmer Press, 1982.

Gleig, George Robert. *A Narrative of the Campaigns of the British Army at Washington, Baltimore, and New Orleans, under Generals Ross, Pakenham, and Lambert in the Years 1814 and 1815; With Some Account of the Countries Visited.* Philadelphia: M. Carey & Sons, 1821.

Hibbert, Christopher. *Wellington: A Personal History.* Reading, Mass.: Perseus Books, 1997.

Hickey, Donald R. *The War of 1812: A Forgotten Conflict.* Urbana: University of Illinois Press, 1990.

Huber, Leonard V. *New Orleans as It Was in 1814–1815.* New Orleans: The Battle of New Orleans 150th Anniversary Committee of Louisiana, 1965.

James, Marquis. *Andrew Jackson the Border Captain.* New York: Grossett & Dunlap, 1933.

Latour, A. Lacarriere. *Historical Memoir of the War in West Florida and Louisiana in 1814–15.* Translated by H. P. Nugent. Philadelphia, John Conrad and Co., 1816. Reprint, Gainesville: University of Florida Press, 1964.

Lord, Walter. *The Dawn's Early Light.* New York: Norton, 1972.

MacManus, Seumas. *The Story of the Irish Race.* Old Greenwich, Conn.: Devin-Adair, 1992.

Markham, Felix. *Napoleon.* London: Weidenfeld, 1963.

McCoy, Drew R. *The Last of the Fathers: James Madison and the Republic*

*Legacy.* Cambridge: Cambridge University Press, 1989.

Meuse, William H. *The Weapons of the Battle of New Orleans.* New Orleans, The Battle of New Orleans 150th Anniversary Committee of Louisiana, 1965.

Moore, G. C., ed. *The Autobiography of Lieutenant-General Sir Harry Smith.* London, 1901.

Muir, Rory. *Salamanca 1812.* New Haven, Conn.: Yale University Press, 2001.

Owsley, Frank Lawrence, Jr. *Struggle for the Gulf Borderlands, the Creek War and the Battle of New Orleans 1812–1815.* Tuscaloosa: University of Alabama Press, 1981.

Parton, James. *General Jackson.* New York: D. Appleton and Company, 1912.

———. *Life of Andrew Jackson.* 3 vols. Boston, 1887.

Rakove, Jack N. *James Madison and the Creation of the American Republic.* New York: HarperCollins, 1990.

Reilly, Robin. *The British at the Gates.* New York: Putnam, 1974.

Remini, Robert V. *Andrew Jackson and His Indian Wars.* New York: Viking, 2001.

———. *The Battle of New Orleans: Andrew Jackson and America's First Military Victory.* New York: Viking, 1999.

———. *The Life of Andrew Jackson.* New York: Penguin Books, 1988.

Roosevelt, Theodore. *The Naval War of 1812.* New York: Modern Library, 1999.

Rutland, Robert Allen. *The Presidency of James Madison.* Lawrence: University Press of Kansas, 1990.

Saxon, Lyle. *Fabulous New Orleans.* New Orleans: Robert L. Crager and Company, 1947.

———. *Lafitte the Pirate.* Gretna, La.: Pelican, 1999.

Schom, Alan. *Napoleon Bonaparte.* New York: HarperCollins, 1997.

Scott, Valerie McNair, Lady Pakenham. *Major-General Sir Edward M. Pakenham.* New Orleans: The Battle of New Orleans 150th Anniversary Committee of Louisiana, 1965.

Walker, Alexander. *Jackson and New Orleans.* New York: J. C. Derby, 1856.

Weller, Jac. *Wellington in the Peninsula.* London: Greenhill Books, 1999.

# INDEX

# ABOUT THE AUTHOR

BENTON RAIN PATTERSON is a former staff writer and editor for the *Saturday Evening Post* and the *New York Times.* He is Emeritus Associate Professor of Journalism at the University of Florida, as well as the author of *Harold and William: The Battle for England, A.D. 1064–1066* and *Washington and Cornwallis: The Battle for America, 1775–1783.*